Corporate Psychology and Its Impact on Diversity, Equity, and Inclusion

Ebtihaj Ahmed Al A'ali
University of Bahrain, Bahrain

Meryem Masmoudi
Applied Science University, Bahrain

Gardenia AlSaffar
Royal Bahrain Hospital, Bahrain

IGI Global
PUBLISHER of TIMELY KNOWLEDGE

A volume in the Advances in Human Resources Management and Organizational Development (AHRMOD) Book Series

Published in the United States of America by
IGI Global
Business Science Reference (an imprint of IGI Global)
701 E. Chocolate Avenue
Hershey PA, USA 17033
Tel: 717-533-8845
Fax: 717-533-8661
E-mail: cust@igi-global.com
Web site: http://www.igi-global.com

Library of Congress Cataloging-in-Publication Data

Names: Al-Aali, Ebtihaj Ahmed, 1957- editor. | Masmoudi, Meryem, 1979- editor. | Alsaffar, Gardenia, 1980- editor.
Title: Corporate psychology and its impact on diversity, equity, and inclusion / edied by Ebtihaj Ahmed Al A'Ali, Meryem Masmoudi, and Gardenia AlSaffar.
Description: Hershey, PA : Business Science Reference, [2024] | Includes bibliographical references and index. | Summary: "This book provides reflections on theories related to diversity, equity, and inclusion, organizational strategies to enhance diversity, equity, and inclusion, and tackles various issues such as racial and special needs issues, gender impacts, age diversity, ethnic and religious diversity, implicit bias, and prejudice, and sexual diversity. It is an essential resource for leaders, human resource managers, academicians, researchers, and students of different disciplines who seek to promote diversity orientations in their future workforce employment and boost diversity, equity, and inclusion in all fields of life. Corporate Psychology and Its Impact on Diversity, Equity, and Inclusion provides a comprehensive understanding of the issues and offers strategies for building a positive corporate psychology that fosters diversity, equity, and inclusion"-- Provided by publisher.
Identifiers: LCCN 2023025850 (print) | LCCN 2023025851 (ebook) | ISBN 9781668490136 (hardcover) | ISBN 9781668490143 (paperback) | ISBN 9781668490150 (ebook)
Subjects: LCSH: Corporate culture--Psychological aspects. | Diversity in the workplace. | Racism in the workplace. | Organizational behavior. | Psychology, Industrial.
Classification: LCC HD58.7 .C67 2024 (print) | LCC HD58.7 (ebook) | DDC 302.3/5--dc23/eng/20230623
LC record available at https://lccn.loc.gov/2023025850
LC ebook record available at https://lccn.loc.gov/2023025851

This book is published in the IGI Global book series Advances in Human Resources Management and Organizational Development (AHRMOD) (ISSN: 2327-3372; eISSN: 2327-3380)

British Cataloguing in Publication Data
A Cataloguing in Publication record for this book is available from the British Library.
All work contributed to this book is new, previously-unpublished material.
The views expressed in this book are those of the authors, but not necessarily of the publisher.
For electronic access to this publication, please contact: eresources@igi-global.com.

Advances in Human Resources Management and Organizational Development (AHRMOD) Book Series

ISSN:2327-3372
EISSN:2327-3380

Editor-in-Chief: Patricia Ordóñez de Pablos, Universidad de Oviedo, Spain

MISSION

A solid foundation is essential to the development and success of any organization and can be accomplished through the effective and careful management of an organization's human capital. Research in human resources management and organizational development is necessary in providing business leaders with the tools and methodologies which will assist in the development and maintenance of their organizational structure.

The **Advances in Human Resources Management and Organizational Development (AHRMOD) Book Series** aims to publish the latest research on all aspects of human resources as well as the latest methodologies, tools, and theories regarding organizational development and sustainability. The **AHRMOD Book Series** intends to provide business professionals, managers, researchers, and students with the necessary resources to effectively develop and implement organizational strategies.

COVERAGE

- Workplace Culture
- Training and Development
- Outsourcing HR
- Executive Compensation
- Employee Relations
- Succession Planning
- E-Human Resources Management
- Performance Improvement
- Compliance
- Strategic HRM

IGI Global is currently accepting manuscripts for publication within this series. To submit a proposal for a volume in this series, please contact our Acquisition Editors at Acquisitions@igi-global.com or visit: http://www.igi-global.com/publish/.

The Advances in Human Resources Management and Organizational Development (AHRMOD) Book Series (ISSN 2327-3372) is published by IGI Global, 701 E. Chocolate Avenue, Hershey, PA 17033-1240, USA, www.igi-global.com. This series is composed of titles available for purchase individually; each title is edited to be contextually exclusive from any other title within the series. For pricing and ordering information please visit http://www.igi-global.com/book-series/advances-human-resources-management-organizational/73670. Postmaster: Send all address changes to above address.

Titles in this Series

For a list of additional titles in this series, please visit:
http://www.igi-global.com/book-series/advances-human-resources-management-organizational/73670

Role of Human Resources for Inclusive Leadership, Workplace Diversity, and Equity in Organizations
Caglar Dogru (Ufuk University, Turkey)
Business Science Reference • copyright 2023 • 421pp • H/C (ISBN: 9781668466025) • US $240.00 (our price)

Policies, Protocols, and Standards for Professionalism in a Diverse Work Environment
Christiana Bevier (Purdue University Global, USA) Barry Regan (Purdue University Global, USA) and Carolyn N. Stevenson (Purdue University Global, USA)
Business Science Reference • copyright 2023 • 300pp • H/C (ISBN: 9781668473085) • US $225.00 (our price)

Global Citizenship and Its Impact on Multiculturalism in the Workplace
Randa Diab-Bahman (Kuwait College of Science and Technology, Kuwait) and Abrar Al-Enzi (Gulf University for Science and Technology, Kuwait)
Business Science Reference • copyright 2023 • 300pp • H/C (ISBN: 9781668454367) • US $240.00 (our price)

Talent Acquisition and Retention Strategies in Global Startups
Neetima Agarwal (Symbiosis International University, India) Leo Paul Dana (Kingston University, UK) and Sujata Khandai (Amity University, India)
Business Science Reference • copyright 2023 • 305pp • H/C (ISBN: 9781668475140) • US $250.00 (our price)

Addressing Corporate Scandals and Transgressions Through Governance and Social Responsibility
Carlos Flórido Lopes (Center for Research in Accounting and Taxation (CICF), Portugal) Augusta Ferreira (Center for Research in Accounting and Taxation (CICF), Portugal) Carlos Ferreira (DEGEIT/LASI/IEETA - University of Aveiro, Portugal) Helena Inácio (GOVCOPP,

For an entire list of titles in this series, please visit:
http://www.igi-global.com/book-series/advances-human-resources-management-organizational/73670

IGI Global
PUBLISHER of TIMELY KNOWLEDGE

701 East Chocolate Avenue, Hershey, PA 17033, USA
Tel: 717-533-8845 x100 • Fax: 717-533-8661
E-Mail: cust@igi-global.com • www.igi-global.com

To our parents, who taught us that life is diversity

Editorial Advisory Board

Table of Contents

Detailed Table of Contents

Microaggressions are small slights, insults, or dismissive actions that members of marginalized or underrepresented groups have to deal with daily. Even though these things may seem minor or unimportant, they can impact the person who gets them and make the workplace hostile and unwelcoming. Many workplaces have microaggressions, which can hurt people's mental health, happiness at work, and overall health. Also, research has shown that microaggressions can hurt people from underrepresented groups, like people of colour and women, more than others, which can worsen workplace inequality. They can also contribute to a hostile and unwelcoming work environment that makes employees less productive, more likely to miss work, and less happy. Microaggressions can be done on purpose or by accident. Even though they are small, research has shown that they significantly impact employees' mental health, job satisfaction, and overall well-being. The exposure to microaggressions can change how employees see the organization, making them less loyal and trusting.

International employment markets have been transformed due to various societal, organizational, and individuals changes these days. The last pandemic of Covid-19 has accentuated the negative impacts of changes leading to under-representation of certain groups in terms of their numbers and in relation to types of positions

This approach is eminently humanistic and places the person at the center of all action, because it recognizes that each person is valuable and has talent—therefore, it is necessary to identify and create conditions for it to flourish. Each person must be respected, regardless of their origin, ability, or identity. In consequence, all educational systems and schools must be creative in the face of diversity, responding with quality and equity, and avoiding discrimination and exclusion in schools. That is why there is a need for strong inclusive leadership. This is possible because of an environment of shared purpose and teamwork, so relationships are ascending, descending, and moving laterally due to the collaborative culture. It is also considered as a shared function that exercises collegiality and collaboratively.

Unconscious bias is a prevalent and persistent issue in the workplace, particularly concerning gender. Even though men and women are getting closer to having the same rights, unconscious bias still keeps women from getting ahead at work. It contributes to the pay gap between men and women, fewer chances for professional growth, and other kinds of discrimination based on gender. Organizations must look at these biases and do something about them to make the workplace fairer and more open to everyone. This chapter will overview unconscious bias and its effects on women in the workplace. First, the authors will discuss unconscious bias and how it works in the workplace. Next, they will examine how women's unconscious bias affects their career growth, pay, and chances of getting ahead. Then, the authors will talk about different tools, strategies, and organizations which can be used to assess and deal with unconscious bias, such as bias interrupters, unconscious bias training, and diversity and inclusion initiatives.

Researchers and policymakers have increasingly recognized the importance of studying diversity, equality, and inclusion in education. These studies can help identify how cultural values influence the learning outcomes of immigrants and inform evidence-based policymaking. This book chapter aims to scrutinize the diversity, equality, and inclusion practices in schools within the scope of Hofstede's cultural values in the sample of the countries participating in the TALIS 2018 survey. The sample consisted of 13,730 schools from 44 countries participating in both studies. The study found that only the masculinity dimension was negatively associated with teachers' diversity beliefs. The study found that DEI beliefs were in many points unrelated to Hofstede's cultural dimensions. Future research could explore multilevel models that include cultural dimensions and diversity and equality beliefs, as well as results from international assessments.

The advancement of the digital landscape has caused organizations to scrutinize their actions and practices through constant re-evaluation of its practices and this has yielded some valuable implications for society. This chapter proposes that effective leadership arises from an individual's capacity to engage in cross-cultural interactions. The study revealed that reward systems, communication processes, and diversity opportunities were three patterns that emerged within the institution under review. Implications for how diversity has the power to impact personal and professional lives in positive ways are examined and recommendations for leadership on embracing diversity initiatives are proposed.

A determination of current and probably future issues is tendered to in four segments. The first area manages the inescapable discussion among relativistic and universalistic introductions. In the second area, the authors talk about how the idea of culture is utilized in experimental investigations, attracting regard for, in addition to other things, the low accentuation on culturally diverse likenesses that rise up out of numerous informational indexes. The third segment addresses three topics that may well turn out to be progressively vital later on, to be specific inquiries concerning the level of soundness in culturally diverse information crossing bigger scopes of conduct, the coordination of discoveries from non-western social orders, and expansion in look into on human improvement in a social setting. The fourth segment stresses the duty of culturally diverse clinicians to apply their ability, particularly to issues of monetary and social imbalance, to add to human prosperity.

Preface

This book examines the impacts of the issues of diversity, equity and inclusion on individuals' behaviors in organizations. The implementations of tools, methods and strategies to enhance diversity, equity and inclusion lead to the development of cultural values. Such cultural values promote unique corporate psychology reflected on members of organizations. The pandemic of Covid-19 has accentuated the issue of under representation of certain groups in organizations. Under representation may be due to differences related to gender, race, ethnicity, age and physical disabilities and other reasons. This highlights the needs to enact strategies to balance the under representation of certain groups in organisations. The issue is contemporary and in some parts of the world is at infancy phase.

The book revolves around the following themes:

Impacts of diversity on organizational cultures
Inclusiveness strategies on women leadership styles
Impacts of inclusiveness strategies on organizational culture
Inclusive leadership and impacts on education
Leadership strategies to enhance diversity, equity and inclusion.
The psychology of diverse cultures
Bias against women in organizations
Microaggressions and work climate

Chapter 1 argues that organizations have to attend the negative impacts of microaggressions practices to enhance diversity, equity, and inclusion.

Chapter 2 illustrates that women inclusivity can add positive values to organizations and at the same time organizational strategies uphold the acts to appoint women in leadership positions.

Chapter 3 shows that building trusts at individuals and organizational levels sustain effectiveness of organizations and employees.

Chapter 4 displays the leadership strategic style of women . It elaborates as well on strategies to enhance women diversity in leadership positions.

Chapter 5 claims that inclusive leadership style focusing on humanistic sides of organisations lead to promote diversity, equity and inclusion.

Chapter 6 illustrates that unconscious biases against women still prevail in organisations. The chapter elaborates on strategies to mitigate the negative impacts of such biases.

Chapter 7 expounds that masculinity dimension is linked negatively with teachers' belief of diversity. The chapter also explicates that diversity, equity and inclusion in many points are not connected to Hofstede's cultural dimensions

In Chapter 8 the authors illustrate that leadership styles play major roles in creating climate for workplace diversity

Finally, Chapter 9 explains that the issues explored in studies reflect one of four premises. The four premises discussed lead to fragmentation of findings and results.

Ebtihaj Ahmed Al A'ali
University of Bahrain, Bahrain

Meryem Masmoudi
University of Bahrain, Bahrain

Gardenia AlSaffar
Royal Bahrain Hospital, Bahrain

Chapter 1
Microaggressions and Equity in the Workplace

Asma Ayari
University of Bahrain, Bahrain

ABSTRACT

Microaggressions are small slights, insults, or dismissive actions that members of marginalized or underrepresented groups have to deal with daily. Even though these things may seem minor or unimportant, they can impact the person who gets them and make the workplace hostile and unwelcoming. Many workplaces have microaggressions, which can hurt people's mental health, happiness at work, and overall health. Also, research has shown that microaggressions can hurt people from underrepresented groups, like people of colour and women, more than others, which can worsen workplace inequality. They can also contribute to a hostile and unwelcoming work environment that makes employees less productive, more likely to miss work, and less happy. Microaggressions can be done on purpose or by accident. Even though they are small, research has shown that they significantly impact employees' mental health, job satisfaction, and overall well-being. The exposure to microaggressions can change how employees see the organization, making them less loyal and trusting.

INTRODUCTION

Microaggressions are minor, everyday insults and slights that target people or groups based on their race, gender, sexuality, religion, or other aspects of their identity (Nadal & Wong, 2017). These things can range from using hurtful words to making gestures or using body language that does not include everyone. When these small

DOI: 10.4018/978-1-6684-9013-6.ch001

events happen over and over, they can have a significant effect on the mental health and well-being of the people who are targeted. This can lead to feelings of isolation, self-doubt, and depression (Fattoracci et al., 2021).

In the workplace, microaggressions can make the environment toxic and unwelcoming, making people less happy at work, less productive, and more likely to leave their jobs (Agarwal, 2019). They can also worsen power dynamics, making it harder for people from underrepresented groups to advance in their careers and get fair treatment at work (Capodilupo et al., 2010).

To deal with these problems, human resource professionals and organizational leaders need to know how common and harmful microaggressions are in the workplace and what strategies and interventions can be used to lessen their effects and promote equity and inclusion (DeAngelis, 2009).

The first part of the chapter will talk about what microaggressions are and give some examples of microaggressions that often happen at work. The chapter will also discuss how microaggressions can be both overt and subtle and the impact they can have on individuals and groups over time. The second part will look at how microaggressions can keep power dynamics and implicit biases and privileges going, it will talk about how people from underrepresented groups may experience microaggressions more often and how this can make them feel less like they belong at work. The third section will discuss different strategies and interventions that can be used to deal with microaggressions and make the workplace fairer for everyone. Then the chapter will talk about how critical organizational policies and training programs are, as well as how leaders can show how to act inclusively and deal with microaggressions when they happen. Finally the chapter will talk about how important it is to keep track of and evaluate efforts to stop microaggressions in the workplace, as well as how important it is to keep educating people and raising awareness about this issue and it's impact on the equity.

Overall, this chapter aims to give HR professionals and organizational leaders a complete understanding of what microaggressions are and how they affect fairness at work. By pointing out how important it is to deal with these issues, we hope to make the workplace more open and welcoming for all employees and, in the long run, help the organization be more successful and grow.

Workplace Microaggressions: Forms and Types

American professor Chester Pierce (Pierce, 1970) came up with the word "microaggression." He used it to describe offensive actions toward people of colour and promote racism (Pérez-Huber & Solorzano, 2015). Pierce coined the phrase "racial microaggression" to refer to "brief and commonplace daily verbal, behavioral, or environmental indignities, whether intentional or not, that communicate hostile, derogatory, or negative racial slights and insults to the target person or group" (Sue, 2007, p. 273). Since then, microaggression has become an umbrella term for describing daily indignities (Einarsen et al., 2003); acts of subtle nature that have derogatory undertones (Forrest-Bank et al., 2015); covert forms of racism (Dover, 2016); and "everyday experiences of perceived discrimination" (Forrest-Bank et al., 2015, p. 66), which may lead to a degradation of "people's mental health, job performance, and the quality of social experience" (DeAngelis, 2009, p. 42).

Microaggressions, microinsults, and microinvalidations are three forms of discrimination or prejudice that can harm individuals from marginalized groups (Sue et al., 2007). Micro-aggressions are intentional acts, such as using racial insults or making sexist jokes. At the same time, micro-insults and micro-invalidations are subtle and unconscious acts that convey disrespect or invalidate a person's experience or identity, such as assuming that a person with a disability needs help with everything or telling a person of colour that they are "too sensitive" when they express their feelings about racism (Brondolo et al., 2009; Nadal, 2011; Forrest-Bank et al., 2015). Microaggressions target specific groups or disseminate stereotypical, generic statements and actions that can unconsciously harm individuals (Sue, 2010; Palmer, Orabi & Harvey, 2019). Recent studies have also addressed women's gender in microaggression research, and theoretical frameworks have been developed to comprehend workplace microaggressions (Capodilupo et al., 2010; Kim Nguyen & Block, 2018).

Microaggressions are also defined as actions or words ***intentionally*** or ***unintentionally*** directed at a marginalized individual or group. They are a subtle prejudice that can harm those who encounter them (Spanierman et al., 2021). Microaggressions are characterized as ordinary, subtle, purposeful, and frequently inadvertent exchanges or acts that reflect a bias toward historically oppressed groups. They are classified into three types: attacks, insults, and invalidations (Palmer et al., 2019). Micro assaults are deliberate discriminatory behaviors, whereas microinsults are subtle snubs or insults, and microinvalidations are actions that exclude or negate marginalized groups' experiences (Sue, 2010).

Responding to microaggressions includes evaluating whether the microaggression occurred, confirming that it is a microaggression, and correctly responding. It is crucial to gain awareness of how widespread and harmful microaggressions are and work to eradicate them from the workplace.

Intentional microaggressions are deliberate discriminatory actions directed towards a minority individual or group (TED, 2019). They are subtle but damaging actions that convey a bias toward historically marginalized groups. Intentional microaggressions include:

- denying the existence of racism,
- when a microaggression hurts the other person, accusing them of being oversensitive, and,
- serving a white person without determining who was there first (Nadal et al., 2011; Nadal et al., 2019).

Intentional microaggressions can be highly damaging to those subjected to them, with serious repercussions such as depression, anxiety, absenteeism, and a hostile work environment (Sue et al., 2007). It is critical to develop a knowledge of how common and detrimental microaggressions are and to strive toward reducing them in the workplace.

Microaggressions in the workplace are ***unintended***, everyday interactions or acts that signal bias toward historically oppressed groups (Torres et al., 2012). They can impact a person's ability to perform their job, sense of security, and overall happiness (Summer et al., 2016). Microaggressions in the workplace include interrupting or rolling one's eyes when a female colleague speaks, complimenting a black student on their "great command of English," referring to women by seemingly endearing names, and telling a colleague from a marginalized group that they are "so articulate" (Nadal et al., 2014). These activities can harm those who witness them and have profound effects such as depression, anxiety, absenteeism, and a hostile work atmosphere. It is critical to develop a knowledge of how common and detrimental microaggressions are and to strive toward reducing them in the workplace. Microaggressions must be interrupted when they occur, and workplace cultures with no microaggressions must be promoted (Wing et al., 2019).

Consequences of Workplace Microaggression

Microaggressions in the workplace are small but hurtful things done to specific groups, like people of colour, women, people with disabilities, and religious minorities (Martinelli et al., 2020). Microaggressions can be said, done, or be a part of the environment (Nadal, 2011). They can cause depression, anxiety, missed work, and a hostile work atmosphere, among other things. So it is essential to understand what microaggressions are and work to fix them (Lipford & Rood, 2020). According to the findings of several researches (Brondolo et al., 2011; Fattoracci et al., 2021; Sue et al., 2007; 2009), encounter with subtle forms of discrimination may have a negative impact not only on cognitive functioning but also on mental and physical health. Because of the damage they cause, microaggressions need to be remedied. Spanierman and his colleagues (2021) say that people who are the targets of microaggressions may use self-defence techniques and group resistance to fight back against the destructive effects of these incidents. They talked about the power of collective (i.e., getting help from family, friends, and the community), resistance (i.e., going against stereotypes and confronting abusers), and self-protective (i.e., self-care) ways to deal with trauma (Medical news today, 2020). Collective coping means getting help from family, friends, and the community. Workplace microaggressions are rapidly becoming an emerging discursive field as corporate organizations, human resource managers, and researchers begin to find subtle forms of discrimination in the workplace (Kim Nguyen & Block, 2018). Given that individuals spend the vast majority of their time at work (Hunter, 2011) and that communications and behavior in such a space lead to the development of their identity, physical-emotional well-being, and individual productivity, identifying the tropes of workplace microaggressions becomes necessary to provide a healthy work environment and to ensure the employees and managers working there have a good quality of life (Pérez-Huber & Solorzano, 2015).

Microaggressions can significantly impact a company's ability to attract and retain talented employees (Lutgen-Sandvik, 2006). Organizations that fail to address microaggressions risk damaging their HR branding and reputation, making it difficult to compete for top talent in the job market. Potential employees may view a company with a reputation for tolerating microaggressions as unwelcoming, unsafe, and lacking in diversity and inclusivity (Einarsen et al., 2003). In contrast, companies that prioritize diversity, equity, and inclusion (DEI) and actively address microaggressions are more likely to attract a diverse pool of talented candidates who value a welcoming and inclusive workplace culture (Kim Nguyen & Block, 2018). Furthermore, employees who experience microaggressions may be less likely to stay with an organization and may actively discourage others from joining (Wing Sue et al., 2019). As a result, companies that do not address microaggressions may experience higher turnover rates and difficulties retaining top talent. Addressing microaggressions is therefore crucial for building a strong HR brand, attracting and retaining talented employees, and maintaining a competitive advantage in the job market (Summer et al., 2016).

Microaggression and Workplace Equity

Microaggressions can affect workplace equity, employee performance, and commitment. Microaggressions have a significant influence on employee performance (Baker College, 2021). They can lead to decreased job satisfaction, lower productivity, and increased absenteeism (HRCI, 2022). Medical News Today (2020) mentioned that microaggressions can also lead to imposter syndrome, negatively affecting an employee's confidence and performance. People who experience microaggressions may feel undervalued and avoid applying for promotions, leading to the loss of organizational talent. Microaggressions can also create a hostile work environment, negatively affecting employees' safety and well-being (Agarwal, 2019). Frequently, the onus of addressing microaggressions and instructing others falls on the victims, which can lead to additional stress and decreased productivity (Lipford and Rood, 2020). Addressing microaggressions in the workplace is essential to creating a more inclusive and welcoming workplace culture that values all employees and promotes their well-being and productivity (Nadal et al., 2011).

Microaggressions can perpetuate systemic inequalities by creating a hostile and unwelcoming environment for individuals from marginalized groups, affecting their sense of belonging, engagement, and commitment (Sue, 2010). Employees who experience microaggressions may feel undervalued and excluded, decreasing motivation, productivity, and job satisfaction. Microaggressions can also lead to adverse health outcomes such as stress, burnout, and absenteeism, affecting the employee's well-being and organizational performance (Nadal et al., 2019). Furthermore, microaggressions can reinforce larger systems of oppression and discrimination, making achieving workplace equity and promoting diversity and inclusion more difficult (Wing Sue et al., 2019). To prevent and address microaggressions, organizations must prioritize training on unconscious bias, diversity and inclusion, and cultural awareness, establish policies and procedures for reporting and addressing microaggressions, provide resources such as employee resource groups and counselling services, and increase diversity in recruitment and promotion processes (Nadal et al., 2014). Organizations can foster employee engagement, commitment, and well-being by creating a more inclusive and respectful work environment, promoting equity and diversity (Pérez Huber et Solorzano, 2015a).

Finally, organizations can improve workplace equity by implementing Employee Resource Groups (ERGs), company policies and rules, and training programs for Diversity, Equity, and Inclusion (DEI). Employee resource groups are a way to create a sense of belonging and community for underrepresented groups in the workplace (Sue, 2010). Employee Resource Groups (ERG) can offer support, networking opportunities, and a platform for advocacy and education. Companies can also establish clear policies and rules to address microaggressions and discrimination in the workplace, such as a zero-tolerance policy for harassment and discrimination (Pérez Huber & Solorzano, 2015b). These policies should be enforced consistently and transparently. Training programs for Diversity, Equity and Inclusion (DEI) can help employees understand unconscious biases and cultural differences, creating a more inclusive and respectful workplace culture (Lipford & Rood, 2020). DEI training can also improve leadership skills, communication, and teamwork. Moreover, organizations can ensure accountability and progress by establishing diversity, equity, and inclusion metrics and regularly reviewing and evaluating progress. By incorporating these strategies, organizations can create a more equitable and inclusive workplace for all employees (Nadal et al., 2019).

Workplace Microaggressions, Inclusion, and Diversity in the Workforce

Microaggressions are a subtle form of discrimination that can significantly impact equity in the workplace. They create a hostile environment for marginalized groups, diminish their professional status and contribution to the organization, and negatively affect team dynamics and productivity (Hunter, 2011). Moreover, microaggressions cause stress and anxiety, leading to absenteeism, burnout, and turnover (Lipford & Rood, 2020). Research by Lutgen-Sandvik (2006) indicates that microaggressions significantly impact employees' job satisfaction and engagement. Another study by Spanierman et al., (2021) shows that employees who experience more microaggressions report lower job satisfaction, higher intentions to leave the organization, and a greater likelihood of turnover (Einarsen et al., 2003). To prevent these adverse outcomes, organizations have implemented various programs and plans to address and deter microaggressions, including training on unconscious bias, establishing policies for reporting and addressing microaggressions, and increasing diversity in recruitment and promotion processes (Fattoracci et al., 2021). By promoting workplace equity and proactively addressing microaggressions, organizations can create a more inclusive and welcoming work environment for all employees.

Addressing microaggressions in the workplace requires a multifaceted approach that involves education, awareness, and accountability (HRCI, 2022). Here are some strategies that organizations can use to address microaggressions in the workplace:

a. ***Education and Training***: Organizations can provide education and training programs to raise awareness of microaggressions and their impact on individuals and the workplace (Lipford & Rood, 2020). Training programs can also provide employees with strategies for responding to and preventing microaggressions. For example, the training could provide employees with the language and skills to interrupt microaggressions when they occur and promote a more inclusive workplace culture. Education and exercise can also help employees understand the importance of diversity and inclusion and their role in creating a welcoming environment for everyone (DeAngelis, 2009).
b. ***Clear Policies and Procedures***: Organizations can establish clear policies and procedures that prohibit microaggressions and provide a mechanism for reporting and addressing incidents of microaggressions. These policies and procedures should be communicated to all employees and enforced consistently (TED, 2019). To promote accountability and encourage people to speak out when they observe or suffer microaggressions, it is crucial to create a clear and open mechanism for reporting incidences of microaggressions (Torres-Harding et al., 2012).

c. ***Diverse Hiring Practices***: Organizations can promote diversity and inclusion by implementing hiring practices that prioritize diverse candidate pools and eliminate implicit bias in the hiring process (Palmer et al., 2019). This can include creating job postings using inclusive language and contacting various candidate pools. Training hiring managers to recognize and eliminate implicit bias in the hiring process is also essential.

d. ***Supportive Workplace Culture***: Organizations can create a supportive workplace culture that values diversity and inclusion. This can include promoting employee resource groups, celebrating cultural events and holidays, and providing employee feedback and engagement opportunities (Sue, 2010). It is essential to have leadership that values and models diversity and inclusion, as this can create a more welcoming and inclusive workplace environment.

e. ***Ongoing Assessment***: Organizations should continuously assess their workplace culture and practices to identify areas where microaggressions may occur and take action to address them. This can include regular surveys, focus groups, and other employee feedback forms (Spanierman et al., 2021). The best way for businesses to combat microaggressions and foster an inclusive environment is to conduct regular cultural assessments that reveal where changes are needed.

Recommendations and Future Research Directions

To prevent and address microaggressions in the workplace, organizations should take proactive steps. This can be achieved by providing training on unconscious bias, diversity, and cultural awareness to increase awareness and promote inclusive behaviors (Pierce, 1970). Organizations should also establish clear policies and procedures for reporting and addressing microaggressions and provide employees with resources such as employee resource groups and counselling services (Wing-Sue et al., 2019). Additionally, organizations should prioritize increasing diversity in recruitment and promotion processes to ensure all employees have equal professional development and advancement opportunities. To ensure progress toward equity goals, organizations should establish accountability metrics and regularly assess the effectiveness of their programs and plans (Summer et al., 2016). By taking these steps, organizations can create a more inclusive and welcoming work environment for all employees, promote equity, and reduce the negative impact of microaggressions on employee well-being, job satisfaction, and retention (Forrest-Bank et al., 2015).

Addressing microaggressions today can be challenging, but it is essential to do so to create a more inclusive and respectful workplace. One way to address microaggressions is to use "I" statements to express how the behavior makes you feel (Nadal & Wong, 2017). For example, "I felt uncomfortable when you made that comment." This approach avoids putting the other person on the defensive and focuses on the impact of their behavior (Forrest-Bank et al., 2015). Another method is to ask questions to clarify the intent behind the behavior. For example, "Can you explain what you meant by that?" This approach can help the person realize their behaviors impact and allow them to correct it (Kim et al., 2018). It is also essential to educate ourselves and others about microaggressions and their impact. By raising awareness and promoting a culture of respect and inclusion, we can reduce microaggressions in the workplace (Spanierman et al., 2021; HRCI, 2022).

While there has been significant progress in the study of microaggressions in the workplace, several areas still require further investigation. In particular, future research should focus on:

a. ***Intersectionality***: People who belong to multiple marginalized identities experience microaggressions differently. Future studies should examine how microaggressions intersect and affect individuals with intersecting marginalized identities, such as those who identify as people of colour (Nadal et al., 2014; Pérez-Huber & Solorzano, 2015; Kim et al., 2018; Martinelli, 2020).
b. ***Organizational Culture***: The corporate culture plays a crucial role in perpetuating or preventing microaggressions. Future studies should examine how organizational culture can either exacerbate or mitigate the incidence and effects of microaggressions in the workplace (Nadal & Wong, 2017).
c. ***Impact on Performance***: While research has shown that microaggressions lead to adverse outcomes such as depression, anxiety, and missed work, there is still a need to investigate the impact of microaggressions on job performance, turnover intention, and job satisfaction (Nadal et al., 2011).
d. ***Perpetrators***: Research should also focus on the perpetrator's role in microaggressions in the workplace. Studies should examine the motivations and intentions behind microaggressions and how they can be prevented or addressed.
e. ***Interventions***: There is a need to develop and implement effective interventions to address microaggressions in the workplace (Spanierman et al., 2021). Future research should examine the effectiveness of various intervention strategies, such as diversity and inclusion training, bystander intervention, and the development of workplace policies and procedures.

CONCLUSION

The purpose of this chapter is to demonstrate that the professional space of the modern-day workplace environment is made up of people from various geographical, cultural, and social backgrounds, with employees of multiple genders, ages, and ideologies who either create or are subjected to stereotypical practices and hurtful communicational behavior, which hinder productivity and positivity at work. This chapter proposes to analyse microaggressions using literary theories to contextualize verbal, nonverbal, overt, or covert microaggressions arising from rising human diversity in the workplace. It also investigates its effects on employees to devise a corrective approach to alleviate socio-psychological problems in the workplace and give them a higher quality of life. Finally, the chapter, shows demonstrate how microaggressions are considered as a form of discrimination that hurts marginalized people or groups. They can be done on purpose or by mistake. Some examples of microaggressions are words or actions that show discrimination against members of a marginalized group in a way that is indirect, subtle, or unintentional. To make workplaces more open and sensitive to different cultures, we need to think about our own biases, become aware of them, and work to reduce them at work. It's essential to stop microaggressions when we see them and encourage workplace settings with fewer of them. In the end, getting better at noticing and reacting to microaggressions is a journey that requires educating staff and students, changing people's actions, and being more aware of how we talk every day.

REFERENCES

Agarwal, P. (2019). *How Microaggressions Can Affect Wellbeing in the Workplace*. Forbes. https://www.forbes.com/sites/pragyaagarwaleurope/2019/03/29/howmicroaggressions -can-affect-wellbeing-in-the-workplace/#18fc6a1973cb

Baker College. (2021). *Examples of workplace microaggressions and how to reduce them*. Baker College. https://www.baker.edu/about/get-to-know-us/blog/examples-of-workplace-microaggressions-and-how-to-reduce-them

BetterUp. (n.d.). The impact of microaggressions in everyday life. *BetterUp*. https://www.betterup.com/en-us/resources/microaggressions

Brondolo, E., Brady ver Halen, N., Pencille, M., Beatty, D., & Contrada, R. J. (2009). Coping with racism: A selective review of the literature and a theoretical and methodological critique. *Journal of Behavioral Medicine*, *32*(1), 64–88. doi:10.100710865-008-9193-0 PMID:19127420

Capodilupo, C. M., Nadal, K. L., Corman, L., Hamit, S., Lyons, O. B., & Weinberg, A. (2010). *The manifestation of gender microaggressions. Microaggressions and marginality: manifestation, dynamics, and impact*. Wiley.

DeAngelis, T. (2009). Unmasking racial microaggressions. *Monitor on Psychology, 40*(2), 42.

Dover, A. M. (2016). The moment of microaggression: The experience of acts of oppression, dehumanization, and exploitation. *Journal of Human Behavior in the Social Environment, 26*(7-8), 7–8, 575–586. doi:10.1080/10911359.2016.1237920

Einarsen, S., Hoel, H., Zapf, D., & Cooper, C. L. (2003). The concept of bullying at work. In S. Einarsen, H. Hoel, D. Zapf, & C. L. Cooper (Eds.), *Bullying and emotional abuse in the workplace: International perspectives in research and practice* (pp. 3–30). Taylor & Francis.

Fattoracci, J., Kwon, P., & Kwon, J. (2021). Intersectional microaggressions and mental health among sexual and gender minority people of colour. *Journal of Counseling Psychology, 68*(2), 179–191. doi:10.1037/cou0000539

Forrest-Bank, S., Jenson, J. M., & Trecartin, R. (2015). Microaggressions and the clinical supervision process. *Journal of Counseling and Development, 93*(4), 427–436. doi:10.1002/jcad.12054

Forrest-Bank, S. S., Jenson, J. M., & Trecartin, S. (2015). The revised 28-item racial and ethnic microaggressions scale (r28rems): Examining the factorial structure for black, Latino/Hispanic, and Asian young adults. *Journal of Social Service Research, 41*(3), 326–344. doi:10.1080/01488376.2014.987944

Human Resource Standards Institute (HRCI). (2022). *Combating microaggressions in the workplace*. HRCI. https://www.hrci.org/community/blogs-and-announcements/hr-leads-business-blog/hr-leads-business/2022/02/14/combating-microaggressions-in-the-workplace

Hunter, R. L. (2011). *An examination of workplace racial microaggressions and their effect on employee performance (Order No. 1503508)*. Available from ProQuest Dissertations & Theses Global. (915679506). https://lavasalibrary.remotexs.in/docview/915679506?accountid=38885

Kim, J., Nguyen, D., & Block, C. (2018). *The 360-degree experience of workplace microaggressions: who commits them? How do individuals respond? What Are the Consequences?* Influence and Implications., doi:10.1002/9781119466642.ch10

Kim Nguyen, H., & Block, C. J. (2018). The impact of microaggressions on mental health: Intersectionality and clinical implications. *Journal of Counseling and Development, 96*(4), 390–400. doi:10.1002/jcad.12222

Lipford, W. J., & Rood, S. A. (2020). That's What "Generation We" Said? The Office Enables Active Learning and Improved Retention in the Modern Human Resource Management Classroom. *Journal of Hospitality & Tourism Education, 32*(3), 178–185. doi:10.1080/10963758.2019.1655435

Lutgen-Sandvik, P. (2006). Take this job, quit, and other forms of resistance to workplace bullying. *Communication Monographs, 73*(4), 406–433. doi:10.1080/03637750601024156

Martinelli, V. (2020). How to Spot and Shut Down Microaggressions in the Workplace. *FAIRYGODBOSS Blog*. https://fairygodboss.com/articles/microaggressions-in-the-workplace

Medical News Today. (2020). Microaggressions in the workplace: examples, responding, and how to help. *Medical News Today*. https://www.ef.com/wwen/blog/language/understanding-microaggressions/

Nadal, K. L. (2011). The Racial and Ethnic Microaggressions Scale (REMS): Construction, reliability, and validity. *Journal of Counseling Psychology, 58*(4), 470–480. doi:10.1037/a0025193 PMID:21875180

Nadal, K. L., Davidoff, K. C., Davis, L. S., & Wong, Y. (2015). Emotional and behavioral responses to racial microaggressions: A closer look at Black Americans. *Race and Social Problems, 7*(1), 17–26. doi:10.100712552-014-9138-5

Nadal, K. L., Griffin, K. E., Wong, Y., Hamit, S., & Rasmus, M. (2014). The impact of racial microaggressions on mental health: Counselling implications for clients of colour. *Journal of Counseling and Development, 92*(1), 57–66. doi:10.1002/j.1556-6676.2014.00130.x

Nadal, K. L., & Wong, Y. (2017). Microaggressions and social work: A review of the literature. *Journal of Ethnic & Cultural Diversity in Social Work, 26*(1-2), 1–17. doi:10.1080/15313204.2016.1268989

Nadal, K. L., Wong, Y., Griffin, K. E., Sriken, J., & Vargas, V. (2011). The impact of racial microaggressions on mental health: Counselling implications for clients of colour. *Journal of Counseling and Development, 89*(3), 338–348. doi:10.1002/j.1556-6676.2011.tb00092.x

Nadal, K. L., Wong, Y., & Sriken, J. (2019). The impact of racial microaggressions on mental health: A systematic review and meta-analysis. *Journal of Counseling Psychology, 66*(6), 637–655. doi:10.1037/cou0000386

Palmer, C. T., Orabi, J., & Harvey, J. B. (2019). The impact of microaggressions on employees' mental health: The role of resilience. *Journal of Occupational Health Psychology*, *24*(2), 246–258. doi:10.1037/ocp0000129

Pérez-Huber, H. L., & Solorzano, D. G. (2015). *Microaggressions in everyday life: race, gender, and sexual orientation*. John Wiley & Sons, Inc.

Pérez Huber, L., & Solorzano, D. G. (2015). Racial microaggressions as a tool for critical race research. *Race, Ethnicity and Education*, *18*(3), 297–320. doi:10.1080/13613324.2014.994173

Pierce, C. M. (1970). Offensive mechanisms. In R. K. Merton (Ed.), *Robert K. Merton: Selected Writings* (pp. 289–316). Free Press.

Spanierman, L. B., Todd, N. R., & Anderson, C. J. (2021). Racial microaggressions: Critical questions, state of the science, and future directions. *Cultural Diversity & Ethnic Minority Psychology*, *27*(3), 357–368. doi:10.1037/cdp0000429

Sue, D. W. (2010). *Microaggressions in everyday life: race, gender, and sexual orientation*. John Wiley & Sons Inc.

Sue, D. W., Capodilupo, C. M., Torino, G. C., Bucceri, J. M., Holder, A. M. B., Nadal, K. L., & Esquilin, M. (2007). Racial microaggressions in everyday life: Implications for clinical practice. *The American Psychologist*, *62*(4), 271–286. doi:10.1037/0003-066X.62.4.271 PMID:17516773

Sumner, E., Scarduzio, J., & Daggett, J. (2016). Drama at Dunder Mifflin: Workplace Bullying Discourses in the Office. *Journal of Interpersonal Violence*, *35*(1-2), 127–149. Advance online publication. doi:10.1177/0886260516681158 PMID:27920361

TED. (2019, December 9). *Eliminating Microaggressions: The Next Level of Inclusion | Tiffany Alvoid.* [Video]. YouTube. https://youtu.be/cPqVit6TJjw

Torres-Harding, S. R., Andrade, A. L., Romero Diaz, C. E., & Garcia, C. (2012). Microaggressions and Latina/o Americans: An analysis of nativity, gender, and subjective social status. *Journal of Latina/o Psychology*, *1*(1), 37–51. doi:10.1037/a0026469

Wing Sue, D., Alsaidi, S., Awad, M. N., Glaeser, E., & Yan, M. C. (2019). Disarming racial microaggressions: Micro-intervention strategies for targets, White allies, and bystanders. *The American Psychologist*, *74*(1), 128–142. doi:10.1037/amp0000296 PMID:30652905

Chapter 2
Impacts of Gender Inclusivity on the Banking Sector in Bahrain:
Culture Perspective

Gardenia AlSaffar
Royal Bahrain Hospital, Bahrain

Ebtihaj Ahmed Al-Aali
University of Bahrain, Bahrain

Meryem Masmoudi
Applied Science University, Bahrain

ABSTRACT

International employment markets have been transformed due to various societal, organizational, and individuals changes these days. The last pandemic of Covid-19 has accentuated the negative impacts of changes leading to under-representation of certain groups in terms of their numbers and in relation to types of positions occupied. Women employment in organizations, as studies indicated, have been greatly influenced. Furthermore, women in leadership positions are still behind in comparison to men. Hence there are societal, organizational and individuals' calls to rectify the situations of women in leadership. Diversity, equity, and inclusion are strategic tools and methods to accomplish such rectification. This research attempts to investigate the issue of inclusivity as reflections of diversity and equity on women leadership styles in banking sector in Bahrain. The research employs qualitative methodology. In-depth interview is the research method to collect information.

DOI: 10.4018/978-1-6684-9013-6.ch002

INTRODUCTION

Diversity, equity, and inclusion are strategic considerations enabling organisations to deal with the contemporary international issues of employment. Such employment issues are transformed in the post COVID-19 era. This leads many social vulnerable groups to be negatively affected in term of inclusivity. Therefore concerns of diversity and equity regarding the inclusion issue are highlighted in relation to women in top leadership positions. The research at hand examines the issue of inclusivity of women top leaders as reflection of diversity and equity. The focus of the research as well is to explore the impacts of inclusivity on organizational culture. This research consists of seven sections. Section two defines the issues of diversity and equity as Organizational approaches to enhance inclusivity. Their impacts on organizational culture are studied in section three. Section four defines women leadership and its impacts on organizational culture focusing on the issue of inclusivity. Section five elaborates on methodology. Section six then presents analysis of information collected. The conclusion and the suggested future researches are mentioned in the final section.

DEFINITION OF DIVERSITY, EQUITY, AND INCLUSION: LITERATURE REVIEW

This section expounds on the definitions of diversity, equity to enhance inclusivity. Benefits of accomplishing inclusivity then are stated. Diversity has received no actions to achieve before the 60s of last century (Allvoices Team, 2022; and Dong, 2021) . They have added as well that diversity training programs in the following decades have failed to meet diversity targets. In a recent experiment conducted by Harvard Business Review study, it is found that white men employees with organizational power have not changed their behaviors as results of attending non- bias training programs (Dong, 2021). This illustrates the need to have clear and solid definitions for the terms diversity, equity and inclusion to take the right actions to achieve. The lack of concrete and clear definitions according to Siri, Leone and Bencivenga (2022) is due to the overlapping meanings assumed . Ebert & Griffin (2019) state that workforce becomes more diverse leading human resources to transform their functions. They explain that race, physical abilities, ethnicity, gender religion, ethics and values shape human behaviors . They expound that diversity is a method to attain competitive advantage which results from hiring the best workforce regardless of any other issue. As a result, Ebert and Griffin (2019) claims that innovation is enhanced. Training is a major role to achieve diversity. Ebert and Griffin implicitly refer to inclusivity for achieving Organizational interests. However they have not highlighted the issue of inclusivity as an ethical act. Dewider, Elmestekawy & Welch (2022) elaborate on the definitions of diversity, equity and inclusion. They define equity as acknowledging the advantages and obstacles related to various identities exist. This acknowledgment enables organizations to enhance diversity and to overcome obstacles leading to the inclusion which means the acceptance and the valuing of all identities.

Koku (2022) states however that diversity, equity and inclusion are used as interchangeable terms by some organisations. This may explain his claim that it is hardly found Organizational reports about such interchangeable terms. Chapman (2021) in Webrecruit Co examines the Organizational barriers to diversity, equity, and inclusion. The first barrier is the budget issue. If diversity, equity, and inclusion concerns are new to the organisations, financial budgets have be allocated. This is to assist in instigating the desirable changes. The second barrier is the absence of support from management and employees to accept and accomplish the changes sought. The last barrier states that there is scarcity of tools to achieve the targets of diversity, equity, and inclusion. The above discussion illustrates two points. The first proposes that diversity, equity and inclusion are used interchangeably or there is an an assumption of overlapping in meanings. This explains the reason behind focusing only on diversity as reflections of equity and inclusion. The second assumes that diversity, equity and inclusion are different targets as stated by Dewider, Elmestekawy & Welch (2022). However little emphasis is mentioned in relation to cultural changes accompanied the implementation of diversity, equity, and inclusion in organisations.

IMPACTS OF DIVERSITY, EQUITY, AND INCLUSION ON ORGANISATIONAL CULTURE

This section probes two issues in relation to research at hand. The first issue presents the definition of Organizational culture. The second issue then explores the impacts of diversity, equity, and inclusion on Organizational culture.

Organisational CULTURE: DEFINITION

The concept of organisational culture was first discussed in 1970s (Negi & Dangwal, 2021). Culture is defined as communal values which identifies a given group from the others (Al-Faihani & Al-Alawi, 2020). They explain that researches state that it is hard to change culture as it develops over time. Ebert & Griffin (2019) differentiate between the broader culture and sub culture. They expound that the broader culture represents the style of life while the sub culture stands for values of a given group or a specific social class. Kinicki & Williams (2020) define culture as the implicit assumptions and taken for granted values underlying behaviors in organisations. They explicate that culture is instigated by drivers. These are values held by founders, the broader environment of every different industry, culture of the country, visions stated and strategies for an organization, and finally styles of leaders' behaviors. This makes the processes of changing culture slow and un easy. Values are stated to guide desirable behaviours leading to achieve organisational visions and objectives (Ebert & Griffin, 2019 and Kinicki & Williams, 2020).

Impacts Of Diversity, Equity, and Inclusion on Organizational Culture

Culture as defined earlier refers to the implicit assumptions underpinning human behaviors. Cultures as well are varied between sub groups. The diversity of work force affect individuals' behaviours and in turn their interactions, perceptions and performances. Moorhead and Griffin (2011) add that diverse work force was attempting to integrate with the majority culture and norms. This was hard to do. Melting different cultures in one is realised to be un realistic . They explain that organisations these days appreciate and encourage diversity that leads to positive performance. Diversity according to Moorhead and Griffin can enable organizations to develop competitive advantage. Organizational diversity, equity, and inclusion according to Koku (2022) are strategic approaches to correspond to stakeholders' changing demands. Such demands are related to values, experiences and identities. This leads to corresponding to what stated earlier as cultures of sub groups and in turn leading to transform the broader cultures and societies. Koku indicates that inclusive culture lead to accommodate to the demands of society and businesses stakeholders.

Rizwan et al. (2016) illustrate that diversity has positive impacts on organisational values. However some negative consequences according to Rizwan et al. can result from diversity based on a few earlier researches. They exhibit that age diversity leads to generation gaps. This in turn instigates clashes and conflict according to some findings. Ethnicity sometimes shows that heterogeneous are less productive than homogeneous groups. Despite all of these negative consequences of diversity, the literature exhibits many positive impacts of diversity on organisational values. Performance of employees is shown by Rizwan et al (2016) is enhanced by diversity. This is due to availability of diverse talents, skills, knowledge and aptitude of critical thinking. Therefore creativity, innovation and profitability is strengthened. These values can be resultant from employing different ethnic groups as well. They confirm that management of differences becomes inevitable in relation to diversity of workforce. Despite the positive values referred to, Rizwan et al. (2016) have not noted the issue of inclusiveness in relation to diversity. Al-Alawi (2016) recommends to enhance awareness of society and culture in relation to importance of gender diversity. He explains that diversity improves performance of organizations and the economy. However Al-Alwai is similar to Rizwan et al. (2016) in respect to overlooking the issue of inclusiveness and its effects on the cultures of organisations.

Siri, Leone & Bencivenga (2022) argue that creating inclusive culture can provide equity to diverse workforce. Inclusiveness according to them is a strategic goal for organisations. They are referring to higher education institutions as organisations. Diversity and equity are aiming to achieve inclusiveness. However their findings explicate that diversity, equity and inclusion are seen to be overlapping and each automatically leads to the other. This is due to the lack of clear and concrete definitions for the terms diversity, equity and inclusion.

Gigliotti, Dwyer & Ruiz-Mesa (2018) propound that diversity leadership is a must to initiate changes at all levels in organizations. Such leadership has to promote diversity visions, to espouse strategies for highlighting diversity, and building climates and cultures nurturing and fostering diversity . This is comparable to Siri, Leone & Bencivenga' (2022) s argument that inclusiveness is strategic goal. Gigliotti, Dwyer & Ruiz-Mesa (2018) examine five strategies to enhance diversity leadership and to foster inclusion . The first asserts that commitments of all organizational levels to diversity is a must to succeed in the process of changes toward diversity and then inclusion. The second contends that the new societal, climate and cultural changes require to conduct diversity audit. This is to say that diversity and inclusiveness are on going processes demanding continuous modification of policies and procedures. The third affirms the importance of training to foster organizational changes in relation to diversity. The fourth concerns with recruitment, mentoring and guiding careers paths for diverse groups. The fifth and the last is to maintain inter group dialogue of expertise. This can refine Organizational climate and improve conflict resolutions. These five strategies according to Gigliotti, Dwyer & Ruiz-Mesa can lead to the desirable styles of diversity leadership which can improve inclusiveness.

There are many advantages for achieving diversity. In their editorial post (2021) the University of St. Augustine for Health Sciences list the advantages of diversity . Many of such advantages are similar to those discussed above by Rizwan et al (2016). The first is to intensifying comfort levels of customers, i.e patients. The second is to improve decisions as consequences of having various perspectives presented by different types of workforce. The result is to improving innovation and creativity. The third is to comprehend and to appreciate values of different sub professional diversity groups. The fourth is to ameliorate communication with customers i.e patients. The fifth is to raise patients' trust as a resultant of the existence of diverse workforce accommodating the need of various customers, i.e patients. The sixth is to lessen discrepancies in rendering services i.e health services for diverse customers. The seventh aims to boosting affiliation of employees and customers with organizations that affect their societies positively. The eighth intends to escalate engagement of lower level employees. This is done trough integrating and appreciating the various sources of diversity. The eight advantages can achieve inclusiveness due to integration targets sought by the organisations.

The discussion of this section exhibits the disadvantages and advantages of implementing diversity in the organizations. The advantages of diversity and inclusivity overlap relying on compatible strategies as illustrated above (Gigliotti, Dwyer & Ruiz-Mesa, 2018 & editorial post, the University of St. Augustine for Health Science, 2021). This is due to the assumption of overlapping in meanings of the terms diversity, equity and inclusion postulated by Siri, Leone & Bencivenga (2022) and Gigliotti, Dwyer & Ruiz-Mesa (2018). Koku (2022) explains as well that diversity, equity and inclusion are used interchangeably. In the following section the impacts of women's leadership on Organizational culture as reflections of inclusivity are examined .

WOMEN LEADERSHIP AND ITS IMPACTS ON ORGANIZATIONAL CULTURE: INCLUSIVITY PERSPECTIVE

Al A'ali & Alazali (2018) mention that the societal roles of males and females are reflected on their organizational roles . Men are assumed to be more competent than women leading the later to be excluded from top managerial and leadership positions . Singha & Sivarethinamohan (2022) claim that women are not empower. They have no access to social and professional networking and therefore they are excluded in the society and in organizations.

Rizwan et al. (2016) and Moorhead and Griffin (2011) illustrate that organisations have tendency to contract male workforce. This is compatible to stereotypes held about males and females stating that the former is more competent than the later . Moorhead and Griffin contend that stereotypes underpinning individual behavior is an obstacle for gender equality. They add that cultures characterised by pluralism in term of workforce can enhance positive values related to diversity and inclusion.

Rizwan et al. (2016) demonstrate that the groups with women based diversity at management and non management posts are found to be collaborative and cooperative. Some researches exhibit that appropriate degree of gender diversity can yield competitive advantages. This is in harmony with Kinicki and Williams (2019) claiming that women, based on some previous studies, are rated to be more effective leaders than men. This is in congruence as well with with Ebert & Griffin (2019) affirming that women exhibit democratic style of leadership and men follow autocratic leadership style. The democratic style is argued to promote cohesiveness among team members. Service sector, it is asserted . will benefit from gender diversity more than assembly manufacturing firms. Kaku (2022) mentions that the International Labor Organization studies in 2019 reveal that businesses with inclusive focus strategies are more innovative and are capable of serving interests of customers. He elaborates stating that McKinsey & Co consulting group 's study confirms that gender-based teams of executives outperform others in relation to profitability.

The above discussion concerning impacts of women leadership as a reflection of inclusivity reveals the existence of positive impacts on organizations. Women can add new ideas leading to innovation and creativity. This can improve profitability. Women exhibit democratic leadership styles and hence they become more effective leaders. The above elaboration as well argue that culture with more gender diversity i.e pluralism values, fosters the appointment of women in leadership positions. In the following section the methodology employed in this research is scrutinised.

THE METHODOLOGY

The supreme council for women in Bahrain commands all public and private organizations to provide equal opportunities for women. The Central Bank of Bahrain requires banks to appoint women at their board of directors (AURORA50,2022). However academic researches concerning diversity, equity, and inclusion is lacked. Due to the contemporary nature of the issue of diversity, equality, and inclusion and the lack of their related researches on Bahrain in general and on banks in specific, this research is employing qualitative methodology.

Denzin and Lincoln (2011) argue that qualitative methodology yields profound apprehensions of the subject being studied from view points of research participants.

Al A'ali & Al-Sarraf (2016) and Al A'ali (2020) claim that qualitative methodology enables as well to seize meanings and perceptions of participants which can shed light and develop more holistic understandings of the subject being examined.

In-depth interview is the research method used. No more interviews are conducted if no new information is generated as a premise of snowballing method to reach participants. Content analysis is the research tool to capture meanings, concepts and ideas presented by interviewees

Six interviews were conducted with Chief Executive Officers of Banks in Bahrain . Four are men and two are women. Each interview lasted from one hour to one hour and a half. The interviews revolve around the following issues:

1- Definitions of diversity, equity, and inclusion and their relationships .
2- Definition of organizational culture
3- Impacts of diversity, equity, and inclusion on organizational culture

4- Impacts of women leadership on organizational culture as reflections of inclusivity perspective.

DISCUSSION AND ANALYSIS OF COLLECTED INFORMATION

Analysis of information collected from interviews based on the above four questions is presented below.

Analysis of Collected Information for Question One in relation to the definitions of diversity, equity and inclusion:

The first question explores the definitions of diversity, equity, and inclusion. The same question then attempts to understand the relationship between such three definitions.

The first interviewee mentions that diversity refers to differences in relation to race, gender, special needs groups, religion and ethnicity. He adds that equity is the premise which human resources practices are based on in banks. Employees are treated fairly based on their performance regardless of their differences resulting from diversity. The first interviewee explains that there are barriers for women's inclusivity in organizations. Such barriers are caused by women themselves resulting from commitments to family responsibilities, being less experienced than men, and for their bringing up processes and related stereotypes. This is similar to the statement of Al A'ali and Alazali (2018) illustrating that stereotypes regarding social roles are reflected on gender organizational roles. The definitions of the diversity and equity according to this first interviewee are in harmony with the definitions discussed by Dewider, Elmestekawy & Welch (2022) and Ebert & Griffin (2019). The interviewee has not presented a specific definition for the term inclusion. However he expounds that women have their own inclusive barriers. The absence of the definition of inclusion given by the interviewee is in agreement with Koku (2022) illustrating that diversity, equity, and inclusion are used interchangeably.

The second interviewee asserts that diversity can be seen from two different angles. The first angle attests that diversity refers to the move of the bank to invest in risky business. The second angle means that diversity implies recruiting individuals regardless of their gender, race, ethnicity, sexual orientation and special needs groups. Equity, according to the second interviewee, is assumed to provide equal opportunities to all employees. The interviewee does not differentiate between the three concepts of diversity, equity and inclusion. He looks at them as naturally leading to each other. This is in congruence to the arguments offered by Siri, Leone and Bencivenga (2022) stating that definitions of diversity, equity, and inclusion do overlap.

The third interviewee explains that heterogeneity in term of ideologies, gender, cultures, religious beliefs and other individual's differences are sources of human resources diversity. Equity as mentioned by this interviewee proposes that individuals should be treated fairly regardless of their differences. This enables organizations to exclude no groups. The same interviewee however provides no definition for the the concept of inclusion. This is in harmony with the definitions of Moorhead & Griffin (2011) and Kinicki & Williams (2020) who refer to the sources of differences attributed to human resources in organisations. However they provide no definition for inclusion.

The fourth interviewee argues that employees in organizations represent the same groups of individuals in the broader society. Equity on the other hand refers to organizations providing equal rights, obligations, opportunities, rewards and compensations to employees regardless of their differences. This leads to foster inclusion. This is similar to the third interviewee' s definition of individual's' differences. However this interviewee illustrates more on the positive impacts of equity on enhancing inclusion which is in accordance with the arguments of Vaughan (2022) stating that equity leads to more inclusion and hence having positive impacts for stakeholders. The fourth interviewee however provides no definition for inclusion which is in accordance with kinick and Williams (2020) who present no definition.

The fifth interviewee exhibits that diversity is any issue that differentiates one group from the other . The interviewee adds that diversity however is gender-free in organizational contexts. This implies that variations between males and females in organizations are not based on gender . Dealing with the differences among groups fairly can promote equity and hence improving performance. This interviewee also mentions that the issue of inclusion has never been an issue to think of . The arguments of the fifth interviewee concerning gender-free diversity and unthinkable status of the concept of inclusion may be ascribed to the relatively contemporary nature of the issue of diversity and inclusivity as mentioned by Allvoices Team 2022 and Dong, 2021.

The sixth interviewee illustrates that diversity refers to origins of differences among members of the organization. Such origins stem from backgrounds variations in term of race, gender, education, ethnic groups and cultures. Organizations, regardless of such variations, have to treat their employees fairly for performance to be improved. Inclusion to this sixth interviewee is not an issue to think of . The definitions of diversity and equity expressed by the sixth interviewee are comparable to those of Moorhead and Griffin (2011) and Kinicki and Williams (2020) . The two interviewees, however, the fifth and sixth, have common perspective concerning the unthinkable status of inclusion.

The above analysis reveals that all of the interviewees share the same definitions of diversity and equity. The majority of Interviewees argue as well that diversity and equity lead to inclusion. However no one of them has provided definition for the issue of inclusion. The lack of the definition of inclusion may be understood in the light of the findings of Kuko (2022) stating that diversity, equity and inclusion are used interchangeably. In addition, Siri, Leone and Bencivenga (2022) claim that diversity, equity and inclusion are assumed to have overlapping meanings . The fifth and sixth interviewees expound that inclusion has never been an issue to think of . This unthinkable stance for the term inclusion is ascribed to the contemporary nature of the issue of inclusivity as discussed above by Dong (2021). This moreover exhibits the absence of the definition of inclusion in the analysis of diversity and equity explored by Moorhead & Griffin (2011) and Ebert & Griffin (2019).

Analysis of the Second Question Regarding the Definition of Organizational Culture

This question is required as it is explores values prevailing in organizations. Such values shapes the behavior of employees.

The first interviewee contends that culture is made of values stating human behavior in the broader society. Organizations develop their own unique cultures that are progressive in nature . The progress reflects organizational learning processes. This leads to modify the culture which occurs slowly. Values are not sex-related. Values are to maintain equity .

The second interviewee affirms that every organization has a unique culture. Values underpin cultures shape behaviors in organizations. The values have to be written in strategies and policies which must be revised and to be updated from time to time due to changes in internal and external environments.

The third interviewee defines organizational culture in term of how employees are expected to act. Values and ethics underlining organizational culture differentiate every organization from the other one. Cultural values are stated by board of directors. This implies that it is hard to change cultural values.

A culture is about values underlining organisational behaviors. The values are related to the well being of stakeholders. Organisational visions according to the fourth interviewee are reflections of the culture . Equity is a natural value once it is followed, diversity emerges.

The fifth interviewee elucidates that cultures are the systems of values underpinning behaviours in organizations in order to predict certain outcomes. Such values does not differentiate between types of sex of employees and their related organizational treatments. All employees are treated equally.

The sixth interviewee states that organizational cultures are made of values and ethics. The values and ethics are needed to shape the desirable behaviors of employees in order to achieve organizational visions and objectives. The values are gender-free and are not easy to change.

All interviewees contend that the organizational cultures are made of values. Cultural values, according to the interviewees, underpin employees behaviours. Such behaviours instigate the achievement of organisational visions and objectives. This is compatible to the definitions of culture stated above by Ebert & Griffin ; Kinicki & Williams (2020) and Faihani and Al-Alwai (2020). The second and the fourth interviewees highlight the factors and roles of internal and external environments and stakeholders in shaping values of organisations. This is stated by Kinicki and Williams (2020) referring to factors leading to changing organizational culture. Values according to interviewees are to accomplish organizational visions and objectives as mentioned by Kinicki & Williams (2020). The majority of interviewees declare that values are gender free which assist to maintain equity in organizations. The majority of interviewees as well confirm that changing cultures requires more time and efforts as illustrated by literature stated above (Ebert & Griffin,2019).

Analysis of the Third Question Concerning Impacts if Diversity, Equity, and Inclusion on Organisational Culture

The third question examines the effects of diversity, equity and inclusion on moulding cultures of organizations.

The first interviewee asserts that diversity and equity enhance inclusivity . This has positive impacts on the culture. However this same interviewee has not described the positive impacts. The assertion of this interviewee is in harmony with Kinicki & Williams (2020) stating that diversity enhances equity and inclusion which they provide no definition for inclusion.

The second interviewee explains that their bank is to enrich human element in Bahrain through focusing on diversity and equity which leads to inclusion of all human resources. This boosts employees' motivation and hence increases productivity and performance. Diversity reduces cost of recruitment and training due to the hiring of the most qualified individuals regardless of gender, race or any other factor. The demonstration of the positive impacts of diversity, equity and inclusion in relation to uphold motivation, to improve productivity and performance of the second interviewee is compatible to the analysis of Rizwan et al.(2016).

The third interviewee argues that diversity endorses by equity leads to promote positive organizational environments. Different groups of employee related to various groups add different values and ideas which improve performance and productivity.

The explanation of the third interviewee is in accordance with Moorhead and Griffin (2011) illustrating that diversity implying inclusion. This instigates high performance and high productivity.

The fourth interviewee assures that equity should be a natural and be a normal value underlying organizational visions, strategies and procedures. The interviewee adds that equity is not an artificial target to reach. It is not a man-made value. Equity means accepting and recognizing the importance of diversity to enhances inclusivity. Diversity unlike exclusion of certain groups, assists organizations to be creative, to be innovative and may reduce the cost of recruiting of the un qualified individuals. This fourth interviewee exhibits the advantages for implementing diversity in organizations as illustrated by Gigliotti, Dwyer & Ruiz-Mesa (2018).

The fifth interviewee expounds that women are similar to men in term of organizational performance and productivity. Both of them can add values in their own ways. Diversity then for this fifth interviewee seems to be gender-free. The interviewee also elaborates that inclusivity is a normal process for males and females leaders. This justifies his statement that inclusivity as an issue is not thought of by himself. The arguments of this fifth interviewee are discrepant with Rizwan et al. 's (2016) assumption that gender variations have impacts on organizational culture.

The sixth interviewee explains that inclusivity as a cultural value leads to certain advantages such reduction of hiring and training costs due to the elimination of bias in evaluation of employees. Inclusion of different groups with different backgrounds can boost creativity and innovation as well. This interviewee similar to the fifth one however states that inclusion as an issue is not thought of . The definitions of diversity and equity of this interviewee are comparable to those stated above by Moorhead & Griffin (2011), Al-Alwai (2016) and Rizwan et al. (2016) who implicitly refer to inclusion. However they present no concrete definition of inclusion.

The majority of interviewees highlight the positive impacts of diversity, equity and inclusion on Organizational culture. They argue as shown above that diversity and equity enhance inclusion which is referred to implicitly. It is worth mentioning that no interviewee presents a definition for inclusion however the majority elaborates on the advantages of inclusion. This supports the claim of Koku (2022) stating that diversity, equity and inclusion are used interchangeably. The majority of Interviewees exhibit that diversity contributes to reducing the cost of hiring and training, enhancing creativity and innovation by introducing new ideas and values presented by different groups, improving performance and productivity and hence develop competitive advantages (Moorhead & Griffin, 2011; Al-Alwai, 2016; Rizwan et al. (2017); Ebert and Griffin, 2018; and Kinicki & Williams, 2020). The fifth interviewee however differs from others by stating that diversity is gender-free. This is incongruent with the deliberations of Rizwan et al. (2016) and Gigliotti, Dwyer & Ruiz-Mesa (2018).

The Analysis of the Fourth Question Examining the Impacts of Women Leadership on Organizational Culture as Reflections of Inclusivity Perspective

The fourth question discusses the impact of inclusivity on promoting cultural values that support women leadership.

The first interviewee argues that the Old generation of women exclude themselves from the cycle of organizational leadership. This is due to their upbringing values which lead them to manage lives differently from men. This deprives them from having access to professional networking. However the present young women seek leadership positions. This is due to their contemporary values acquired from their schooling and education that stress the importance of diversity and equity. Organizations as well change their perspectives about leadership. Leadership at the present are not gender- based. Organizational values support and promote inclusivity . The first interviewee explains that social roles and stereotypes hindered women from being leaders in the past. This is in accordance with Moorhead & Griffin (2011) and Al A'ali & Alazali (2018) 's statements concerning the impacts of women social roles and related stereotypes on their organizational roles. The declaration of this same interviewee about women being denied from having access to professionals networks is in harmony with Singha & Sivarethinmohan (2022) ' saying that women are excluded from societal and Organizational networking for they are not empowered. They (2022) however are still arguing that women are still have no access to networking due to their social roles unlike the explanation of this interviewee showing that women ' s situation has changed in the organisations.

The second interviewee claims that appointing women in leadership positions can have qualitative impacts on work. The impacts are positives. Inclusion of women as leaders can improve the quality of languages used at the board levels. Besides, innovation and creativity can be reinforced . The cultural impacts of women in leadership positions mentioned by the second interviewee is comparable to the Koku (2022) attesting that inclusive strategies can enhance creativity and innovation. This leads to improve the general environment qualitatively for following pluralism culture (Moorhead & Griffin,2011).

The third interviewee exhibits that women have sixth sense which men lack. Women leaders promote better relationships with their employees and stakeholders in general. They develop more collaborative teams. Women make better decision-makers by adding new values and new perspectives. So women can have positive impacts on organizations as a consequence of inclusivity. The explanations of the third interviewee are corresponding to Rizwan et al. (2016) and Moorhead and Griffin (2012) ' interpretations that women leadership improves collaboration and cooperation between team members which boosts competitive advantages. This is also similar to the Kinicki & Williams (2019)'s classification that women are more effective than men in relation to leadership styles.

The fourth interviewee illustrates that women leaders create collaborative teams. Such teams enable to serve all types of stakeholders. This leads to develop long lasting relationships with the present customers and can attract potential ones. Inclusivity then has positive impacts on women leaders who in turn supports efforts for inclusivity. The fourth interviewee agrees with the third interviewee in relation to the abilities of women to the development of cohesive teams (Kinicki and Williams, 2020) . The same interviewee as well supports the comprehension of the third interviewee in relation to the talents of women to advance better relationships with customers and stakeholders as Koku (2022) displays.

The fifth interviewee illustrates that women leaders go by the book which makes them good for certain jobs. Inclusivity as stated above by the fifth interviewee is not an issue to think about. Therefore women as leaders have no different effects than that of men on organizational culture. This interviewee seem to diverge from the understandings of all other interviewees and the literature stated above in relation to inclusion and impacts of women leaders on Organizational culture. The interviewee does not acknowledge the existence of inclusion and hence does not recognise its related impacts on culture.

Women can add values according to the sixth interviewee as a result of inclusivity. Women are multitasks unlike men who are sequential thinkers. Women leaders hence are more effective than men. Women create more different ideas which can be integrated together to enhance motivation,

creativity, innovation and performance. Organizations therefore become more resilient to the environmental changes. The sixth interviewee 's analysis conforms to the Kinicki & Williams (2019) 's elucidations that women are more effective than men. The interviewee as well states women leaders add values to the organisations which enrich innovation, performance and productivity. This is compatible to the findings of McKinsey & Co. Koku (2022)' description of such findings affirming that gender-based teams outperform others.

The majority of interviewees acknowledge the existence of positive impacts of women leadership on Organizational culture which in turn supports such existence. This is to say that there is a reciprocal positive impacts between women leadership and organizational values related to inclusivity. The majority of interviewees state that women are seen to be more effective than men (Moorhead & Griffin, 2011), to build cohesive team with better relationships with stakeholders (Kinicki & Williams, 2020), to be more creative and innovative and to outperform other organisations with no diversity in leadership (Koku, 2022). The fifth interviewee opposes the other interviewees' arguments in relation to impacts of women leaders as reflection of inclusivity on Organizational culture. The same interviewee believes that men and women have equal impacts on cultures of organisations and inclusivity is not a target to seize. This also disagrees with the literature referred to above in the literature review.

CONCLUSION AND SUGGESTED FUTURE RESEARCH

The issues related to diversity, equity and inclusion are relatively contemporary in general. Besides, Studies and researches on such issues are lacked in Bahrain. This research therefore attempts to explore the impacts of gender inclusivity on banking sector in Bahrain. It also explore the effects of gender inclusivity on Organizational culture. The research on hand is based on qualitative methodology due to the lack of research on the issue of gender inclusivity on banking sector in Bahrain. The methodology helps to promote holistic apprehensions about the issues being examined. In-depth research method is employed to collect information. Six Chief Executive Officers contribute to this research. Four questions have been investigated. The first question has strived to scrutinize the definitions of diversity, equity and inclusion. All of the interviewees state that diversity refers to the differences among human resources such as race, gender, age, ethnic groups, religion's marital status and education. Equity according to the interviewees are to treat employees fairly. No interviewee presents concrete definitions for inclusion. Two interviewees state that inclusion is never thought of as a target. This is attributed to the contemporary nature of the issue of inclusivity and the assumption as shown above by literature that diversity, equity and inclusion are used interchangeably. The second question is an endeavor to study the interviewees' perceptions of organizational culture. All interviewees express that organizational culture is made of values underpinning human behaviors in organizations. Cultures, interviewees add, are hard to change. The third question then is concerned with the impacts of diversity, equity and inclusion on culture. Though interviewees present no definition for the term of inclusion, the majority explain that diversity and equity enhance inclusivity in organizations. This leads to promote positive consequences on the cultures of organizations. The last question then explores the impacts of women leadership on organizations as reflections of inclusivity. The last question reveals that women leadership styles have positive impacts on organizational values and cultures which in turn support those leadership styles as reflections of inclusivity values.

SUGGESTED FUTURE RESEARCH

The research on hand illuminates that the issue of inclusivity in organizations are not investigated thoroughly in literature. This is due to the assumptions either concerned to the overlapping meanings or for the interchangeable definitions for the terms diversity, equity and inclusion. Besides, the impacts of women leadership on cultural values as reflections of inclusivity are not studied in the context of Bahrain. Therefore the following are suggested future researches to promote holistic understandings for the issues of organizational cultures, women leadership styles in banking and inclusivity.

- examining in depth the styles of women leadership in banking in Bahrain for the majority of the studies focus on barriers encountering women to reach leadership positions.
- Scrutinizing the definitions of diversity, equity and inclusion held by Chief Executive Officers in other industries besides banking.
- Investigating in depth the effects of the reciprocal relationships between women leadership and organizational inclusivity.
- Replicating the same research by employing quantitative methodology may yield different results and findings.

REFERENCES

Al A'Ali, E. (2020). The Role of Auditing Firms in Promoting Ethical Consumerism. In E. A. Al-A'Ali & M. Masmoudi (Eds.), *Ethical Consumerism and Comparative Studies Across Different Cultures* (pp. 39–52). IGI GLOBAL. doi:10.4018/978-1-7998-0272-3.ch004

Al A'ali, E., & Al-Sarraf, A. R. (2016), Ethical Consumerism: Contextual Issues Of Ethical Decision-making Processes: An Exploratory Study. In Ethical and Social Perspectives on Global Business interaction in Emerging Markets (pp.133-149). IGI Global

Al A'ali, E., & Alazali, R. (2018). Gender Differences in Relation to Organization Sources of Power. In E. Al-A'ali, M.M. Al—Shammari & H. Masri (Eds) Arab Wimen and their Evolving Roles in Global Business Landscape. IGI Global. doi:10.4018/978-1-5225-3710-6.ch001

Al-Alawi, A. I. (2016). Status of Bahraini Women in the Banking and Financial Sector: Challenges and Opportunities. *Journal of International Women's Studies, 17*(4), 210–228. https://vc.bridgew.edu/jiws/Vol17/iss4/15

Cooper, D. R., & Schindler, P. S. (2008). *Business Research Methods* (10th ed.). McGraw Hill.

Denzin, N. K., & Lincoln, T. S. (2011). *The SAGE handbook of Qualitative research*. Sage.

Dewidar, O., Elmestekaway, N., & Welch, V. (2022). Improving equity, diversity, and inclusion in academia in Research Integrity and Peer Review. *2020 International Conference on Data Analytics*.

Ebert, R. J., & Griffin, R. W. (2019) Business essential. New York: Pearson (12ed.)

Gigliotti, R. A., Dwyer, B., & Ruiz-Mesa, K. (2018). Campus Unrest in American Higher Education: Challenges and Opportunities for Strategic Diversity Leadership in J. L. Chin; J. E. Trimble & J. E. Garcia (Eds) Global and Culturally Diverse Leaders and Leadership: New Dimensions and Challenges for Businesses, Education and Society. (pp.211-229), UK: Emerald Publishing Limited

Kinicki, A., & Williams, B. K. (2020). Management (ninth edition). New York: McGraw-Hill Education

Koku, P. S. (2022). *Critical Perspectives on Diversity, Equity, and Incy in Marketing: The case of Business Schools in the United States*. IGI Global. doi:10.4018/9781-1-6684-3590-8-ch008

Moorhead, G., & Griffin, R. S. (2011). *Organizational Behavior* (11th ed.).

Negi, P. S., & Dangwal, R. C. (2021) *Identifying the aspects of organizational culture: a study of Indian banking industry*. Emerald Insights. https://www.emerald.com/insight/2399-1747.htm

Rizan, M.,, Khan, M.,, & Nadeem, B., & Qalb, A. (2016). The Impacts of Workplace Diversity Towards Employee Performance. *Evidence from Banking Sector of Pakistan in American Journal of Matketing Research*, 2(2), 53–60.

Singha, S., & Sivarethinamohan, R. (2022). Social Inclusion, Equity, Leadership, and Diversity to Attain Sustainable Development Goal 5 in the Indian Banking Industry. *Journal of International Women's Studies*, *23*(5), 135–142. http://VC.bridgew.edu/jiwa/vol23/iss5/9

Siri, A., Leone, C., & Bencivenga, R. (2022). Equality, Diversity, and Inclusion Strategies Adopted in European University Alliance to Facilitate the Higher Education-to-Work Transition. *Societies (Basel, Switzerland), 12*(5), 140. doi:10.3390oc12050140

Chapter 3
Leadership Strategies and Tactics for Diversity, Equality, and Inclusion Determinants of Organization Effectiveness

Evgeny Rudnev
Private Institute Moscow Economic Institute, Russia

ABSTRACT

The chapter addresses the issue of diversity and equity at the group and individual levels in an organization and presents a classification of the determinants of organizational effectiveness–trust, choice of strategy for work with personnel, involvement, and work at individual level. Particular attention is paid to issues of involvement and work of management with staff, decision-making, and personnel policy issues that ensure diversity, equality, and inclusion, as well as properties on strategic development of organization.

INTRODUCTION

Organizational studies focused on equality, diversity and inclusion are distinguished by different understandings of who is included in the work process, what diversity is and how equality manifests itself. Nevertheless, researchers agree that the personnel policy of organizations in the 21st century is based on strategic multi-stakeholder collaborations, holistic talent management, change leadership, inclusive knowledge sharing (Mukhuty et al, 2022), an engagement with employees' understandings of organizational culture and their place or otherwise within it, without this employee

DOI: 10.4018/978-1-6684-9013-6.ch003

engagement, many wellintentioned diversity initiatives may go awry, in order to be successful an inclusion strategy needs to embrace both minority and majority perspectives (Cassell et al, 2022). In addition, there is a need to consider specific contexts and conditions, relevance and applicability to their (policy) specific situations, and who will benefit from them (Aguinis et al, 2022). Thus, managing equality, diversity and inclusion is not limited to ethnic or gender characteristics, which requires the development of strategies and tactics for working with personnel and different behavior from leaders of organizations.

Trust for Diversity, Equity, and Inclusion

Trust is a fundamental social characteristic. It determines the quality of management decisions, their successful implementation, eliminates resistance to change. Where trust reigns, people come to work with desire, joy, and show initiative. It all depends on level of trust in organization. What undermines trust? How to raise it? What should managers and employees do to achieve this?

Trust is foundation of happy life for every family. While raising us, parents treat us with trust, but also control our actions. Such an attitude is based on knowledge that the world is full of dangers and surprises. But, nevertheless, children are brought up in openness to the world and people, on which a person's success in life, career, family, and general feeling of satisfaction with life largely depend. A person brought up in trust better understands the reasons for behavior of other people; in a difficult situation, he\she trusts not only himself\herself, intuition, but also people, and this helps to find the most acceptable way to solve, to overcome the situation. A sign of distrust is doubt in actions of others, which causes alienation.

Interpersonal trust is an interactive process in which people learn to establish and maintain trustworthiness under conditions set by organizational (contextual and structural) parameters and directly subject to policies. Trust can only be built when both people are driven by action, the desire to maintain the relationship, and to abandon opportunism. Trust depends on the perception of mutual and respectful treatment with mutual vulnerability turning into stable expectation, that is, norms and values should emphasize these points leading to practical interest in relationship (Six, Sorge, 2008).

In organizations with low level of trust, as a rule, people are isolated from each other, all professional procedures are formal, everyone is for himself, does not express opinion at meetings. In such organizations, nothing is discussed jointly and no collective decisions are made. This organizational culture is not conducive to creativity. And quite another - where the trust of people reigns. When making decisions, managers do not have hidden motives, people will not be deceived in their expectations, and any actions of administrators will not entail any losses, for example, an unfair assessment of work. Whereas, fairness forms a stronger predictor of trust in organizations where HR practices are less developed (Searle et al, 2011). Trust enhances social capital, promotes the development of such values as humor, the ability to speak frankly, to be critical of one's own and activities of colleagues, and to have a right to make mistakes. And most importantly, there is a collective search for ways to improve work, employees show responsibility for overall result, create creative communities to solve complex problems. In an organization with high level of trust, colleagues are not afraid to be critical of decisions they make. One of factors that reduce the level of trust is fear of being punished for one's ideas or actions, which manifests itself in negative reaction of leader. Fear fetters initiative and does not at all evoke a sense of respect for leader, as some believe, but gives rise to depression and oppression. In this state, a person is unlikely to become more energetic and show higher performance. Most likely, he\she will close, will be silent, afraid to shake friendly relations with colleagues, to hurt someone's self-esteem. And other will agree in everything with opinion of administration: "The management can see it!", thereby removing responsibility for results of work. It's easier, no need to think ..." The silence of employees has detrimental consequences. A study of 231 white-collar workers from China found that perceived stress mediated the relationship between employee silence and task performance and deviant behavior. In addition, the trust of colleagues softens the relationship between employees (Dong, Chung, 2021).

Trust satisfies basic human needs - security, belonging to group, self-respect. No one wants to go to work in such team, where they are constantly faced with petty attacks, accusations of incompetence, superiority of others and humiliation. Such working atmosphere causes neither satisfaction, nor positive emotions, nor the desire to be responsible for results of work. And while dynamics of control and trust are unclear to date (Long and Sitkin, 2018), it has been proven that people who engage in (reliable, local) reasoning activities are better at (re)producing institutional trust (Fuglsang, Jagd, 2015). Among the conditions of trust are risk and interdependence, as well as altruism, fairness and reciprocity. Altruistic behavior and cooperation are a mystery to evolutionary biologists. Hamilton (1964) proposed a kinship mechanism called inclusive fitness. A bird wich gives warning about predators increases the chances of not only the survival of relatives, but also own chances of survival. A form of reciprocity suggests that by increasing the survival of others, conspecifics make the survival of warning birds more likely (Fichman, 2003).

At the same time, role of leaders is not unambiguous in different cultures. For example, studies in South Korea show that trust in leaders is especially important for high-performing employees, as they expect to receive high resources - rewards, shares, and opportunities, and may consider leaving organization or withhold knowledge when they lack of confidence in leader. Thus, HR managers need to highlight the critical role of leaders in encouraging high performers to stay and share knowledge (Kim, 2019).

Research in Africa has shown that politics of diversity, equality, and inclusion must be sensitive to relational imperatives (e.g., informality, collectivism, sharing, belonging, and reciprocity) in an ethnically diverse setting. National structures play an important role at macro-national level, while at meso-organizational level, rules are defined by organizational processes, rituals, and routine behaviors strongly associated with core values, meanings, and identities (Umeh et al, 2023).

Research shows that levels of trust are positively associated with cultures with high individualism and long-term orientation, while cultures with high power distance and uncertainty avoidance appear to have a lower pressure on overall levels of trust. Thus, ideal culture for trust to promote effective client-consultant interaction and collaboration includes low power distance, high individualism, low uncertainty avoidance, and high long-term oriented culture (Thanetsunthorn, Wuthisatian, 2020).

However, speaking about differences and connection between culture and trust, one should probably take into account the ethical aspect. To build employee trust in organization, leaders must not only be "moral managers" (for example, infuse organization with ethical principles and hold employees accountable for this), but also be "moral people" (for example, be honest and caring), deal with ethical dilemmas (Xu et al, 2016).

Nicholai Roerich, Russian philosopher, noted: "Trust is so much a feeling that it does not need evidence. One can feel trust in something or someone without ever seeing that deed or that person. In its own circumstances, trust is like persuasiveness. Just as persuasiveness appears as the highest vision, as immutability. It has both faith and consciousness of present reality. The same circumstances are indispensable in formation of trust". The "top-down" view reduces level of trust, does not create an opportunity for developing the skill of a critical attitude towards one's work, for adequate self-esteem, does not leave employee a place for self-development, deprives of right to individuality.

In this process, communication matters - symmetrical or asymmetrical.

Symmetrical communication plays an important role in determining the positive character of benevolence (warmth, empathy and honesty), enterprise (modernity, adventure and courage) and competence (conscientiousness, motivation). Symmetrical internal communication has a positive effect on quality of employees – organization relations. Managers and subordinates engage in dialogue and listen to each other, and information is shared to promote mutual understanding and employee awareness. Leaders respond to employee feedback, value their input, and care about the interests and well-being of employees. It includes two-way interactive channels and tactics, develops a collective organizational culture and organic structures, forms a favorable corporate character, and cultivates the quality of employee-organization relationship. In contrast, asymmetric communication tends to use one-way top-down communication, persuade or control employee behavior to achieve management goals, is associated with a centralized and mechanical organizational structure, and an authoritarian culture where there is little opportunity for workers to make organizational decisions. Organizations with symmetrical communication are willing to respond to the concerns and interests of public by changing themselves, rather than persuading the public to change their attitude and make them behave the way the organizations want. Thus, symmetrical communication promotes understanding, cooperation, responsiveness, and creation of long-term and mutually beneficial relationships. Organizations that advocate symmetrical communication behavior listen to public opinion and keep an eye on the ever-changing business environment (Men et al, 2022).

However, trust and distrust can act both as a substitute for and as a complement to each other through three interrelated dynamics: undermining, stimulating and compensating. Studies of firms working in areas of complex products and systems in Sweden have shown that dynamics evolve and interact recursively through inter-firm interactions within individual projects and in wider network. The interplay of trust and distrust can have both positive and negative effects on pursuit of project-based relationship. For example, faith, rethinking, and recognition, combined with disclosure, trust, and accomplishment, are active processes of trust, and not just passive assessments of trustworthiness - measurements of reliability/insecurity - of partners. In addition, they are different in nature and can coexist in relationships. For example, trust motivated the disclosure of critical information for the successful completion of projects, but at the same time distrust motivated the withholding of confidential information, which was often an important source of competitive advantage.

It is important to distinguish between trust and distrust, as they guide firms in interactions differently. When trusting, organizations interact with optimism about opportunities for interaction, and when they show distrust, they demonstrate vigilance about such opportunities. Trust and distrust can complement each other in some situations and substitute for each other in others, but mostly as a complement to basis of two dynamics. Behavioral mechanisms of trust create conditions conducive to cognitive mechanisms of distrust, and vice versa (activating dynamics). At the same time, the cognitive mechanisms of distrust compensate for shortcomings the behavioral mechanisms of trust, and vice versa (compensating dynamics). Thus, trust and distrust motivate firms not only to use the resources and opportunities present in their current connections, but also to explore hidden connections in network and create more opportunities for future projects with others. In context of inter-firm networks, this means that firms need not only to reflect, but also to adapt to their behavior and actions of their partners, as well as consequences of these actions for firm and others in wider network. This allows other "ways of looking" and questioning self-evident assumptions in midst of action that can constructively address the potential limitations of misplaced trust and unjustified optimism, as well as misplaced distrust and unjustified vigilance (Kostis et al, 2022).

Wage issues tend to generate the most controversy, and if they are not related only to workload, these are always decisions in field of strategic management. Changes in surcharges determine the priorities of organization, direction of its further development. If they do not affect the nature of management strategy, this is perceived by team as indifference to people, leading to cooling of relations, manager's interest in work of individual employees and attention to those for whom the head of organization has more sympathy, access to additional resources of limited circle of workers. This situation dramatically reduces the level of trust in the team. There are groups of individuals. They can be quite conscientious workers who have reason to discuss the unfair actions of management.

It has been found that employee self-efficacy has a positive effect on job satisfaction, task performance and organizational civic behavior, but at the same time increases the employee's desire to leave organization when organizational conditions are unfavorable, for example, in case of low trust in organization. In particular, employees who have high levels of self-confidence may be at higher risk of employee turnover when they are dissatisfied with organization. The motivational value of self-trust is stronger to extent that workers also have high system trust, while low system trust neutralizes the motivational benefits of self-efficacy (Ozyilmaz et al, 2018). The other side of organization and leadership - working with newcomers.

Research on socialization and creativity shows that newcomers who are encouraged by organization to express, rather than repress, their personality and personal characteristics, with strong sense of self-creativity with participation of supervisors and behavior of supervisors that meet need for such workers for self-consistency, with more likely to successfully adapt to new job. Furthermore, self-validation of supervisor's perception of newcomer creativity cannot lead to successful adjustments without reinforcing control behaviors that maintain authenticity, and that such attributes are valued and encouraged within organization. The central role to facilitating creativity among employees who see themselves as capable of generating creative ideas but who also face increased ambiguity in introductory period is the trust of executives who invest in exploiting the creative potential of employees from start of their careers, and creativity positively impacts work-related outcomes, are highly valued by organizations and newcomers alike (Dufour at el, 2020).

In organizations with high level of trust, the formal and informal structures are the same. This is difficult to achieve. Status and position are achieved over the years, which is called labor and sweat, but they are lost very easily. People are sensitive to status differences. In low-hierarchical organizations, a person is valued not so much for status, but for abilities, talent, and contribution to solving the common problems of organization. This creates a special reputation for person. Trust cannot arise only from the fact that someone knows more, has more experience or regalia. Trust is always informal in nature. Conciliation procedures contribute to cultivation of trust.

Honest and trusting relationships, in which the individuality of participants in common cause is manifested, have a psychotherapeutic effect. Being yourself is profitable and very productive. Distrust breeds manipulation, the use of other people to achieve their own goals. This corrodes the organizational fabric, social contacts between people. At the same time, delegation to an employee is more likely if employee trusts management. Employee trust in management allows relationships/ implicit contracts to be established to improve company value by making better use of their knowledge and skills (Meagher, Wait, 2020).

Negative communication experiences are formed as a result of people colliding with each other. One did something, and other was asked to evaluate it without the permission of first, because someone conveyed a negative assessment of his\ her work to management. Such "mediation" saves manager from self-assessment of colleague work and decision-making. In this case, the leader deliberately puts the subordinate in situation of guilty, leaving no chance for justification. In this situation, employees do not feel psychologically protected. This forms a special type of behavior, develops a defensive position.

The processes of restoring trust in an organizational structure are fundamentally different compared to interpersonal contexts. These are sense-making, regulation and formal control, ethical culture, informal control transparency and accountability (Bachmann at el, 2015). In an inter-organizational network after a crisis, trust is achieved by ensuring the coordination of network participants in relation to network goal and clearly articulated responsibilities so that organizations can trust the structures and protocols of network and depend on institutional trust. The strategy for restoring trust that lead organization follows begins by not apologizing for failures. The absence of apologies successfully convinces organizations that future will be better. At the same time, restoring trust is an opportunity for constructive change, and accepting times of crisis is the way to ensure the effectiveness of network (Owen, Currie, 2022).

Research shows that there are three ways to maintain trust - cognitive bridging, emotional embodiment and inclusiveness of acceptance, that is, the demonstration and understanding by members of organization and their ability to mobilize to maintain it, actively manifest and expand, and in destructive contexts - and transforming existing trust practices (Gustafsson et al, 2021).

At the same time, the Fourth Industrial Revolution is changing the focus of interpersonal trust and requires a rethinking of trust models and fundamental changes - (1) what form organizational trust takes, (2) how it is created, and (3) who is to be trusted. This is due to the fact that trust is likely to become more impersonal and systemic, trust between people is increasingly being replaced by trust in a system based on digital technologies, strengthening the production of trust based on institutions will become increasingly important. In addition, despite the movement towards trust, there is a need to trust certain individuals, not interoperability partners, but rather third parties in charge of technological systems and data. New objects of trust are coming to fore - developers providing information flows and data holders, organizations making decisions in the field of software that automate many of processes traditionally performed by people using technology (Lumineau et al, 2023).

However, these processes cannot be associated with discrimination, and choice of employees who receive trust due to such a role depends on national, age, gender characteristics and rather reflects education, professional level, or experience. It is worth recognizing that in this case, IT specialists receive more power, while it is compensated by the ability to negotiate and conclude an agreement with the client by other specialists (Figure 1).

Choice of Strategy for Work With Personnel

One of the reasons for the low effectiveness of leader is that organization has established a certain order of work, which prevents it from achieving its best results. Often it is determined by what strategy of work with personnel the head will choose. This choice depends on ability to understand the behavior of staff, as well as to adjust the motivation system in time. Skills can be taught, but culture fit is harder (Ogbonna, 2019). Let's look at few cases.

Figure 1. Determinants of organization effectiveness

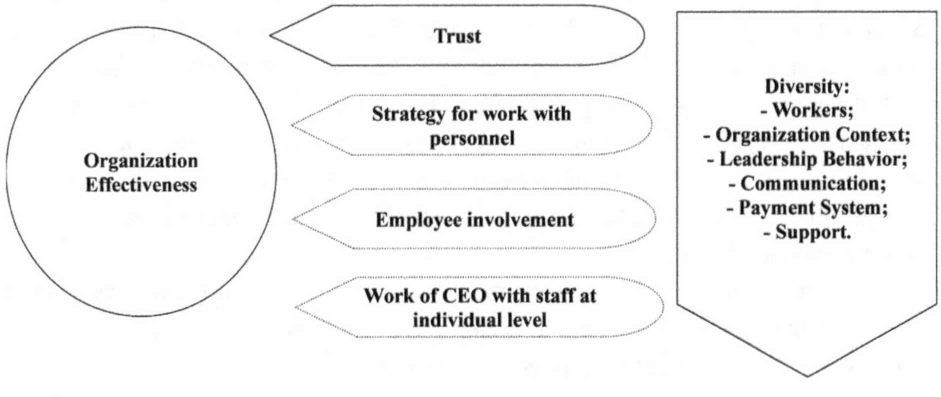

Case 1: Choice of a Pay System

The company formed a friendly team, with whom they started working together. To develop the business, the CEO decided to take a project-based approach, in which groups of employees were formed to work with customer orders. For a while it worked. However, the manager was faced with the fact that at completion of each new project, employees demanded an ever-higher level of payment. Finally, the day came when the CEO could not meet their requests. The number of orders began to fall, the number of people wishing to participate in project groups decreased. The employees who actively supported the CEO at the stage of implementation of idea were no longer enthusiastic.

This case is typical for companies operating in the service sector. Employees quickly get used to increase in wages and begin to take remuneration for granted.

There are two main systems of remuneration: fixed and piecework. The disadvantage of the first is that it requires additional incentives to constantly maintain the motivation of employees. The downside of piecework system is that employees have a feeling of anxiety, uncertainty about the future, a feeling of instability.

If in production organizations the processes and a quantity of product produced are fixed, then work in service companies does not have a clear labor standard, and therefore it is advisable to use a mixed payment system in them. Such a system assumes that employees receive remuneration as the project passes certain stages or achieves its goals. The main advantage of mixed system is a decrease in level of dependence of manager on employees (even if the latter are highly professional and quite interested in work), employees are deprived of opportunity to manipulate the manager.

How is this payment system implemented? First, the manager, when performing work, indicates the total cost of project. Secondly, an additional payment is established for passing the stages of project. Thirdly, in case need to perform additional tasks, hourly wages are indicated in amount, as a rule, corresponding to the average market (depending on type of work). The advantage of this approach is that in this case, employees cease to associate the solution of problems with a constant increase in level of payment. They develop an understanding that the performance of work is clearly tied to result and its quality: in order to get paid, effort and work are needed, while any work is paid, and high-quality work is paid higher. The advantages of this system also include the fact that in work of manager, control becomes more pronounced and objective.

To introduce a mixed wage system is possible after employees have gained experience in project work. The main risk in this case lies in the possible layoffs of workers who are accustomed to fixed pay system.

For personnel who have adopted the new system, not only material incentives become important, but also the opportunity to master new types of work, which requires energy, the development of new skills and abilities. A mixed remuneration system allows to introduce an element of game into work, when getting a result becomes an achievement not only for team, but also for employee, as it helps to gain new professional experience.

Case 2: Working With Creative Employees

The future CEO has long dreamed of opening a beauty salon. First, she graduated from management courses, then began to take lessons from the masters, tracked the novelties on market, and only after that decided to start her own business. She decided to hire masters of different classes. She managed to hire master who had wealth of professional experience, including work in the salons of famous brands. Then three more employees showed up. The first one had little experience, but a rich imagination and desire to find an individual approach to each client. The second received a good education and constantly improved her skills, which indicated the desire for continuous growth. The third, the youngest employee, did not have a higher education. In addition, the CEO has hired an employee who can work with any client and satisfy any request. She had the opportunity to observe how he communicates with clients, as she had previously addressed him herself.

The organization was quite successful, but after a while, employees began to express dissatisfaction with the fact that their contribution to the overall reputation of organization is not the same: some clients come and go, while others create a permanent base.

Personnel management in companies dominated by employees engaged in creative work has its own specifics. It is related to the fact that such employees tend to show individuality and usually want to work on a flexible schedule. Establishing contact within the team may be hindered by seemingly insignificant differences between employees: in education, work experience, and individual characteristics. In this case, for different employees, can set a different order and schedule of work, depending on their personal characteristics and methods of working with clients.

The working hours of the staff must be coordinated in such a way that there is always one of the employees in the salon. It is better when employees are aware of colleague's work specifics and respect the differences between them. For example, an employee earns more because her customers are willing to pay more. Another employee earns by serving clients of different categories with different tastes. The third employee has several clients with special tastes and requirements.

Such differences can be discussed at the workshop, and ideally, they should be fixed in the employment contract. This will reduce tension in relations between employees, avoid mutual reproaches and develop a norm for open discussion of issues.

Case 3: Employees Search for Senior Positions

The general manager has been working at factory as a production manager for more than ten years. If there was need to appoint a new employee to managerial position, he preferred to look for personnel in labor market. However, after the appointment of new chief accountant, as well as middle managers (managers of production processes), some ordinary workers left. As a result, orders began to be regularly fulfilled with violation of deadlines, and some customers preferred to choose another manufacturer.

The reason for the decline in performance, as a result, the loss of customers was due to the fact that CEO hired new employees instead of dismissed managers, not considering specialists working in organization as candidates. He did not take into account the factor of professional growth of staff: there were workers at factory who could potentially take the place of departed manager.

In this case, the leader's action should be to first evaluate possible candidates within organization. The frequent layoffs of employees after departure of middle managers suggests that they may have had ambitions to take a leadership position. The leader of organization should first offer a position to an ordinary specialist (perhaps the latter will need support in form of training) and only if the ordinary employee refuses to resort to an external resource. The frequent failure of employees in such situations should lead to reflection on why people do not want to take on more responsibility. As a rule, the reason is related to manager's management style: the level of involvement in decision-making, encouraging the manifestation of initiative, participation in planning changes.

The advantage of appointing an employee already working in the organization to a vacant position is savings by reducing the cost of adapting a new person to the workplace. In addition, promotion increases the self-esteem of employee, increases his\her responsibility. The leader, by his actions, demonstrates real career opportunities to other employees. If it becomes the norm in an organization to look for middle managers in labor market, then ordinary employees as a whole are less motivated to work. A new line manager may be viewed by subordinates as a careerist who, after some time, will be promoted or take a similar position elsewhere.

There may be two or even three candidates for promotion. In this case, it is advisable to assess which personal characteristics or professional skills of each of them are most significant: the skills of easy communication with subordinates, knowledge of production technologies. In other words, it is necessary to understand what human virtues and how will contribute to business development. When choosing from staff, the likelihood of dismissal of unappointed candidates should also be taken into account. This problem can be avoided if organization has the opportunity to allocate a special area of work to other ordinary employees who have grown professionally (or initiate a new project).

Case 4: Career Prospects for Employees

The CEO organized his own production: he purchased equipment, hired workers, launched processes. Over time, he found that many employees left the organization, and those who remained, in his opinion, did not differ in special responsibility and abilities. The company experienced a staffing shortage. The CEO also hired people who previously worked for the organization and left. However, after working for some time in the same position, such employees left again.

One of the principles of hiring employees is to inform them about career opportunities. Often people can conclude about career prospects in company only after they have already entered into an employment relationship. As a rule, they discover restrictions for promotion.

However, moving up the career ladder can be a motivating factor. This factor is used by European companies: when hiring an employee, they talk about the content of work and level of payment, and also inform about conditions under which the payment can be higher. This approach is reminiscent of surviving system of discharges from Soviet Union system. Its disadvantages include the fact that employee himself must initiate the issue of his professional development and promotion is primarily associated with material gain. In addition, novice specialists, as a rule, have little idea of the differences between work of varying complexity. In this case, the manager is required to understand the features of production processes: which operations are more labor-intensive, which stage requires more payment, what causes differences in level of payment.

How does this approach keep the human motivated? First, the employee sees that can professionally grow and develop. Secondly, after receiving information about career prospects, can evaluate them and make an independent decision about professional development. Thirdly, the employee has a better idea of future.

Depending on the specifics of organization's activities, it is advisable to determine the possible trajectory of employees' career development: horizontal or vertical. In manufacturing organization, one of the options for career growth can be a horizontal trajectory, during which an employee masters the three main stages of production, after which moves along a vertical trajectory and takes up managerial position.

Thus, using this approach, can reduce staff turnover, organize work better and increase the level of trust in team.

Case 5: Interaction With New and Old Employees

The CEO, who has a diploma from a prestigious university and twenty years of management experience, took more than one year to start making a profit in his business. However, after some time he found that the level of profit is not as high as a few years ago. The CEO decided to invest in the development of company. People who came to organization quit. At first, the manager explained this by the incompetence of new employees. However, when the number of people hired and fired on their own initiative increased, he began to ask employees why they left and received approximately the same answer: "There is no field for activity - you have a lot of good employees!".

This case is typical for mature organizations in which a certain order of work has developed, and business is consistently profitable. This situation is dangerous because no changes are taking place in company: old employees, satisfied with the existing state of affairs, do not allow newcomers to make decisions. Typically, this is because the backbone of organization is a group of people who have proven loyalty to company, received promotions and recognition, and the leader feels comfortable around them. A negative signal may be some economic loss due to loss of competitiveness of a product or service. Employees who cannot fit into the team pose a threat to existing system of distribution of resources or power.

What management tactics can be applied in this case? It is necessary to make it clear to honored employees that the company is interested in their work, but is in need of changes. At the same time, it is necessary to involve new employees in solving problems, give them the opportunity to prove themselves and pay them additionally. At the same time, new and old employees should not feel the difference in the requirements and system of remuneration, which will avoid tension and favoritism in professional relations.

At the same time, new and old employees should not feel the difference in the requirements and system of remuneration, which will avoid tension and favoritism in professional relations. To do this, it is necessary to introduce the system of benefits and compensations for employees who have proven loyalty to organization. This can be, for example, an additional increase in unpaid vacation days for each year worked, free trip abroad without production purposes after five to seven years of work at expense of enterprise, payment for training or participation in prestigious seminar, payment for dental clinic services after three years of work in organization.

In this case, it is advisable to amend the collective agreement. All of these measures will allow new employees to join the organization, and deserved ones will be motivated to achieve new goals.

Employee Involvement and Organizational Effectiveness

Involvement has different aspects. By itself, the inclusion of workers in processes does not guarantee high productivity. However, knowledge of some patterns of leader's behavior in organization and support processes can improve organizational efficiency. What factors should a manager consider when considering engagement as a tool to improve organizational effectiveness?

In 2011, Harvard University professor Michael Norton, Duke University professor of economic behavior Dan Ariely, and University of California marketing researcher Daniel Mouchon published "The "IKEA Effect": When Labor Leads to Love". Their work draws interesting conclusions about how people feel about what they do, and what effect this has on the perception of results of their work. The article emphasizes that there is a lot of research indicating that work is directly related to well-being, with a sense of satisfaction from its results - important for many people. For example, people deprived of opportunity to work not only suffer economic losses, but also experience negative psychological consequences. The researchers suggested that work leads to formation of love, if it is successful. The basis of experiment was the ability to successfully produce in their environment the desired results, with help of which people achieved the goal by managing objects and property. The researchers suggested that work leads to the formation of love, if it is successful. The basis of experiment was the ability to successfully produce in their environment the desired results, with help of which people achieved the goal by managing objects and property. According to the researchers, only when people successfully complete labor-intensive tasks do, they value labor more highly. To test the hypothesis, three experiments were proposed to determine success. In first case, an assessment was made of what people had done. In second, in comparison with similar work of other people, it was proposed to lend products of their labor. In third, an assessment was carried out if the product was destroyed or not produced in proper form to end. As part of these experiments, participants built with IKEA boxes, folded origami, and created some objects using Lego. In first experiment, it turned out that participants who collect utility products value them more than identical products collected by other people. The second experiment showed that people are willing to pay more or invest more in what they have made themselves than in products made by others. In third experiment, when the product was assembled and then taken apart, or people were not able to complete the assembly process, it was found that their assessment of their work did not increase.

Various hypotheses arose during the experiment, for example, it was assumed that the state in which participants created their creations increased their sense of ownership, and that the value of their product was increased by physical contact with it, this increased appreciation. However, this hypothesis was refuted in third experiment, as people showed a steady decrease in motivation to do work in event of product failure. Another indirect hypothesis was that the rating went up due to customer satisfaction with a well-executed product.

Additional research has shown that the desire to pay more for manufactured product and show it to other people is most likely associated with the degree of its social utility. Thus, when people fill products with their own labor, their efforts increase the value of this work in their own eyes, at the same time, a poorly executed product alone can lead to overvaluation of labor. This phenomenon was called the IKEA effect by the authors after Swedish furniture manufacturer, the production or assembly of which requires collective participation.

The identification of IKEA effect shows that involvement of personnel in labor process, its completeness and social usefulness are significant factors that increase productivity, motivation and profit of company as a whole.

In a real working environment, when it would seem that everyone is busy and involved in work process, it is difficult to understand how realistically the company's employees are included in work. There are several signs of engagement problems that can be detected by observing employee behavior.

- Non-compliance with work schedule - employees come late and leave work earlier.
- Shifting responsibility to each other - "these are not my duties", "this is not my business", "this is not part of my job competencies."
- Periodic handover of well-known tasks to people with managerial authority: ordinary employees cannot understand who to turn to solve a standard, previously performed task by themselves or to agree on program of action. Only the appearance of work is created, the profit company receives due to self-control, enthusiasm and self-control of individuals dedicated to work.
- The reaction of manager or employees with experience to appeal of newcomers or ordinary employees: "Wait, I'm busy now." If repeated repeatedly, this indicates poorly established communications or, in general, an attitude towards taking the initiative, creating barriers to communication. Thus, energy can be lost, possible solutions of a better order or way of doing work.
- Setting different tasks for different performers: everyone moves in his\her own direction, although outwardly everyone is involved in work. The management

is overloaded with work, but at the same time the process of collective action is not formed, it is not generally determined who, how and what does.

- One-sided assessment of content and results of work by the head - it is not customary to give a general assessment of work done by employees.

Richard Goodman, Consultant and Director of Global Graphic Arts Research at The Technical Assn. of Graphic Arts emphasizes the importance of building people's sense of respect for organizational needs and process change based on an inspiring challenge. For example, leadership is more effective when it supports employees who think like the customer—their needs and interests—and act like the owner—committed to mission of organization and its values. In this regard, leaders and managers, in order to achieve this behavior, it is advisable to allow employees to consider the problem or ask questions when something seems wrong to them (Goodman, 2005, 36).

In literature, an individual's involvement is associated with level of psychological identification with specific content of work in which he or she is engaged or absorbed (Kanungo, 1982a). Participation in work has positive organizational consequences affecting the degree to which an individual maintains organizational goals and thereby increases productivity and efficiency (Brown, 1996). However, empirically this phenomenon, as emphasized in one of latest studies (Zhang. 2014, 165), has been little studied. A study conducted in Taiwan in 2005 among medical personnel showed that a significant influence on level of "organizational citizenship" (commitment to values, mission of organization) is influenced by support of leader and the role of judge in performance of work. Interesting insights about engagement come from a very different kind of activity: policing. According to research results, the participation of citizens in law enforcement increases the efficiency of police work, enhances security and level of crimes detection (Gultekin, 2009, 175). At the same time, Morisson (1994) found evidence for gender differences. In particular, women are more likely to perceive role behavior, which suggests that they better internalize social expectations and perceive common work, helping behavior within workplace, facilitating the solution of issues or problems in process of work, supporting others in achieving a common goal. although they do not differ from men in performance rankings (Lovell et al (1999). In another study (Zhang, 2014) conducted on a Chinese sample, coping and helping behaviors are associated with altruism, kindness, and lack of complaining over trifles, which are more characteristic of "sports behavior" aimed at achievement, the absorption of a person by goal, which turned out to be more pronounced in men than in women. In particular, it is indicated that interested people tend to complain less. Zhang's research found that men who are actively involved in work exhibit these behaviors more than women.

Sharif and Skandura (2014) pay attention to ethical factor, in particular they say that leadership with unethical behavior can lead to negative attitudes of employees, in which case the involvement is significantly reduced. The transparency of leadership in process of change confirms the ethical nature of leader. Employees trust leader in the future if they participate in organizational change, for example, by actively discussing the change with management (Morgan, Zeffane, 2003). An earlier study (Noble, 2000) showed the relationship of financial results with reliance on resource of teams, and involvement acts as a resource of control. It is emphasized that, firstly, the formation of team creates a financial incentive to work together in order to strengthen performance and receive bonuses. Second, the team has an incentive to identify and punish members or employees in workplace who do not cooperate for benefit of the group. Therefore, the practice of employee participation in labor processes - discussing changes, setting standards of behavior, taking collective action, in combination with group financial plans, determines higher productivity than when attracting employees only on the basis of compensation incentives. In addition, an organization emphasizing a group organizational culture should see greater transfer of tacit knowledge between employees necessary for effective job performance, and facilitate access to networks that enable greater information and knowledge sharing between employees, which serves as an important component of organization social capital and improves overall performance (Mohr et al, 2012). At the same time, in order to create a set of shared values and beliefs, practices must be adopted in firms to encourage employees to be passionate about learning, open to innovation, trust, collaboration, and willingness to share their knowledge with each other. These methods include, for example, organizing a community of practice, sharing knowledge during meetings, motivating learning and preparation through examinations, building trust through teamwork, and encouraging a high tolerance for unexpected outcomes of innovative ideas (Liu et al, 2021).

Change creates difficult and unpopular decisions that leaders must implement. However, employees who believe that their manager is acting correctly from a moral point of view are more likely to respond positively to decisions made and results obtained. Ethical leaders demonstrate consistency and act as role models, rewarding ethical behavior and punishing unethical behavior (Brown et al., 2005). Consequently, employees may feel more job-satisfied, more likely to adopt organizational citizenship, and perform their duties well (Sharif, Scandura, 2014, 186). Ethical leadership reduces the level of uncertainty during a period of change, which allows employees to feel more secure. In this case, leaders act as consultants for employees, explaining how work is organized. Furst and Cable (2008) noted that employees who play an active role in organizational change efforts tend to have positive feelings towards change. Leaders who encourage employees to provide help or suggestions in process of change typically reap the benefits of high employee commitment to task and perceptions of leadership effectiveness (Higgins et al, 2003; Yukl, Tracey, 1992).

Sharif and Skandura (2014) have proven that ethical leadership is a strong indicator of organizational commitment and performance, and is even more important in the context of change. For employees experiencing change, ethical leadership was more associated with performance outcomes compared to employees not involved in change. This suggests that in change, employees are more likely to be organizationally committed when they feel that their leader is making ethical choices and acting as an ethical role model. In addition, they are more likely to improve their performance. This may be due to an increase in trust in a fair and ethical leader. Ethical leadership also provides stability for employees who struggle with changes in organizations. Ethical leaders can instill a positive attitude towards work in subordinates. Thus, leaders who actively involve subordinates in organizational process are more likely to benefit from increased participation of subordinates in change.

Low involvement leads to alienation of employees from the organization, loss of profit, decrease in motivation and quality of work. There are several ways to solve this problem.

First way. Discussing the real problems of the company with organizers of work and key performers and developing solutions. Problems such as falling profits, developing a network or divisions in another region, improving the quality of service in order to obtain new competitive advantages and company income can be discussed. It is necessary to invite employees of different departments for joint discussion - marketers, HR specialists, key deputies, representatives of personnel reserve, accountant or commercial director, and ordinary employees. It is known that decisions that are made without their direct executors are not perceived and do not become a value, i.e. are not fulfilled. When making decisions, top managers may find individual ideas more attractive and resourceful, while members of organization may see the solution to problem differently. In this connection, there will be resistance to decision taken or even cause its failure. Therefore, when making decisions and their further implementation, it is advisable to provide an opportunity to put forward ideas with participation of direct executors and evaluate them jointly. What ideas are more interesting, non-standard, attractive, and therefore will allow organization to gain competitive advantages? Which are best resourced (financial, human, informational, legal, etc.)? (Monjaro method) The most attractive ideas are those that receive a high total score for both attractiveness and resourcefulness. The most dubious ideas are those that have high appeal but low resource endowment and vice versa. The second most valuable idea is rated as having high attractiveness but medium resource endowment or high resource endowment but medium attractiveness. All other ideas are also dubious. This procedure helps to release the energy of staff. Sometimes people working in other departments can express quite productive ideas and see solutions that other employees do not find, but which are not accepted by company leaders, since development of such solutions is outside the scope of these employees' job responsibilities. Sometimes people working in other departments can express quite productive ideas and see solutions that other employees do not find, but which are not accepted by company leaders, since development of such solutions is outside the scope of these employees' job responsibilities. It is known that by nature each of us is given several roles or various abilities that are waiting in e wings for disclosure and development. Thus, the involvement of people in affairs of company is enhanced, skills and abilities are developed to understand the essence of problem, to find and put into practice solutions developed jointly. However, there are employees in company who do not want to work in team. It is advisable for such people to formulate separate tasks or offer them other ways of doing work, for example, remote work, which is acceptable in creative professions while maintaining the value of work and level of payment.

Second way. Evaluation of line managers work by ordinary employees. To do this, need to ask personnel service employees to develop a simple questionnaire that will allow to find out how line managers react to questions from ordinary employees about labor safety, rest rights, initiatives to improve processes, if an ordinary employee sees a solution option (less actions and costs for more productive work), timeliness of payments and additional remuneration, promotion. Managers who are interested in doing quality work are also interested in improving processes to better achieve organizational goals.

Third way. Development of product or service with approbation on employees of organization and potential consumers from different social groups, comparison and analysis of these estimates. Of course, in this case are not talking about clinical trials of medicines that require other methods of testing and distribution. This method can be implemented by applying the method of expert assessments, discarding the lowest and highest results. Evaluation of product by an indirect consumer can provide more critical view of whether a product is needed or not. For example, software product for training leaders in leadership can be evaluated by ordinary employees of organizations, and new food and hygiene products for children can be evaluated by students, future parents. Indirect consumers can contribute to dissemination of information about product (service) being developed or already provided by company through informal communication channels.

Fourth way. Joint analysis of work done by line manager and executor, providing an opportunity to analyze the work performed by employee, designing the work to be done in future. In this case, manager can listen and ask questions: what and how can you change in the work, process in order to improve the result? In other words, can help the subordinate recognize mistakes and plan future behavior, and then give a positive assessment. As a result, the self-esteem and motivation of employee increases, professional development takes place in workplace, and responsibility for work increases. The manager is in control of situation. The company develops due to ideas that arise from employee, contributes to embodiment of their talents.

- Let's look at several reasons for decline in engagement and organizational effectiveness.
- Violation of general rules of discussion, inability to listen and speak, pause in communication, encourage the expression of ideas, ways to solve the problem, fix it in writing, pay attention, bring the work started to end.
- Endless rewriting of rules, when employees do not have time to learn the accepted procedure, and therefore, to receive an adequate assessment of work. In addition, in this case it is not clear how a career is built in an organization.
- Take an initiative or a new idea and punish it if it fails. In this case, it is advisable for management to coordinate key actions with leader of initiative and provide intermediate control and support from management.
- The use of paternalistic management model, where manager knows more about personal lives of employees and encourages them to speak out about it, rather than being interested in their opinion about work and its performance.
- Insufficient assessment of labor: contribution to organization's activities in orm of ideas and their implementation is not supported financially, employees get the feeling that they are being exploited, and, as a result, feeling of emptiness and injustice. The inability to give a qualitative assessment, emphasizing the merits of proposals, behavior, teamwork in an informal conversation, to see the differences in contribution to common cause from different employees and to emphasize publicly the value of such differences.
- The inconsistency of material and non-material incentives: one - gratitude, the other - bonuses.
- Changes in composition of participants when discussing ideas, making and implementing decisions, as a result, the perception by employees of new procedure temporality, as a result of which decisions are made on incomprehensible grounds, staff does not know what behavior is welcome, promotes career growth, and what can lead to dismissal.

The involvement of personnel in labor processes is facilitated by working with personnel at the individual level. **(Table 1)**

The Work of CEO With Staff at Individual Level

T.Washington argued: "There is hardly a more effective way to help an person than to lay responsibility on him, thereby showing confidence." A person "burns" or not

Table 1. Diversity, equality and inclusion and organizational effectiveness

Typology of workers	Type of support	Actions of CEO
High level of enthusiasm Low level of professionalism	Directive	Analysis of professional experience, career planning
Low level of enthusiasm High level of professionalism	Motivational	Belief
High level of enthusiasm High level of professionalism	Directive Motivational	Interest in the future, soft assistance in building a career, conditions creating for the transfer of experience
Low level of enthusiasm Low level of professionalism	Directive Motivational	Evidence based dialogue on performance, change of career trajectory in the organization

can be understood by how responsibly he\she approaches the work. At the same time, I understand responsibility as a combination of enthusiasm and professionalism. Enthusiasm is manifested in desire to do something, and professionalism in possession of necessary methods of action to perform a certain job. Whether employees show responsibility or not, whether they become productive or not, depends on how enthusiastic and professional they are. An employee may have high level of enthusiasm but low level of professionalism, or vice versa. An employee can work in an organization both with high level of professionalism and with high level of enthusiasm. In order for responsibility on part of employee to be maximum, general director will also have to work. This job is to provide support. Only when the manager is able to provide support adequate to levels of professionalism and enthusiasm, many sparks in organization will become an unquenchable flame, and the tasks facing it will be solved much faster and more efficiently.

There are two types of support - motivational and directive.

Motivational support is needed when an employee has low level of enthusiasm. Such workers seem disinterested and apathetic. They need it to help them decide to devote themselves to achieving their own goals. This type of support is probabilistic in nature. It is important for leader to understand that what motivates and stimulates one person to work does not motivate another. Thus, more complex level of tasks performed may motivate employees with high level of aspirations and achievements and not affect the increase in motivation in person with low level. Motivational support also consists in identifying the needs of employees and creating conditions for their satisfaction. Directive support is needed when an employee shows strong desire to succeed, and has set goal, but does not know how to competently achieve it. He\she makes efforts, but does not get results. Workers who need directive support tend to experience frustration due to their lack of skills in setting goals and determining how to achieve them. Often this type of support is needed by ambitious but not yet professionally mature employees. It lies in the fact that a person is helped to build professional career - they clarify his\her plans and "draw" the immediate prospects. The main thing for him\her is to answer the questions "what is my goal and what needs to be done to achieve it?". Thus, person with low level of enthusiasm and low level of professionalism needs both motivational and directive support. I would talk to such an employee and ask: does he\she like his\her work? He\she asked if he\she would like to change something in it. I would also ask other questions: how would you feel if you successfully achieved the goals set for you? What are your immediate plans regarding work? What do you plan to take as the first, second and subsequent steps?

When person is productive enough, it is better not to interfere with his\her professional activities, so as not to reduce motivation. A move that can be taken in cooperation with such an employee is professional curiosity: will you surprise us with something else in the near future, if so, with what? To emphasize the significance and success of work with such an employee, can invite he\she to describe an experience in form of article and contribute to publication in journals. Can also involve he\she in improving the skills of colleagues both in organization and for other companies. In the case when the employee is all right with professionalism, but low level of enthusiasm, persuasion should be applied. Perhaps employee will feel that he\she is not alone and that management is interested in his\her activity. Another option - employee is motivated, but level of his\her professionalism needs to be increased, and therefore directive support is required. Its absence can lead to the fact that ambitions will increase, and level of development of action methods are necessary for job performing for leadership position, remain at same level. This is fraught with numerous conflicts, from which everyone will lose: both employee and management. I would analyze together with such an employee his\her managerial experience. He\she noted what worked and what sees as a secret of success, and what failed and why. I would wonder what this employee would do if he\she had similar situations again.

Without supportive leadership, it is extremely difficult to establish a culture of innovation that can lead to product innovation (Park et al, 2021).

CONCLUSION

In this way, choosing HR strategy and cultivating talent can not only help promote equality, diversity and inclusion for employees and leaders of organizations, but also achieve goals, increase productivity and employee satisfaction, and take the business to new level of development.

The leader's behavior determines involvement of people in processes, content of work and effects of changes in organization. Removal of responsibility, multidirectional action, ignoring the initiative, one-sided assessment of content and results of work indicate a decrease in level of personnel involvement, and, consequently, the effectiveness of organization. Ethical behavior and symmetrical communication contribute to more positive perception of change on part of employees. To solve strategic problems, collective methods of making and evaluating the implementation of decisions, analyzing the results of work by a line manager and designing the future together with an employee can be used, and involving employees in assessing the behavior of management and consumers can affect the effectiveness of organization. Lack of communication skills, frequent changes in norms and rules, ambivalent and paternalistic behavior of leaders, unbalanced assessment and encouragement, ambiguity in the norms of behavior leading to career growth, entail a decrease in staff involvement. Showing interest and building trust at both the personal and organizational levels helps to maintain the effectiveness of the organization both in working with high-performing employees and creative newcomers, and the work of the leader with employees at the personal level enhances equality, diversity and inclusion.

REFERENCES

Aguinis, H., Jensen, S. H., & Kraus, S. (2022). Policy Implications of Organizational Behavior and Human Resource Management Research. *The Academy of Management Perspectives, 36*(3), 857–878. doi:10.5465/amp.2020.0093

Bachmann, R., Gillespie, N., & Priem, R. (2015). Repairing Trust in Organizations and Institutions: Toward a Conceptual Framework. *Organization Studies, 36*(9), 1123–1142. doi:10.1177/0170840615599334

Brown, M. E., Treviño, L. K., & Harrison, D. A. (2005). Ethical leadership: A social learning perspective for construct development and testing. *Organizational Behavior and Human Decision Processes, 97*(2), 117–134. doi:10.1016/j.obhdp.2005.03.002

Brown, S. P. (1996). A meta-analysis and review of organizational research on job involvement. *Psychological Bulletin, 120*(2), 235–255. doi:10.1037/0033-2909.120.2.235

Cassell, C., Watson, K., Ford, J., & Kele, J. (2022). Understanding inclusion in the retail industry: Incorporating the majority perspective. *Personnel Review, 51*(1), 230–250. doi:10.1108/PR-02-2020-0083

Dong, X. T., & Chung, Y. W. (2021). The Mediating Effect of Perceived Stress and Moderating Effect of Trust for the Relationship Between Employee Silence and Behavioral Outcomes. *Psychological Reports*, *124*(4), 1715–1737. doi:10.1177/0033294120942914 PMID:32674670

Dufour, L., Maoret, M., & Montani, F. (2020). Coupling High Self-Perceived Creativity and Successful Newcomer Adjustment in Organizations: The Role of Supervisor Trust and Support for Authentic Self-Expression. *Journal of Management Studies*, *57*(8), 8. doi:10.1111/joms.12547

Fichman, M. (2003). Straining towards trust: Some constraints on studying trust in organizations. *Journal of Organizational Behavior*, *24*(2), 133–157. doi:10.1002/job.189

Fuglsang, L., & Jagd, S. (2015). Making sense of institutional trust in organizations: Bridging institutional context and trust. *Organization*, *22*(1), 23–39. doi:10.1177/1350508413496577

Furst, S. A., & Cable, D. M. (2008). Employee resistance to organizational change: Managerial influence tactics and leadermember exchange. *The Journal of Applied Psychology*, *93*(2), 453–462. doi:10.1037/0021-9010.93.2.453 PMID:18361644

Goodman, R. (2005). Risks in process control. Graphic Arts Monthly. *Arts & Humani-ties*, *77*(8), 32–36.

Gultekin, S. (2009). Citizen Involvement and Law Enforcement: Does Oproduction Affect Organizational Efficiency and Organizational Effectiveness? Dissertation Doctor of Philosophy, University of North Texas, Denton.

Gustafsson, S., Gillespie, N., Searle, R., Hope Hailey, V., & Dietz, G. (2021). Preserving Organizational Trust During Disruption. *Organization Studies*, *42*(9), 1409–1433. doi:10.1177/0170840620912705

Higgins, C., Judge, T. A., & Ferris, G. R. (2003). Influence tactics and work outcomes: A meta-analysis. *Journal of Organizational Behavior*, *24*(1), 89–106. doi:10.1002/job.181

Kanungo, R. (1982a). Measurement of job and work involvement. *The Journal of Applied Psychology*, *67*(3), 341–349. doi:10.1037/0021-9010.67.3.341

Kim, S. L. (2019). Enticing high performers to stay and share their knowledge: The im-portance of trust in leader. *Human Resource Management*, *58*(4), 341–351. doi:10.1002/hrm.21955

Kostis, A., Bengtsson, M., & Näsholm, M. H. (2022). Mechanisms and Dynamics in the Interplay of Trust and Distrust: Insights from project-based collaboration. *Organization Studies*, *43*(8), 1173–1196. doi:10.1177/01708406211040215

Liu, G., Tsui, E., & Kianto, A. (2021). Knowledge-friendly organizational culture and performance: A meta-analysis. *Journal of Business Research*, *134*, 738–753. doi:10.1016/j.jbusres.2021.05.048

Long, C. P., & Sitkin, S. B. (2018). Control-trust dynamics in organizations: Identifying shared perspectives and charting conceptual fault lines. *The Academy of Management Annals*, *12*(2), 725–751. doi:10.5465/annals.2016.0055

Lovell, S. E., Kahn, A. S., Anton, J., Davidson, A., Dowling, E., Post, D., & Mason, C. (1999). Does gender affect the link between organizational citizenship behavior and performance evaluation? *Sex Roles*, *41*(5–6), 469–478. doi:10.1023/A:1018883018719

Lumineau, F., Schilke, O., & Wang, W. (2023). Organizational Trust in the Age of the Fourth Industrial Revolution: Shifts in the Form, Production, and Targets of Trust. *Journal of Management Inquiry*, *32*(1), 21–34. doi:10.1177/10564926221127852

Meagher, K. J., & Wait, A. (2020). Worker Trust in Management and Delegation in Organizations. *Journal of Law Economics and Organization*, *36*(3), 495–536. Advance online publication. doi:10.1093/jleo/ewaa008

Men, L. R., & Sung, Y. (2022). Shaping Corporate Character Through Symmetrical Communication: The Effects on Employee-Organization Relationships. *International Journal of Business Communication*, *59*(3), 427–449. doi:10.1177/2329488418824989

Mohr, D. C., Young, G. J., & Burgess, J. F. Jr. (2012). Employee turnover and operational performance: The moderating effect of group-oriented organizational culture. *Human Resource Management Journal*, *22*(2), 216–233. doi:10.1111/j.1748-8583.2010.00159.x

Morgan, D. E., & Zeffane, R. (2003). Employee involvement, organizational change and trust in management. *International Journal of Human Resource Management*, *14*(1), 55–75. doi:10.1080/09585190210158510

Morrison, E. W. (1994). Role definitions and organizational citizenship behavior: The importance of the employee's perspective. *Academy of Management Journal*, *37*(6), 1543–1567. doi:10.2307/256798

Mukhuty, S., Upadhyay, A., & Rothwell, H. (2022). Strategic sustainable development of Industry 4.0 through the lens of social responsibility: The role of human resource practices. *Business Strategy and the Environment, 31*(5), 1–14. doi:10.1002/bse.3008

Noble, D. S. (2000). Human Resource Management Strategy: The Dual Pursuit of Employee Involvement and Workforce Adaptability. Dissertation Doctor of Philosophy, Wayne State University, Detroit.

Norton, M. I., Mochon, D., & Ariely, D. The «IKEA Effect»: When Labor Leads to Love. — https://www.hbs.edu/faculty/Publication%20Files/11-091.pdf

Ogbonna, E. (2019). The uneasy alliance of organizational culture and equal opportunities for ethnic minority groups: A British example. *Human Resource Management Journal, 29*(3), 309–327. doi:10.1111/1748-8583.12227

Owen, G., & Currie, G. (2022). Beyond the Crisis: Trust repair in an interorganizational network. *Organization Studies, 43*(8), 1273–1295. doi:10.1177/01708406211031732

Ozyilmaz, A., Erdogan, B., & Karaeminogullari, A. (2018). Trust in organization as a moderator of the relationship between self-efficacy and workplace outcomes: A social cognitive theory-based examination. *Journal of Occupational and Organizational Psychology, 91*(1), 181–204. doi:10.1111/joop.12189

Park, N., Cho, M., & Lee, J. W. (2021). Building a culture of innovation: How do agency leadership and management systems promote innovative activities within the government? *Australian Journal of Public Administration, 80*(3), 453–473. doi:10.1111/1467-8500.12474

Searle, R., Den Hartog, D. N., Weibel, A., Gillespie, N., Six, F., Hatzakis, T., & Skinner, D. (2011). Trust in the employer: The role of high-involvement work practices and procedural justice in European organizations. *International Journal of Human Resource Management, 22*(5), 1069–1092. doi:10.1080/09585192.2011.556782

Sharif, M. M., & Scandura, T. A. (2014). Do Perceptions of Ethical Conduct Matter During Organizational Change? Ethical Leadership and Employee Involvement. *Journal of Business Ethics, 124*(2), 185–196. doi:10.100710551-013-1869-x

Six F., & Sorge A. (2008) Creating a High-Trust Organization: An Exploration into Organizational Policies that Stimulate Interpersonal Trust Building. *Journal of Management Studies 45*(5). doi:. 00763.x doi:10.1111/j.1467-6486.2007

Thanetsunthorn, N., & Wuthisatian, R. (2020). Trust and culture: Applications for organization development. *Organization Development Journal, 38*(1), 33–43.

Umeh, C., Cornelius, N., & Wallace, J. (2023). Exploring equality, diversity, and inclusion in multiethnic settings: A context-sensitive approach. *Human Resource Management Journal*, *33*(1), 148–169. doi:10.1111/1748-8583.12441

Xu, A. J., Loi, R., & Ngo, H. (2016). Ethical Leadership Behavior and Employee Justice Perceptions: The Mediating Role of Trust in Organization. *Journal of Business Ethics*, *134*(3), 493–504. doi:10.100710551-014-2457-4

Yukl, G., & Tracey, J. B. (1992). Consequences of influence tactics used with subordinates' peers, and the boss. *The Journal of Applied Psychology*, *77*(4), 525–535. doi:10.1037/0021-9010.77.4.525

Zhang, S. (2014). Impact of Job Involvement on Organizational Citizenship Behaviors in China. *Journal of Business Ethics*, *120*(2), 165–174. doi:10.100710551-013-1654-x

Chapter 4
Diversity in the Banking Sector:
Impacts on Women's Leadership Styles

Ebtihaj Ahmed Al-Aali
University of Bahrain, Bahrain

Meryem Masmoudi
Applied Science University, Bahrain

Saleh Hussain
Saleh Hussain Consultancy, Bahrain

ABSTRACT

Previous studies on women leadership in Bahrain focus on situational factors. The earlier studies have attempted to analyze factors either enhancing or impeding women occupying leadership positions . This research, however, is an endeavor to examine styles of leadership followed by women in banking industry in Bahrain. The leadership styles of women are explored in the light of the present organizational contexts which are shaped by the contemporary employment issues of diversity, equity, and inclusion. Strategies developed to cope up with the requirements of diversity implementation and improvement are studied as well. The research is based on qualitative methodology. In-depth interview is the research method used to collect information from six CEOs in banking industry in Bahrain.

INTRODUCTION

The presentation of women in leadership positions in banking sector are still behind in comparison to that of men in the developing world as researches indicate. This

DOI: 10.4018/978-1-6684-9013-6.ch004

highlights the importance of organizational strategies, procedures and actions concerning gender diversity, equity and inclusion. The focus of this research is to examine the issue of women in leadership positions as a reflection of gender diversity in banking sector in Bahrain. The impacts of gender diversity on women leadership styles is examined. Strategic tools, methods and procedures to enhance the positions of women in leadership positions are explored as well. The research on hand comprises of seven sections. The definitions of diversity, equity and inclusion are discussed in section two. Section three examines the literature review concerning leadership and on women leadership styles. Section four explores the situation of women leadership in banking sector in Bahrain. The elaboration on strategies, procedures and actions to promote and to enhance women leadership in banking sector are scrutinized in section five. Methodology and analysis of information collected are probed in section six. The last section then illustrates the conclusions and suggested future research.

DEFINITIONS OF DIVERSITY, EQUITY, AND INCLUSION

Kinicki & Williams (2020), Vaughn in Relias (2022), Moorhead and Griffin (2011) and Rizwan et al. (2016) define diversity in term of sexual orientation, special needs groups, religion, ethnicity, gender, age and race. Diversity affects individuals' behaviours and in turn their interactions, perceptions and performances. Moorhead and Griffin add that diverse work force was attempting to integrate with the the cultures and norms of the majority. This was hard to accomplish. Melting different cultures in one unified is realised to be un realistic goal . Now days, according to Moorhead & Griffin, organizations cherish differences and welcome various perceptions, ideas and views. Kinicki and Williams (2020) explain that different affirmative acts related to diversity issues have instigated changes in organisations and institutions. Factors related to diversity, according to Kinicki and Williams, can be classified as external or internal to organizations. Internal factors related to diverse work force are said to be primary such as race, age, gender and physical abilities. These are beyond being controlled. The external factors are secondary reflecting the acquired nature for work force. These are related to family situations, work experiences, educational levels, religion and other factors. They discuss as well obstacles to the achievement of diversity and their related negative consequences. Obstacles are resultants from resistance to change. The first obstacle is concerned with prejudice and stereotypes. This jeopardizes the need for various qualities and ideas required for innovation. The second then is the resistance of the majority groups to diversity programs. This resistance reflects the fear of creating reversed discrimination. The third obstacle is employees' resistance due to their focus on their present work. The fourth reflects the feeling of the existence of negative diversity climate as results of perceptions of organizational fairness to all groups of in the organization. The fifth is the absence of support from family especially to women . The last obstacle then is related to the hostile work environment. Such environment is against diversity. Equity for Moorhead & Griffin and Kinicki & Williams is to provide equal treatment, opportunities and responsibilities to all employees. This assists to enhance organizational performance and productivity. Despite of elaboration on the issue of diversity and equity, Moorhead & Griffin (2011) and Kinicki & Williams (2020) provide no definitions for the issue of inclusion. This, according to Siri, Leone and Bencivenga (2022), is due to the supposition that the definitions of diversity, equity and inclusion do overlap . This can be ascribed as well to the contemporary nature of the issues of diversity, equity and inclusion. Vaughan however (2022) provides definitions for equity and inclusion. Equity assures treating stakeholders in fair manner to satisfy their requirements. Inclusion states that stakeholders have voices to improve their own and Organizational situations . She adds, based on her findings on health care institutions research in 2021, that 90% of organizations examined provide training for enhancing initiatives for diversity, equity and inclusion. However, only 40% of those organisations require managers to participate in such training. She clarifies that such training are meant to develop cultures leading to improve communication, commitment, employees' retention and loyalty and promoting customers' orientation.

DEFINITION OF LEADERSHIP AND WOMEN: LITERATURE REVIEW

This section elaborates on the definitions of leadership. Then it examines women leadership styles

Definition of Leadership: Literature Review

There is plethora researches and studies on Organizational leadership and it's related issues. Yukl (1989) states that leadership as a phenomenon has been around since A.D. 1300. However he adds that there is no precise definition for the word leadership. The phenomenon of leadership was investigated first in the beginning of last century. Many different theories have been developed looking at leadership from various angles. Theories of leadership, according to Ebert and Griffin (2019); Kinicki & William (2020) Al A'Ali (2009); Hellriegel, Slocum, & Woodman (2001) ; Creto & Creto (2019) and Jones & George (2003) can be studied based on their focus. There are universal, contingency (situational), and the emerging leadership styles . Below is brief presentations of leadership theories based on earlier references.

The Universal Theories

Theories in the first focus are based on universality perspective. There are two groups of theories attributed to the universality perspective. The first group is named trait approach assuming that all effective leaders exhibit certain physical, mental and psychological traits. This group fails to show the relationships between traits assumed, behaviors and effectiveness of the leaders. The second is called behavioural perspective based on universality. Two researches are attributed to to the behavioural perspective. This perspective postulates that behaviour of effective leaders differ from non effective leaders. These behaviours are said to be valid to all leaders regardless of individuals and situational differences. Michigan is the first research stating that leaders display either job- centred or employee-centred focus. The two focuses can not be exhibited at the same time. The second research presenting the behavioural perspective is Ohio Studies. The behaviour of the leader is a combination of initiating and consideration. Initiating behaviour is similar to job-centred behaviour focusing on the job and performance. The consideration is similar to employees-centred behaviour revolving around employees' needs. It was assumed that effective leaders would exhibit high on initiating and consideration behaviour. This assumption changed with further researches.

The trait and behaviour perspectives overlook uniqueness of situations and individuals. These two perspectives therefore are not related to to the present situation.

The Contingency Theories

These theories realize differences of individuals and situations un like universal theories discussed earlier. The fist is the least preferred coworker of Fiedler theory. This theory according to Creto & Creto (2019) and Moorhead and Griffin (2011) postulates that leadership is either task or relationship motivation. Task leadership is task oriented focusing on the job and performance. Leadership motivation is employee-centered rotating around employees satisfaction. The leader exhibits one of these behaviors. The least preferred coworker however states that there are situational factors leading to the emergence of eight situations at which leaders have to deal with. If there is mismatch between constant leadership style and situational factors, the theory suggests to initiate changes to situational factors. The premise that leadership is fixed overlooks the uniqueness of individuals.

The other contingency theories are Path Goal theory ; Vroom-Yetton-Jago decision tree Model and transactional and transformational leadership (Moorhead

& Griffin, 2011) ; Ebert and Griffin (2029) ; kinicki & Williams (2020); and Al-A'ali & Alazali (2022)) .

The revised path-Goal theory states that leadership styles depends on two groups of factors. The first group focuses on employees' traits such as their need for achievement; clarification of path leading to achieve the goals; experience and employees' locus of control. The second group is named environmental referring to the degree of the structure of the task and group dynamics. Leaders based on interactions with these two groups can exhibit six styles. These are supportive, achievement oriented, facilitator, team and group facilitator, group decision making and positively presenting the groups and adding values.

The Vroom-Yetton-Hago model contends that the leadership results from interactions between three groups of factors. The first group is concerned with leaders' information and communication and competencies . The second group is associated with employees' expertise and support; competencies of teams and the degree of commitment. The third group then reflects the decision's importance. Leadership followed illustrates the degree of employees' participation in the decision-making processes.

The charismatic leadership motivates employees through making rewards available to employees. The availability of rewards desired enhances employees' performance and then assist to achieve organizational goals. Transformational leadership differ than transactional. Transformational leadership set organizational visions based on anticipations of future, conveying the visions to employees to adopt, improve organizational learning through utilization of rewards and providing training for leaders. Hellriegel, Slocum & Woodman (2001) and Kinicki & Williams (2020) illustrate the benefits of using combination of transactional and transformational leadership styles. The combination can lead to superior individuals' performance and then excel in achievement of organizational goals .

EMERGING LEADERSHIP STYLES

Ebert and Griffin (2019) discuss three emerging leadership models. They are examined below:

The first is named strategic leadership model. The strategic model examines the organizational internal and external environments. The purpose of examination is to analyze strengths, weaknesses and internal culture in order to match to opportunities and threats imposed by the external environment. The analysis can assist to deal with the present and future economic situations.

The second is ethical leadership. The current requirement for corporate governance upholds the need for organizations to recruit top managers with high ethical standards.

The high ethical standards leaders demand their employees to abide by ethics. Leaders as well are held accountable for their actions.

The last is called virtual leadership stating that leaders and followers interact electronically. Interactions and communication between leaders and employees are not based on face to face. Employees work for a few dates at the office or they work from homes. This makes it hard for leaders to develop strong relationships with employees due to the absence of non verbal communication. Therefore leaders may resort to employ personal words illustrating valuing and reinforcing employees as required.

THE WOMEN LEADERSHIP STYLES

There is a need to mention that studies and researches conducted to explore leadership styles of women are based on leadership theories advanced by scholars of organizational behavior (Harriman, 1985; Al Al A'ali, 1991; & Al A'ali, 2009). Al-A'ali (2022) contends that elementalism underpins theories of Organizational behaviour including leadership. The elementalism in relation to leadership theories is manifested through different ideas, concepts, behaviours and attitudes. Harriman (1985) summaries these manifestations. She states that Schein (1975) claims that management traits are compatible to masculinity. So it is the male/female stereotypes . She elaborates adding that Hennig and Jardim (1977) view women leadership in the light of their upbringing which is assumed to be different than men. Harriman explains that most of research on women leadership, according to her research, are based on trait leaderships theories. She illustrates as well that it was argued previously that men are job focus and women are relationships oriented. She however indicates that kanter (1977) asserts that women leadership styles differ than those of men cause their jobs are characterised by powerlessness. Differences between men and women are attributed to structural factors. This however has changed with situational theories showing that no gender differences between men and women in relation to leadership styles. This is upheld by Al A'ali (2009) ' findings. She concludes her research stating that Women ' leadership styles reflect premises of two main situational theories. These theories are path-Goal theory and Vroom-Yetton-Jago Model. In conclusion the contemporary findings related to women's leadership contend that no differences exist between men and women in relation to leadership styles. women however are seen to be more democratic than men who are found to be autocratic (Ebert & Griffin, 2019). This enables to promote cohesive teams leading to improve performance and productivity.

Women Leadership in Banking Sector in Bahrain

Bahrain is a financial hub consisting of 376 institutions by the end of 2020 comprising of conventional, islamic, offshore banks, insurance companies and other investment institutions. The Standard Chartered Bank was the first to open in 1920s by the the name Eastern Bank Limited. This was followed by the British Bank to open in 1944. The national bank of Bahrain totally owned by Bahrainis was established in 1957 (Gulf Insider, 2023; The standard Chartered Bank, 2023)).

Despite the long history of banking sector in Bahrain, a few women are found to occupying leadership positions. Sinha (2020) illustrates that the boosting number of women at leadership posts in banking sector are due the efforts of the Supreme Council of Women, the governmental policies and the demands of the Central bank of Bahrain . The reasons for having a few women in leadership positions in banking sector may be caused by three factors according to Alhalwachi (2021) and Haward (2019). The first is organizational factors which are lack of mentorship systems and leadership training programs, absence of women role models and discrimination and bias. The second factors are individual referring to the absence of leadership traits, lack of mentorship and needed training and education, and personal fear of failure. The last factors are societal ascribing to stereotypes, and culture clashes. These organizational, societal and individual factors affecting women progression to leadership posts are similar to those found by Al-Alawi & El Naggar (2018). Al—Alawi & El Naggar recommend to initiate gender-free human resources practices, to provide leadership training for women, to enact laws, procedures and plans to encourage the appointment of women in top leadership posts, and to acknowledge the value- added that women can exert on organizations. Such recommendations can institute for cultural changes to accept and appoint women at leadership positions. Studies examining women leadership styles in general are available as mentioned above however there is a lack of studies on women leadership styles in banking sector in Bahrain.

Strategies to Enhance Women Leadership: Literature Review

Organizations, legislations, and gender policies affect women leadership styles which is influenced as well by women's skills, capabilities and confidence (Howard, 2019).

Bullough et al. (2015) and Ngunjiiri & Gardiner (2017) & Haward (2019) highlight the importance of promoting diversity that leads to the evolution of supportive culture to strengthen women leadership styles. They elaborate on strategies to enabling greater gender diversity in relation to leadership positions. The strategies elaborated on are:

1 Flexible work arrangements and environment. Telecommuting, work- life balance programs, and flexible working hours assist women to over come roles conflicts .
2 Organisational policies and procedures to address discrimination and bias against women which may obstruct women from reaching leadership posts .
3 Fostering organisational diversity through setting goals and goals for boosting representation of women in leadership positions. This include promoting succession plans to open opportunities for women to reach leadership positions.
4 Instituting mentorship programs to allow women to have access to professional networks and to acquired required skills, talents and capabilities for leadership positions.
5 Organising, offering and managing programs for leadership development in order to assist women to build up self-confidence, personality traits and knowledge needed by leaders. Such programs can be in the form of coaching and training.

METHODOLOGY

The subject of diversity, equity, and inclusion as stated above still needs to be examine thoroughly. Impacts of such subject on organizational strategies, processes and policies are still being investigated. There is a lack of researches and studies on the subject of diversity, equity, and inclusion in Bahrain in general and on women leadership in specific. Therefore the research on hand employs qualitative methodology for the contemporary nature of the subject. Al-A'ali (2020) argues that the qualitative methodology apprehends the ideas, perceptions and mental constructs of participants to the research. AlSaffar & Al-A'ali (2021) propound that qualitative methodology enables to promote more comprehensive understandings for the subject being studied. In-depth interview is the research method used to collect information . Six Chief Executive Officers of banks participated to this research.

The research attempts to explores four major issues as follows:

1 probing the definitions of diversity, equity, and inclusion and their relationship
2 scanning the definitions of leadership
3 examining the styles of women' leadership in general and in banking sector in specific
4 discussing organizational strategies, policies and procedures to enhance women' diversity in leadership positions.

ANALYSIS OF COLLECTED INFORMATION

The analysis of issues investigated is presented below.

Discussion and Analysis of the First Question in relation to the definitions of diversity, equity and inclusion

The first question probs the definitions and relationships between the terms of diversity, equity and inclusion.

The first, the second, the third and the fourth interviewee state that diversity refers to sources leading to individuals' differences. The sources could be religion, ethnicity, gender and groups of special needs. This is congruent to the definitions. of diversity stated by Moorhead & Griffin (2011) and Kinicki & Williams (2020). Equity on the other hand refers to treat all employees fairly regardless of individual's' differences. The third and fourth interviewees add that treating individuals in organizations fairly in term of responsibilities, rewards, obligations and opportunities lead to upholds inclusion. However, the third and fourth present no specific definition for inclusion. The definition of equity expressed by all interviewees are comparable to the arguments of Moorhead & Griffin (2011) and Vaughan (2022). The later states that equity is to fairly treat the diverse stakeholders who should determine their own and organizational situations as reflections of inclusion. The third and the fourth interviewees however provides no specific definition for inclusion though they state that equity can boost inclusion. The two interviewees also explicate that equity has positive impacts on employees' performance and productivity. This is in harmony with the explanations of Kinicki and William (2020) and Moorhead & Griffin (2011) of diversity and equity but they have no definition for the term inclusivity. The lack of the definition of inclusion could be attributed to the arguments of Siri, Leone, & Bencivenga (2022) ' exhibiting that the meanings of diversity, equity and inclusion overlap.

Diversity for the fifth and sixth interviewees results from background differences among organizational members. Background differences come from gender, age, race, education, and ethnic issues. This is in harmony with the definitions of diversity mentioned by Moorhead & Griffin (2012) and Kinicki and Williams (2020) . Equity according to fifth and sixth interviewees are similar to the views of the other interviewees. Equity is to treat organizational members fairly in term of payments, rewards and opportunities. The fifth and the sixth interviewees highlights the importance of promoting values of equity to improve performance. The fifth and sixth interviewees however contend that inclusivity is never an issue to consider.

The above analysis reveals that though all the interviewees present definitions for diversity and equity, no one of them express concrete meaning for the issue of inclusion. The third and the fourth interviewees mention the importance of employees as stakeholders in relation to the issues of diversity and equity which is similar to the discussion of Vaughan (2022). The same interviewees as well asserts the importance of equity as cultural value to foster inclusion but no definition of inclusion is given as Vaughan does. This can be attributed to two reasons. The first is due to the contemporary nature of the issue of inclusivity in general and in Bahrain in specific. The second is the assumption as shown above concerning the overlapping meanings of diversity, equity and inclusion as postulated by Siri, Leone & Bencivenga (2022).

Definition of Leadership

The second question studies the views of interviewees concerning the definitions of leadership.

The first interviewee asserts that leadership is about setting a vision which is communicated to organizational members. Leaders then develop strategies, policies and action plans to implement the visions. They are strategic designers and are overseeing implementations of organizational objectives.

The second interviewee defines leadership in term of art and science. In the past leadership was depending greatly on art and less on science. At the present leadership counts on science more than art. Leadership theories and knowledge are advanced now . This benefits individuals who practice leadership. However the major roles of leadership are developing visions, designing policies and procedures, communicating the visions to employees and overseeing implementations.

The third interviewee describes leadership in term of leading by examples. Leadership is about setting visions which is communicated to all members of the organizations. It is the commitment of leadership to the vision, encouraging employees to be innovative and creative and to practice fairness. This intensifies, according to this interviewee, the leaders roles as examples.

The fourth interviewee expounds that leadership is not management. Leaders are to provide space to others to manage themselves after illustrating the ways to do the needed jobs. It is to sell the visions and objectives to employees who should adopt and implement. Leaders are to solve problems, to be visionary learners, risk takers and having empathy.

The fifth interviewee states that leadership is about identifying organizational stakeholders and developing visions and settings objectives which are communicated to all in organization. This is to meet the present and future requirements of stakeholders.

Leadership, according to the sixth interviewee, is the ability to influence others without no previous intention to do so. Leaders have visions, set objectives and make decisions.

All interviewees embrace the definition of strategic leadership style. To the interviewees, leadership is about setting visions which should be communicated to employees, designing procedures and policies and and overseeing the implementations. Such definitions are in harmony with the Ebert & Griffin (2019) elucidation of strategic leadership stated above. However there are variations in the elaboration of the strategic leadership style. The third interviewee states that leaders should set themselves as examples for their employees. The fourth highlights the importance of empathy for employees. The fifth accentuates the significance of meeting the demands of stakeholders. This is in accordance with assertions of Ebert and Griffin(2019) in relation to the significance of meeting the demands of stakeholders who exert influence on organizations.

Women Leadership Styles

The third question explores the definition of women leadership styles.

The first interviewee states that the essence of leadership is the same for men and women. Therefore women leadership styles are similar to those styles of men. Such styles revolve around strategies designing and implementing.

The second interviewee confirms that leadership styles for men and women are the same. Leadership is about developing visions which should be communicated to all in organizations and then setting goals to achieve. Equal payment is assured for both women and men by organisations.

The third interviewee states that men prefer to appoint other men as leaders leading to exclude women. This self fulfilling prophecy is attained in many banks. This is in accordance with Alhalwaci (2021) ' discussions that there are organizational, social and individual factors leading to exclude women from top leadership positions. However women leadership according to the third interviewee can add values to organizations. Women are more calculative making them better decision makers . They are ready as well to take risk and to build better relationships with their employees. However the essence of leadership is the same for men and women.

The fourth interviewee expounds lthat women are deprived from networking needed for leadership development and appointment. Women are empathetic and develops cohesive teams . Women follow democratic leadership style. However many women lack exposure required for leadership posts.

Women leadership styles are un like the styles of men's according to the fifth interviewee. Women go by the book making them good only for certain jobs like human resources, legal and retail business. Women are mor rule-minded.

The sixth interviewee propounds that women leadership styles in essence are similar to those of men's styles . Leadership is about developing and implementing the visions. However women are more democratic than men who are autocratic. Women adopt consultative attitudes leading to the evolution of challenging work environments. The interviewee adds that women are assertive and risk takers as well.

The majority of interviewees argue that the essence of leadership is the same for men and women. Leadership is about developing visions which should be implemented. However there are disparities in relation to the reasons for exclusion of women from the top leadership posts. The third interviewee ascribes the exclusion of women from leadership post to men's self fulfilling prophecy. This is consistent to the arguments of Alhalwachi (2021) and Haward (2019). They explain that the absence of role-models, mentorship programs and biases and discrimination hinder women from reaching the top positions. The fifth interviewee claims that women are rule-minded which disagrees with the view of the sixth interviewee asserting that women are democratic while men are autocratic. The view of the fourth and the sixth interviewees about women being democratic and men being autocratic is compatible to the declaration of Ebert and Griffin (2019).

The third and fourth interviewees mention the benefits of having women as leaders. They state that women can add values in relation to the teams development and can make better decision makers. This is upheld by the arguments of Moorhead & Griffin (2011) stating that women can build cohesive teams which boost performance and productivity.

Organisational strategies to enhance diversity for enhancing women leadership

The last question is to elaborate on strategies to enhance diversity for women leadership in organizations. Such diversity is assumed to improve performance and productivity.

The first interviewee states that strategies for enhancing women leadership in organizations in general and in Bahrain in specific are triggered by different sources. These sources are the office of his Majesty the Prime Minister, the Supreme Council for Women and Central Bank of Bahrain. Such sources outline for Banks actions to initiate and promote diversity for boosting women leadership.

The second interviewee emphasizes the importance of the strategic vision of the bank that endorses women leadership. This leads the bank to appoint women in leadership posts. Mentorship programs can assist women to promote their knowledge and skills.

Succession plans are required to consider women for leadership positions as stated by the third interviewee. The interviewee adds that the problem is not to set strategies to include women in leadership posts rather than implementing such strategies due to males and some females' resistance to change. This illustrates the importance of training and mentorship programs in order to change organizational values for the favorite for women.

The fourth interviewee expounds that creating a culture based on values of diversity and equity, rotation programs for women to enhance exposure, formal and informal mentorship plans, opening networking channels, training and flexible work arrangements are strategies to strengthen diversity for women leaders.

The fifth interviewee believes that women in their path to reach leadership positions encounter many possible exits. Exits are related to marital status, children and society demands. Hence there must be methods to assist women in their endeavors to reach the top. Such methods are provided by the kingdom's rules represented in the regulations of the Supreme Council for Women and Central Bank of Bahrain. Organizations can create working environments and cultures inducing women to reach the top positions. This is related to work arrangements, children day take caring and others.

The sixth interviewee emphasises the importance of policies of Central Bank of Bahrain and in GCC in general to increase the number of women leaders in financial and banking sectors. Such guidelines enable banks to set annual measurable targets in relation to the progress of women to top leadership posts. Human resources strategies contribute to achieve fair representation of women at top leadership through developing succession plans, career development systems, and mentorship programs.

The first, the second, the fifth and the sixth interviewees emphasize the important roles of The Supreme Council for Women and the government's development targets, and the the Central Bank of Bahrain objectives and the visions of organizations to foster the appointment of women in leadership positions. This is in agreement with Howard (2018) ' demonstration in relation to the influence of organizations, the state 's legislations and gender policies on increasing the number of women in leadership posts.

The third and fifth discuss the active roles of organizational values and cultures to initiate diversity changes to accelerate the progress of women in organizations. Bullough et. al. (2015) and Nugunjiiri & Gardiner (2017) call for cultural changes to promote women in top leadership posts . The majority of the interviewees clarify that human resources policies and practices reinforce the appointment of women in top leadership positions. Human resources policies like telecommuting and flexible working hours eliminate obstacles which women encounter to reach top leadership positions as stated above by AlAlwai $ El Naggar (2018). The majority of interviewees as well highlight the significance of mentorship, training programs to deal with discrimination and biases, leadership development programs to enabling women to acquire skills and knowledge required for leadership positions and succession plans as discussed by Nugunjiiri & Gardiner (2017).

CONCLUSION

There are studies focusing on women in banking sector in Bahrain. The same studies examine the factors impeding women from being leaders and making suggestions to foster the advancement for women to the top of organizations.

The research on hand however differs as it attempts to comprehend women leadership styles in banking sector in Bahrain. The impacts of espousing diversity in organizations on women leadership styles are investigated as well. The strategic methods, policies and procedures are explored in this research in order to apprehend approaches supporting women to reaching top leadership positions. The research employs qualitative methodology. Qualitative methodology enables to grasp the meanings held by interviewees. Such methodology assists to develop better understandings of the contemporary issues being studied. Diversity is a current issue in Bahrain. Six Chief Executive Officers contribute to this research. In-depth interview is the research method used. Each interview lasts between one hour to two hours. The research explores four questions. The first aims to scrutinize the definition of diversity. The definitions of diversity of all the Interviewees is in harmony with the definitions stated by the literature review. Diversity refers to the sources of individual differences either are primary as race, sex and ethnic groups or secondary like education, experience and family situations. Equity is stated by interviewees as treating employees fairly. Though a few of interviewees refer to the term of inclusion as a consequence of practicing equity but no one of them provided a definition for that term . The second question scans the definition of leadership. The majority of interviewees embrace the definition of strategic leadership which has to setting the visions, communicating the visions to all employees and overseeing the implementation. The third question then surveys the the interviewees' perspectives of women leadership styles. Most of the interviewees state that the nature of leadership is the same for men and women. Women leadership style based on the majority is strategic. However one claim that women are rule-minded which makes them autocratic. This has been un substantiated by more than one interviewees who argue that women are better team member and are more democratic. The last question reviews organizational strategies to enhance women diversity in top leadership positions. Human resources arrangements, leadership development programs, training plans to dealing with biases and discrimination, cultural changes, succession plans and mentorship programs are all strategies expressed by interviewees to enhance the progress of women to top leadership positions.

FUTURE RESEARCH

The literature review reveals the scarcity of research about women leadership styles on banking sector in Bahrain and about the issue of diversity. To develop better comprehension about women leadership styles and the effects of diversity on organizations, the following future research are suggested:

- conducting more studies to develop in depth understandings of women leadership styles
- Examining thoroughly the banking cultures to identify values encouraging women or impeding women to reaching top leadership positions.
- Employing quantitative methodology to triangulate findings of different research methodologies

REFRENCES

Al-A'ali, E. (1991). *The Phenomenon of women in Management: An alternative Perspective and its Implications in the Case of Bahrain*, [Unpublished PhD thesis, University of Lancaster].

Al A'ali, E. (2009). Women Leadership Styles. In *Scientific Journal for Business and Finance. Vol. No. 1.* Tanta University press.

Al A'ali, E. (2020). The Role of Auditing Firms in Promoting Ethical Consumerism. In E. Al A'ali & M. Masmoudi (Eds.), *Ethical consumerism and Comparative Studies Across Different Cultures.* IGI Global., doi:10.4018/978-1-7998-0272-3.ch004

Al A'ali, E. (2022). Human Behaviour in Organizations: An Enhancement perspective. In. E. Al A'ali & M. Masmoudi (Eds), Religion and Its Impact on Organizational Behavior. IGI Global. DOI: doi:10.4018/978-1-7998-9319-6.ch001

Al-Alawi, A., & El Naggar, N. F. (2018). Factors Affecting Women Leadership to Reach Top Management and Its Impact on the Economy: The Case of the Kingdom of Bahrain. In E. Al-A'ali, M. M. Al-Shammari & H. Masri (Eds), Arab Women and Their Evolving Roles in the Global Business Landscape. IGI Global. doi:10.4018/978-1-5225-3710-6.ch005

AlSaffar, G., & Al A'ali, E. (2021). Psychiatry in the midst of the Pandemic:A Narrative Perspective. In E. Al A'Ali & M. Masmoudi (Ed's), Global perspectives on change Management and Leadership in the post -Covid 19 Era. IGI Global. doi:10.4018/978-1-7998-6948-1.ch002

Bullough, A., De Luque, M.S., Abdelzaher, D., & Heim, W. (2015) . Developing women leaders through entrepreneurship education and training. *Academy of Management Perspectives, 29*(2) 250-270.

Creto, S. C., & Creto, S. T. (2019). *Modern Management: Concepts and Skills (global edition).* Pearson Education Limited.

Ebert, R. J., & Griffin, R. W. (2019) Business essential., New York: Pearson (12ed.)

Harriman, A. (1985). *Women/Men/Management*. Praeger Publications.

Hellriegel, D., Slocum, J. w. Jr, & Woodman, R. W. (2001). *Organizational Behavior* (9th ed.). South-Western College Publishing.

Jones, G. R., & George, J. M. (2003). *Contemporary Management* (3rd ed.). McGraw-Hill.

Kinicki, A., & Williams, B. K. (2020). *Management (ninth edition)*. New York: McGraw-Hill Education https://www.relias.com/blog/how-diversity-equity-inclusion-influence-healthcare https://www.fdic.gov/about/diversity/pdf/dei2021.pdf

Moorhead, G., & Griffin, R. S. (2011). *Organizational Behavior* (11th ed.).

Ngunjiiri, F. w., & Gardiner, R. A. (2017). Future Strategies for developing women as leaders. In *Handbook of research on gender and leadership* (pp. 423–437). Edward Elgar Publishing. doi:10.4337/9781785363863.00038

Rizan, Muhammad, Khan, Mula Nazar, & Nadeem, Babar & Qalb e Abbas. (2016). The Impacts of Workplace Diversity Towards Employee Performance. *Evidence from Banking Sector of Pakistan in American Journal of Matketing Research*, *2*(2), 53–60.

Sinha, C. (2020), Women in the Bahraini Financial Sector: Opportunities, Challenges and Strategic Choices. In SAGA Journals. doi:10.1177/0049085719901069

Siri, A., Leone, C., & Bencivenga, R. (2022). Equality, Diversity, and Inclusion Strategies Adopted in European University Alliance to Facilitate the Higher Education-to-Work Transition. *Societies (Basel, Switzerland)*, *12*(5), 140. doi:10.3390oc12050140

Yukl, G. A. (1989) Leadership in Organizations. New Jersey: Prentice-Hall International.

Chapter 5
Inclusive Leadership:
Vital Element to Achieve Equity and Inclusion in Education

Humberto Javier Rodriguez
Escuela Normal de Especializacion, Mexico

ABSTRACT

This approach is eminently humanistic and places the person at the center of all action, because it recognizes that each person is valuable and has talent—therefore, it is necessary to identify and create conditions for it to flourish. Each person must be respected, regardless of their origin, ability, or identity. In consequence, all educational systems and schools must be creative in the face of diversity, responding with quality and equity, and avoiding discrimination and exclusion in schools. That is why there is a need for strong inclusive leadership. This is possible because of an environment of shared purpose and teamwork, so relationships are ascending, descending, and moving laterally due to the collaborative culture. It is also considered as a shared function that exercises collegiality and collaboratively.

INTRODUCTION

The challenges posed by the twenty-first century are abundant and multifaceted: Violence in all its forms and global warming are just two of them. On the other hand, the digital age and globalisation lead us to new ways of living and interacting. That is why we need people who assume an active role in the face of new challenges.

However, when considering it as inclusive, it takes a new perspective, because it has as its centre, the human being, and his well-being. A community that promotes

DOI: 10.4018/978-1-6684-9013-6.ch005

inclusive values such as compassion, respect, tolerance, empathy, among others. A community made up of global citizens who understand their specific and local action, but with a broad framework.

A common tendency in the face new paradigms is to try to understand them with the same concepts and actions as before. This generates great confusion. Such is the case with leadership and the need for it to be inclusive.

What we do or don't do now will have an impact on generations to come. The human being in the rescue of his humanity, seems to be a valid premise that encourages us to be leaders and act in education as a means of transformation and consolidation of our fundamental values. Definitely, each region of the world has achievements and also limitations. We occupy inclusive leaders who assume their task with vision and purpose. That is why this chapter brings together various ideas, offering elements for reflection and debate on leadership. Its core of its action is diversity, equity, and inclusion, which undoubtedly represent the social and educational ideal. The debate, it seems to me, must analyse not only the subject but also its context, and its mission in the new social imaginary of the twenty-first century. Without doubt are benefits of inclusive leadership in terms of personal, organizational, and societal levels.

The purpose of this chapter is describe inclusive leadership as a vital component in achieving equity and inclusion in education. The fundamental premise is that the present twenty-first century demands new actions from each of the members of society to advance the ideal of a more just and equitable society. It is therefore intended to provide frameworks for reflection and action.

According to the Inclusive Leadership Handbook an inclusive leadership (IL) approach "appreciates diversity" invites and welcomes everyone´s individual contribution, and encourages full engagement with the processes of decision-making and shaping reality, capable of listening, communicating a vision, and building consensus among diverse stakeholders.

The chapter has the following issues:

1. Challenges on present century. This section introduces some challenges for the human being while describing humanity´s desire for a just and egalitarian society
2. Equity and Inclusion. Presents a new educational community having the global Agenda 2030, and describing the equity and inclusion in education and their social impact.
3. Inclusive leadership in education. Make an explanatory about the concept of inclusive leadership, its role, and the new profile of the inclusive society in the 21st century.

4. Dimensions of Inclusive leadership. In this section introduces diverse elements characterize the leadership: dialogic perspective, personal disposition, professional capacities, and social responsibility, and
5. Inclusive Leadership action frameworks. The last topic frames the components that are core to inclusive leadership: Human rights, diversity, community, learning environment, communication and collaboration and finally, welfare.

CHALLENGES ON PRESENT CENTURY

According to UNESCO (2020), the present century is absolutely characterised by three characteristics: uncertainty, complexity, and precariousness. It seems to me that the health pandemic, which we have just experienced, allowed us to understand this concept more deeply. In the same manner, the complexity in the current problems and the precariousness, which forces us to be able to more efficiently. Besides, the OECD (2019) identifies four megatrends that are transforming our environment: globalisation, digitalisation, migration, and demographic trends. Today, more than ever, collaboration between the different spheres of society must be effective.

That is why it is essential to transform the conception of education, its purposes, and its structure. Several authors, for example, point out that the idea of an individual teacher, locked in the classroom, separate the social responsibility of education and school in front of families and classrooms, is in crisis (Garcia-Huidobro, 2001). Under this approach, the World Bank's Development Report (2018) argues that schooling without learning is a wasted opportunity and identifies three dimensions of the learning crisis: the student doesn't have basic competences and the children often arrive in school unprepared to learn, also teachers often lack the skills or motivation to be effective and the action on behalf of the head of the school, don't improve teaching and learning. On the other hand, despite increasing access to education, recent studies reveal that many young people, especially those who are poor or marginalised, are leaving schools unequipped with ever the foundational skills they need for life.

Irina Bokova (former UNESCO director) said "There is no more powerful transformative force than education, to promote human rights and dignity, to eradicate poverty and to build a better future for all, but the changes in the world today are characterised by new levels of complexity and contradiction". (2015) Vulnerability, inequality, exclusion, and violence have increased throughout the world. The aspiration of sustainable development requires us to resolve common problems and to recognize new horizons.

According to Luna-Scott (2014), the education of the 21st Century needs to include new approaches and perspectives like the following: the role of teachers will be extended as mentors, mediators and guides, facilitators, learning coordinators, assessors and designers and compilers of learning tools. The purpose is to promote actions more personalised and customised to reflect students' individual needs and interests. Informal learning opportunities will become recognized alternatives to traditional formal education. Schools will remain but classrooms will become more open to diverse learning experiences and instruction will likely move out the community. Technology will support personalised learning processes and facilitate inclusion and equity.

Without doubt, society lives immersed in accelerated changes in all fields of human activity. The idea of a changing world (UNESCO, 2015) is a reality and requires new patterns of thinking and action, in the face of continuous challenges.

EQUITY AND INCLUSION IN EDUCATION

Inclusion and equity can be used to guide a process of strengthening the capacity of an education system to reach out to all learners in the community. These means that they must be seen as some overall principles that guide educational policies and practices, the education as a basic human right and the base for a more just society; serving all children and young people, with a particular accent on those who have traditionally been excluded from educational opportunities- such as learners with impairments, children from ethnic and linguistic minorities, and so on.

Inclusive education is an approach to provide equal education experience for all students no matter what age or grade they are in, or needs they have. This concept can help in achieving five sustainable development goals: No poverty, quality education, gender equality, inequalities and maintaining peace and justice.

According to General Comment # 4 of the Committee on the Rights of Persons with Disabilities (2016), it states that Inclusive Education is indispensable for the formation of inclusive, peaceful, and just societies.

It is clear that inclusion is a transformative process that ensures full participation and access to quality learning opportunities for all children, young people and adults, respecting and valuing diversity, and eliminating all forms of discrimination in and through education. In this sense, the learning environments should be safe, welcoming, free of all forms of violence, ensuring a high level of motivation, engagement, and learning outcome for everyone. (UNESCO,2019)

The Education 2030 Framework for Action has been adopted by the global education community to advance progress towards SDG4 and its targets. The framework stresses the need to eliminate all forms of exclusion. The definition of inclusion involves four key elements: 1) A process search to find ways of responding to diversity, learning from differences, 2) Is concerned with the identification and removal of barriers, 3) Is about the presence, participation and achievement of all students, and 4) involves a particular emphasis on those groups of learners who may be at risk of marginalisation. Quality, equality, equity, and diversity are interconnected in this important approach. Therefore, are principles that values the well-being of all learners, respects their inherent dignity and autonomy, and recognizes people's needs and their effective ability to be included and contribute to society.

Research suggests that inclusive education is more successful in contexts with a culture of collaboration allowing us the preparation of the environment that is favourable for collaboration, overcoming possible obstacles. (Galkienė, 2021)

Dialogue, and mutual vision of empowering staff through co-operative teamwork, leading by example, stimulate self-questioning, creativity, and action for the wellness of all students. Without a doubt, this is the great challenge that must be faced.

In this direction, the society needs a more humanistic and global education, which identifies the person, their needs, interests and expectations and that generates a model that encourages collaboration and solidarity with others and live in harmony with your surroundings. Currently, there is a great social demand to recognize the human rights of all, freedom to be, express themselves and live according to their personal conviction.

On the same consideration, the Guide for Ensuring Inclusion and Equity in Education (UNESCO, 2017) highlights that leaders at all levels must articulate consistent policy goals to develop inclusive and equitable educational practices. In the same guide stresses, the needs to address all form of exclusion and marginalization, enable education systems to serve all learners, with particular focus on those who have traditionally been excluded from the poorest households, ethnic and linguistic minorities, indigenous people, and personas with disabilities. It is important to consider what is the meaning of inclusion and equity: Inclusion is a process that helps overcome barriers limiting the presence, participation and achievement of learners and equity is about ensuring that there is a concern with fairness, such that the education of all learners is seen as having equal importance.

According to UNESCO (2020) human interaction and wellbeing must be given priority in education. The centre of any educational process is the human relationship.

The humanist perspective invites us to recognize the different areas of the human being, for example, public health and public education are closely interconnected as they show undeniable necessity of collaboration, solidarity, and collective action for the common good. In fact, the new vision about schools is places where we can encounter, not like ourselves, others whom we learn from and with, others who expand our understanding of the global variety of ways of being human.

Under this paradigm, an equitable, inclusive, and quality education must consider comprehensive care for each and every student. UNICEF (2020) We must also take care, support, and protect the mental health of children and young people and bring an end to abuse, gender-based violence and neglect in childhood.

The emotional and social aspects of all members of the educational community are important, so they must be taken care of. Concern for the person must be a global and integral aspect.

Facing this challenging situation, is aspirated to a more just and egalitarian society; that recognizes diversity and promotes inclusive values. The values are fundamental guides and prompts to action. When involving particular values into action in education and society, inclusion forms a coherent approach to educational and social development; equality, respect, sustainability, non-violence, responsibility, collaboration, as essential components of the educational community.

As we know, inclusive education arises from the great movements to defend the dignity of each person and make effective the exercise of their rights, as well as to receive quality education with equity for all.

The evolution of inclusive education has enabled new areas of knowledge such as the *inclusive pedagogy*, whose purpose is improving teaching, recognizing diversity and the need to promote inclusion and equity in education. Requires that educators and leaders embrace their students as whole human beings consisting of mind, body, and soul and create interactive and dynamic environments that inspire deep and meaningful transformational learning (Tuitt et al.,2016). It embraces a view of individual difference as the source of diversity that can enrich the lives and learning of others (Hockings, 2010). Through inclusive pedagogy we can support the success of all students regardless of background and ability (Salazar et al. 2009)

Diversity and Collaboration are two aspects linked in the inclusive vision Teaching is conceived as a collective action, exchange of knowledge, ideas, and experiences to facilitate learning for all. Some authors frame the collaboration in terms of co-planning, co-teaching, and co-evaluation (CEC,2012, Rodríguez,2014) Other authors describe the need for teacher accompaniment, under the perspective of intervention, facilitation, and cooperation as elements for peer teaching work. (Nieto, 2001). Below this field we can locate personalised learning.

Other emerging field is the *inclusive research that* requires teachers to enter dialogues with children and with their colleagues about how to develop lessons that respond positively to learner differences. Central to the strategy is the involvement of students as researchers, gathering information from their classmates to assist in processes of lesson planning. (Ainscow, 2020) which seeks to arrangement a methodology for all members of the community to participate in the implementation of actions to strengthen the learning of all. Its purpose is to encourage dialogue among teachers and students. In the definition de Lodge (2005) dialogue is about engagement with others through talk to arrive at the point one would not get alone. It is important to consider that knowledge is socially constructed by all the people who participate in the research and that perceptions of reality are modified through the process of study.

In consequence, all educational systems and schools must be creative in the face of diversity, responding with quality and equity; avoiding discrimination and exclusion in schools. That is why we need strong inclusive leadership. (UNESCO, 2019) In my perspective: we cannot understand diversity if we do not first understand what equity is. Recognize that each person is unique and that we live in a plurality.

According the Guide for Ensuring Inclusion and Equity in education (2017) diversity is defined as people´s differences which may relate to their race, ethnicity, gender, sexual orientation, language, culture, religion, mental, and physical ability, class, and immigration status.

INCLUSIVE LEADERSHIP IN EDUCATION

Conceptual approach:

An inclusive leadership is built on the next premises:

- Recognize the basic human rights as fundamental
- Foster attitudes and actions to break down barriers for people at risk of being discriminated and excluded form society.
- Call for collaborative work and nurturing dialogue
- Opinion and feelings of all are taken into account in decision-making.

According to *the Inclusive Leadership Handbook* an inclusive leadership approach "appreciates diversity" invites and welcomes everyone´s individual contribution, and encourages full engagement with the processes of decision-making and shaping reality.

Certainly, inclusive leadership is positioned as a quality that must be distributed, and shared and offers us a new conceptual perspective. This is possible because of an environment of shared purpose and teamwork, so relationships are ascending, descending and lateral due to the collaborative culture. It is also considered as a shared function that is exercised collegially and collaboratively. (Lorenzo, 2005). This does not mean that formal leadership is not required, but it encourages the development of distributed leadership. (Harris, 2012). Keeping this in mind, all contribute though opinions, experiences and cultural resources because there are no experts who possess all the social and cultural knowledge.

Promoting an educational environment favourable for the participation of all is a priority in. However, for this, to become possible, leadership with a clear inclusive vision is required. A leadership opposite the hierarchical power structure, because seeks only efficiency and a single leader rather than a team and community approach, and exclude.

Leadership needs to have a clear inclusive vision. A new perspective, foster equitable and horizontal relationship and promote a collaborative work.

This approach is eminently humanistic and places the person at the centre of all action; because it recognizes that each person is valuable, has talent, therefore, it is necessary to identify and create conditions for it to flourish that is why each person must be respected, regardless of their origin, ability, or identity.

The best conditions for leadership development is developed from various fields: Firstly, legislation which provides the articulation of principles and rights that is needed for creating a framework for inclusion. Second, the articulates the inclusive practices that will facilitate equity. Third, ensure effective communication among stakeholders. Four, a culture of inclusion and equity in education requires a shared set of assumptions and beliefs is valuing differences, believing collaboration, and offering opportunities for all students.

Central Role

Inclusive leadership must recognize that every child is unique, and every school must be prepared to respond to a broad and unique variety of children. The diversity of learners facilitates the dialogue and collaboration of cultures but also accelerates the becoming of social justice. (Florian, 2019).

Based on the above, leadership must be inclusive to achieve the society and education we want; educating for autonomy, cooperation, participation, and solidarity (Savater, 1997), thereby ensuring the right to education of all people, within a framework of equal opportunities and non-discrimination, particularly those who present some condition of vulnerability.

According to various studies, the role of inclusive leadership has a special development through collaborative approaches, such as mentoring, networking, study groups, school´s visits, and peer coaching, but the most important thing is to be proactive, resourceful, seeking advice for professional improvement, taking initiative, looking for evidence, planning, anticipating needs and finding solutions, often beyond the call of duty. One of these perspectives is collaborative work, promoting co-responsibility as a team.

The role of the leader is vital for any organisation, but when it is linked to equity and inclusion, it acquires a deeper meaning and great transcendence.

Without a doubt, education in undergoing multiple changes. Next, some recommendations are presented on behalf of international organisations, which the role of inclusive leader should consider.

UNESCO Recommendations: (2020) Commit to strengthening education as a common good. Broadening the definition of the right to education to address the importance of connectivity and access to knowledge and information We must create conditions that give educators autonomy and flexibility to act. Protect the social spaces offered by schools. Make free and open-source technologies available to teachers and students.

UNICEF Recommendations (2020): Ensure that all children can learn, including bridging the digital divide. Support and protect the mental health of children and young people and end abuse, gender-based violence and neglect. Strengthen efforts to protect and support children and families living in situations of conflict, disaster, and displacement.

CALI commitment to equity and inclusion in education (UNESCO,2019): Establish alliances with other sectors to strengthen broader collaboration and thus strengthen the sense of well-being of the members of their community. Implement diversified programs considering all aspects inherent to their students; their needs, interests, expectations, seeking to strengthen not only the cognitive aspects, but also the affective and social ones, with a strong vision of caring for the environment, in addition to respect and acceptance of diversity, as a principle for coexistence and the development of a culture of peace and non-violence. Promote coexistence, solidarity, and collaboration as essential elements of a humanistic education through inclusive methodologies such as service learning, among others.

In this point of view, inclusive leadership has a transformative meaning. According to Giroux (1990) the leader is a transformative intellectual, committed to their time and to the situations of social injustice that are generated in their environment. His language is always accompanied by the language of possibility, working with the community, dialogue with families and get closer to their lives. (Macedo,1994).

DIMENSIONS OF INCLUSIVE LEADERSHIP

Dialogic Perspective

One aspect to keep in mind, is that dialogue transforms the context, in this sense dialogic learning is enhanced in the diversity of levels, gender, cultures, ways of learning, and aims to overcome social inequalities, solidarity must be one of its fundamental elements. From the dialogic perspective, it is understood that the meanings we give to social reality have been created in interaction, neither are given by systems nor leave our interior, but both systems and our interior have been generated by interactions. People continually create and recreate meanings about reality that are the result of intersubjective agreements reached through communicative processes. (Flecha, et al, 2001)

Addressing this perspective requires leadership with a clear vision about the community. In consequence, the following actions place the social context as a centre:

- Foster collaboration and strive to create an atmosphere of trust and make each person feel capable (Kouzes and Posner,2017) and learn interaction, as well as social and cultural participation. (Galkienė, 2021).
- Maximises the efforts of others, towards the achievement of a goal (Kruse, 2013).
- Work with teachers and other staff for the improvement of school results. (Pont, 2020).
- Provide support and follow-up to students who present some condition of vulnerability.
- Create synergy across the relevant variables (Louis et al.,2010).
- Focus on learning through the plan, and coordinate and evaluate the curriculum
- Develop people, providing support and mentoring opportunities. (Leithwood et al,2020)

Certainly, inclusive leadership is positioned as a quality that must be distributed, and shared and offers us a new conceptual perspective. It is important to explain that multiple people serve as a leadership; collective goals but in different levels. In words of the Global Education Monitoring Report the impact of leadership is oriented to equality, respect, engagement, harmony, cohesion, solidarity, justice, innovation, sustainability, resilience, satisfaction, and well-being. (UNESCO,2020).

Personal Disposition

It is important to highlight some traits of inclusive leader in terms of build an inclusive culture, in this sense, I take again what is indicated by the inclusive leadership handbook:

- Visible commitment. The diversity and inclusion are a personal priority.
- Humility. Listening all voices and proposals
- Curiosity about others. Work with multicultural people, promoting tolerance, respect and inclusion.
- Cultural intelligence. It is sensitive to diverse cultures.
- Effective collaboration. Identify talents, and promote positive attitudes.

The personal disposition (Gonzalez, 2004) is oriented to promote the well-being of all, seeking to eliminate barriers that impede the right to education. In this aspect I consider it of utmost importance, to review the being, from the Bio-Psycho-Social-Cultural and Spiritual unity, in which various positions converge that complement this vision. Each of the components is explained:

- Biological being. It is made up of healthy lifestyles that have as their centre, self-care, prevention, food, health, among others.
- Psychological being. Centre of behaviour. This is where emotions are located but also attitudes, thoughts, and knowledge in which each person must seek a balance so that these are enhanced for the well-being of himself and those around him.
- Social being. Interpersonal relationships and the role plays in different contexts assume vital importance. The relationship and bonds with others are and will always be a key part of an inclusive leader.
- Cultural being. A person located in his environment, that is, he shapes his identity and participation within a social collective in which he influences and is influenced by the collective.
- Spiritual being. Denotes a vision and life project in which he incorporates values that allow him to review his transcendence as a leader; solidarity, respect, tolerance, among many others, make up this great component.

Undoubtedly, maintaining a positive attitude is an indispensable element of an inclusive leader. This does not mean ignoring or hiding the bad or inadequate situations that happen, on the contrary, they allow us to face them in a better way, always seeking the improvement or solution of these situations promoting a "global" vision, that is, a broad and globalised knowledge, but with a specific action in the local.

An indispensable element in the leader is proactivity, which allows us to re-imagine the future we want, document possibilities and experiences and look for actions in the present and future.

One of the actions of every leader is the elaboration and implementation of a plan. Some authors place planning as the rational application in decision-making, based on knowledge of reality and directing all action to achieve the purposes set. In this sense, a lesson that the COVID-19 pandemic has left us is the need to be flexible, identify when it is necessary to adjust, recognize what does not work and change it quickly (Samoilovich, 2020). This sensitivity and flexibility are a characteristic of every inclusive leader.

Professional Capacities

A pertinent aspect is that the leader must develop a set of professional competencies that qualify him for the performance of the function as a leader. The purpose of this section is not to highlight any leadership program, but to review some of the actions that will undoubtedly allow you to be more assertive. In this regard, some aspects pointed out by Linda Darling-Hammond (2020) and it seems to me, that they are indispensable elements in the preparation: Leadership adapts to environment and defines goals (executive functions) planning, flexible thinking, regulation of emotions, among others. Communicates effectively through various means. Adequately manages the interaction between personal, behavioural, and environmental factors (self-regulation). He faces obstacles and uncertainty because of his resilience, perseverance, and resourcefulness. Because of their interpersonal skills, works with others and participates effectively in cross-cultural contexts (cultures that have contact with and influence each other). Learn independently, with curiosity, creativity, and originality. Finds, analyses, synthesises, and applies knowledge to new situations. Reflects on their learning processes which allows them to plan and make decisions (Metacognitive Skills).

Social Responsibility

The leader understands the transcendence of his decisions and actions. Undoubtedly, the performance of an inclusive leader has as its fundamental task to promote a deep sense of community. In the words of Daniel Samoilovich (2020) To ensure the physical and mental well-being of students and teachers, a sense of community is imposed, maintaining a sense of common purpose." This indicates that the physical and mental well-being of all is closely linked to the formation of the sense of community. Therefore, it seeks to promote a safe environment for all, has high expectations and carries out monitoring and evaluation as planned. It also always seeks to maintain a positive relationship with families and various external agents. The processes of research and obtaining reliable information, allows you to perform an effective management to respond to the various approaches of the members of your educational organisation.

Another important element of their performance is that they have the ability to build collaboration based on a shared vision of teaching and learning. A vital element is the formation of structures for consensual and effective decision-making. Undoubtedly, the development of evaluation and research are two inherent pillars of the inclusive leader.

INCLUSIVE LEADERSHIP ACTION FRAMEWORKS

How it has been expressed in previous sections, inclusion is the fundamental element to consider inclusive leadership. But what are the elements that underpin the actions of the inclusive leader? Below, I will present some of the most important frames of reference for actions of the inclusive leadership:

- **Human rights**. This perspective is at the heart of all action and is supported by legal and regulatory instruments. This recognition has taken a long process starting in 1948 with the Universal Declaration of Human Rights, through the United Nations Convention on the Rights of the Child (1989) to recent instruments, to sustain access and participation in education for all. In 2016 with General Comment number 4 on article 24 of the United Nations Declaration on the Rights of Persons with Disabilities, it states that inclusive education is fundamental to achieving high quality education for all students, which must be implemented at all levels and for all students, without discrimination and on equal terms. In this sense, the phrase gains strength: every learner matters.
- **Diversity.** It is necessary to recognize that each of us is unique and that we move in a plurality. Diversity must be accepted and recognized. Therefore, any action should recognize this plurality and privilege the development of each person.
- **Community**. The participation of all agents of the educational environment is of vital importance for the formation of communities dedicated to learning and the well-being of all. Values such as solidarity are important in interpersonal processes and in the sum of efforts to achieve a common good.
- **Learning Environment.** This conception is vital in the development of communities, recognizing that we must act for our educational organisations to be physically safe, emotionally healthy, and psychologically empowering and in a certain way this sets the tone for leadership performance by clearly establishing the orientation of the various actions and programs that are implemented in their educational organisation. This element it is also essential to identify and eliminate barriers to learning and participation.
- **Communication and Collaboration**. These components are fundamental. The full participation of all members of the community and the sum of efforts and talents are necessary to advance in the construction of projects of benefit for all. Already from the fundamental elements for the education of the XXI century, collaboration and communication appear as elements that must be promoted in any educational organisation. This component is vital among teachers to address the diversity of their students also for the development of

effective professional development actions, under the paradigm of inclusion that bets on trans-disciplinary models of collaboration and co-teaching.

- **Welfare.** The ultimate goal of all action is to contribute to the well-being of all. This requires obtaining data and information on the profile of the community and pinpointing the challenges and challenges it presents. It also requires management for the improvement of the building, equipment, support and human resources, materials, among others. and the inherent aspects of each situation. The link with instances external to the organisation itself is vital to advance in this regard. Also in this direction, joint work with other instances takes on special interest and need for inclusive leadership.

All this leads us to consider that each educational organisation is the meeting space and exchange of ideas, knowledge, stories, and life projects of each of its members. This gives a strong dynamism for dialogue, reflection and the construction of new relationship guidelines based on respect, empathy, tolerance, among others. In this order of ideas, I do not omit to consider the need to always provide educational services that are *accessible* (without any barrier) *affordable* (that what is required exist), *adaptable* (to the conditions of each one) and *acceptable* (culturally appropriate and free of all types of violence) (UNESCO, 2019).

CONCLUSION

Ensuring the right to inclusive education leads to the transformation of culture, policy, and practice in all formal and informal educational settings to accommodate the different needs and identities of each learner, as well as a commitment to removing barriers to this possibility (UN, 2016)

Teachers will require preparation in health and safety protocols, as well as psychosocial support to manage stress and learn how we should support students and other teachers. Promote learning environments, physically safe, emotionally healthy, and psychologically empowering.

For this reason, Inclusive leadership, place the well-being of all at the centre of all action. Its purpose is the creation of learning environments that allow access, permanence, participation, and achievement for all. In this same sense, the development of policies that consolidate inclusion and equity, in addition to the promotion of inclusive culture are fundamental actions.

The education as a human right should be more humanistic and global, recognizing the person, their needs, interests, and expectations and that generates a model that encourages collaboration and solidarity with others and living peace in mind with all including the environment and nature. Inclusion and equity can be used to guide a process of strengthening the capacity of an education system to reach out to all learners in the community.

Undoubtedly, the inclusive leader occupies a very important role in the current period because it contributes to the consolidation of educational organisations that strive to provide quality education with equity for all its members and thus achieve the ideal of an increasingly just and egalitarian society.

In consequence, this approach is eminently humanistic and places the person at the centre of all action; Because it recognizes that each person is valuable, has talent, therefore, it is necessary to identify and create conditions for it to flourish that is why each person must be respected, regardless of their origin, ability, or identity.

In my perspective we need understand equity then diversity, all are unique and that we live in a plurality. Under inclusion quality, equality, equity, and diversity are interconnected. Diversity is recognized as a natural component of every human group and dialogic learning as a vital strategy. The processes of dialogue allow us to learn from each other and can involve various people, but all with the same purpose: to promote learning for all.

In this sense, the learning environments should be safe, welcoming, free of all forms of violence, and exclusion or discrimination, ensuring high level of motivations, engagement, and learning outcome for everyone and promotes inclusive values.

The inclusive leadership must be distributed, and shared, in consequence the relationships are ascending, descending and lateral due to the collaborative culture. Also has high expectations and carries out monitoring and evaluation as planned. He also seeks at all times to maintain a positive relationship with families and various external agents. Establish alliances with other sectors to strengthen broader collaboration and thus strengthen the sense of well-being of the members of their community.

Create conditions that give educators autonomy and flexibility to act and provide support and mentoring opportunities for teachers. Protect the social spaces offered by schools and provide support and follow-up to students who present some condition of vulnerability.

Work with teachers and other staff for the improvement of school results. make each person feel capable.

The benefits of inclusive leadership are diverse, some of them are:

Sense of belonging and purpose in a safe environment, share vision and co-responsibility, empower Individuals and development more empathic and compassionate with all as an inclusive culture.

REFERENCES

Abtar, D., & Moustafa, H. (2017). *In pursuit of Smart Learning Environments for the 21st Century*. IBE-UNESCO.

Ainscow, M. (2016) Collaboration as a strategy for promoting equity in education possibilities and barriers. *CSC JES*. https://www.cscjes-cronfa.co.uk/api/storage/2a6d51d2-92c2-45e3-97a8-2567619e7fb6/Ainscow-paper-for-JPCC-February-2016.pdf

Ainscow, M., & Messiou, K. (2017). *Engaging with the views of students to promote inclusion in education*. Springer.

Aiscow, M. (2016). *Diversity and Equity: A Global Education Challenge*. Springer.

California University. (2021). *El ser biopsicosocial y espiritual*. California University. www.socialwelfare.Berkeley.edu

CEC. (2012). *Co-Teaching and Collaboration. A collection of Articles*. CEC.

Collet, J., & Grinberg, S. (2021). hacia una escuela para lo común. Debates, luchas y propuestas en América Latina y España. Madrid: Morata.

Darling-Hammond, L. (2020). *Implications for educational practice of the sciences of learning and development.* Taylor and Francis. doi:10.10.1080/10888691.2018.1537791

Etling, A. (2005) Liderazgo efectivo, técnicas, recursos y actividades didácticas en la dinámica de grupos. *The inclusive leadership handbook.*. Association. https://inclusiveleadership.eu/

Flecha, R. (2010). *Aprendizaje dialógico en la sociedad de la información*. Hipatia.

Florian, L., & Camedda, D. (2020). Enhancing teacher education for inclusion. *European Journal of Teacher Education*, *43*(1), 4–8. doi:10.1080/02619768.2020.1707579

Forlin, Ch. (2012). *Future Directions for Inclusive Teacher Education*. Routledge. doi:10.4324/9780203113585

Galkiené, O. M (eds). (2021) Improving Inclusive Education through Universal Design for Learning. inclusive learning and Educational Equity 5. doi:10.1007/978-3-030-80658-3_1

Garcia- Huidobro, J. (2001) Conflictos y alianzas en las reformas educativas: siete tesis basadas en la experiencia chilena. Santiago: PREL/CIDE

Giroux, H. (1990). *Los profesores como intelectuales*. Paidós.

Harris, A. (2012). *Liderazgo y desarrollo de capacidades en la escuela*. Fundación Chile.

Howard, G., & Laskin, E. (1998). *Mentes líderes. Una dicotomía del liderazgo*. Paidós.

Kouzes, J., & Posner, B. (2017). *The leadership challenge: How to Make Extraordinary Things Happen in Organizations*. Wiley and Son, Inc.

Kruse, K. (2013) What is Leadership? Cited by the Article: Effective Leadership in the 21st Century. *Open Journal of Social Science, 4*(2).

Leithwood, et al (2004) *How Leadership Influences Student Learning*. University of Minnesota: Carei.

Lodge, C. (2005). From hearing voices to engaging a dialogue: Problematizing student participation in school improvement. *Journal of Educational Change, 6*(2), 125–146. doi:10.100710833-005-1299-3

Lorenzo, M. (2005). El liderazgo en las organizaciones educativas: Revisión y perspectivas actuales. *Revista Española de Pedagogía, 232*, 367–388.

Louis, K. (2010). *How Does Leadership Affect Student Achievement? Results from a National US Survey*. University of Minnesota. doi:10.1080/09243453.2010/486586

Luna-Scott, C. (2015) The futures of Learning 3. *What kind of pedagogies for the 21st Century?* Working Papers, No 15. Paris. UNESCO.

Macedo, D. (1994). *Literacies of power: what Americans are not allowed to know*. Paradigm.

Nieto, C. (2004) Modelos de asesoramiento a organizaciones educativas En: Jesús Domingo Segovia (coord.) Asesoramiento al Centro Educativo: colaboración y cambio en la Institución. Barcelona. Octaedro-EUB pp.147-166

OECD. (2019). *Skills Strategy 2019. Skills to shape a better future*. OECD. doi:10.1787/9789264313835-

Opertti, R. (2017). *15 Clues of Analysis Reflecting Upon the Education 2030 Agenda*. IBE-UNESCO.

Pont, B. (2020). A Literature Review of School Leadership Policy Reforms. *European Journal of Education, 52*(2), 154–168. doi:10.1111/ejed.12398

Prospects 151. (2009) *Inclusive Education: controversies and debates*. UNESCO-IBE.

PROSPECTS 159. (2011) International Developments in Teacher Education for Inclusive Education: issues and challenges. UNESCO-IBE.

Rodríguez, F. (2014) *La co-enseñanza, una estrategia para el mejoramiento educativo y la inclusión*. Educrea. https://educrea.cl/wp-content/uploads/2017/08/DOC- co_enseñanza.pdf

Salazar, M. (2009). Weaving promising practices for inclusive excellence into the higher education classroom. In LB. Nilson and J: E Miller (Eds.) to improve the academy.

Samoilovich, D. (2020) *Liderazgo en tiempos de Covid-19*. UNESCO. https://www.iesalc.unesco.org

Savater, F. (1997). el valor de educar. Barcelona. *Ariel*.

Spillane, J. Paquin, R. y Asmaa Al-Fadala (2019). Educational Leadership: A Multilevel Distributed Perspective. *Wise Qatar*. www.wise-qatar.org/educational-leaderhip-a-multilevel-distributed-perspective

Tuitt, F. (2016). *Race, Equity, and the learning environment: the global relevance of critical and inclusive pedagogies in higher education*. Stylus Publishing, LLC.

UN. (2006) *Convention on the rights of persons with disabilities*. NY: ONU www.social.desa.un.org

UN (2016). *Observación General No. 4 sobre el derecho a la educación inclusiva*. UN.

UNESCO. (2015). *Rethinking Education. Towards a global common good?* UNESCO.

UNESCO. (2016). *Reaching out to All Learners: A Resource Pack for Supporting Inclusive Education*. UNESCO-IBE.

UNESCO. (2017). *A Guide for Ensuring Inclusion and Equity in Education*. UNESCO.

UNESCO. (2019a). *The UNESCO Salamanca Statement 25 years on. Developing inclusive and equitable education system*. UNESCO.

UNESCO. (2019b). *Final Report of the international forum on inclusion and equity in education Paris*. UNESCO.

UNESCO. (2019c). *Futures of Education Initiative*. UNESCO. **www.es.unesco.org/futuresofeducation/**

UNESCO. (2020). *Education in a post- COVID world: nine ideas for public action. International Commission on the Futures of Education*. Paris: UNESCO. https://en.unesco.org/futuresofeducation

UNESCO. (2021). *Garantizar la enseñanza y el aprendizaje inclusivos para la recuperación educativa: formas prácticas de avanzar*. UNESCO.

UNESCO. (2023). *Global Education Monitoring Report on leadership and education.* UNESCO.

UNESCO-GEM. (2020). *Inclusión y Educación. Mensajes clave y recomendaciones. América Latina y el Caribe*. UNESCO. https://en.unesco.org/gem-report/LAC202

UNESCO-IESALC. (2020). *COVID-19 and Higher Education: Today and Tomorrow. Impact analysis, policy responses, and recommendations. April, No.9 Paris.* UNESCO.

UNESCO-UIS. (2012). *A Place to Learn. Lesson from Research on Learning Environments.* Paris, UNESCO. http://www.uis.unesco.org/

UNICEF. (2020). *Averting a lost COVID generation. A six-point plan to protect our children*. UNICEF.

World Bank. (2018). *Learning to Realize Education's Promise*. WBP.

Chapter 6
Unconscious Bias Against Women at Work

Asma Ayari
University of Bahrain, Bahrain

ABSTRACT

Unconscious bias is a prevalent and persistent issue in the workplace, particularly concerning gender. Even though men and women are getting closer to having the same rights, unconscious bias still keeps women from getting ahead at work. It contributes to the pay gap between men and women, fewer chances for professional growth, and other kinds of discrimination based on gender. Organizations must look at these biases and do something about them to make the workplace fairer and more open to everyone. This chapter will overview unconscious bias and its effects on women in the workplace. First, the authors will discuss unconscious bias and how it works in the workplace. Next, they will examine how women's unconscious bias affects their career growth, pay, and chances of getting ahead. Then, the authors will talk about different tools, strategies, and organizations which can be used to assess and deal with unconscious bias, such as bias interrupters, unconscious bias training, and diversity and inclusion initiatives.

INTRODUCTION

Women are underrepresented in companies worldwide, and the number of women gets smaller as you move up the corporate ladder (Cooper et al., 2018). Many things make it hard for women to advance in a company and become leaders. These things include discrimination based on gender and unconscious gender bias (Fiske et al., 2002). Many companies have shown they care about gender equality by making

DOI: 10.4018/978-1-6684-9013-6.ch006

rules that are good for families and making it easier for women to get jobs and join professional networks (Eagly & Karau, 2002). Still, women are affected by unconscious gender bias in the workplace, and more needs to be done to help highly skilled women get into leadership roles.

This study overviews unconscious gender bias and how it can stop women from succeeding in their careers. It then discusses how to avoid and deal with unconscious gender bias in the workplace. The first part of this chapter note talks about unconscious gender bias and gives examples of how it can make it hard for women to advance in their careers. In the second part, the chapter looks at how practical the mitigation steps have been. The third section discusses what managers' groups can do to help their members lessen the effects of unconscious bias.

UNCONSCIOUS GENDER BIAS IN THE WORKPLACE

Unconscious gender bias is when your mind automatically makes gender-based connections based on traditions, norms, values, society, or past experiences (Gul & Lynn, 2021). Automatic links help us make decisions, so we can quickly judge someone based on their gender and gender stereotypes. Organizations can take steps to fight gender bias and other types of discrimination, which means that just because a person has unconscious gender bias doesn't mean that the workplace will also have preferences.

The International Labour Organization Bureau (ILO) for Employers' Activities talked to many companies to determine the most significant problems for women who want to lead. *Women in Business and Management: Gaining Momentum*[1], a global report (2015), shared the findings. Five factors are identified as obstacles that stop women from being leaders: discrimination and unconscious bias based on gender. The social roles of men and women came up as the second most-mentioned barrier in the study. Respondents also said that most people think management is a job for guys. Masculine company culture was the third most-mentioned problem. The respondents also discussed stereotypes about women and gender bias in hiring and promotion. In the same way, a study by McKinsey and Company showed that invisible barriers, glass ceiling, are holding women back. More work needs to be done to eradicate unconscious gender bias so that women and men have equal chances of advancing into leadership roles (Ayari, 2018). Many organizations have made it easier for women to network and advance their careers, but there is still work to be done to eliminate unconscious gender bias.

Gender Bias in Organization Practices and Structures

In recent years, women have made substantial strides in the workforce. They have entered and excelled in many formerly male-dominated industries and disciplines. Despite advancements in gender equality, structures and practices in the workplace that favor men still occasionally disadvantage women. This section provides an overview of human resources practices and other factors that may impede women's career advancement due to implicit bias.

Performance Appraisal

Methods and tools based on traditionally male values inevitably disadvantage women and diminish their opportunities (Glick & Fiske, 1996). Some talent management policies may be biased towards masculinity, for example, by including talent management standards and competencies defined in terms of their appeal to males. For example, the McKinsey report *Women Matter*[2] cited "*unfailing availability and total geographical mobility*" as a leadership criterion for one company's performance indicator (2017). Generally, men's reduced domestic responsibilities make them more available and mobile geographically. Consequently, this criterion has a pro-male, pro-childless prejudice and penalizes women, especially working mothers (Gaucher et al., 2011).

Project Responsibilities

Employees' visibility and competitiveness for promotion rise when they lead or participate in a significant project. There are typically two methods for assigning workers to tasks. Projects with high visibility, high implications, essential duties, and highly particular skill sets or capabilities often require senior executives or teams of people to be involved in the assignment decision. Business unit managers or selected personnel often make arbitrary assignments to lower-profile initiatives (Ely et al., 2020). Both conscious and subconscious prejudices can affect the judgment of who should be given a particular task (Ayari, 2018). Rather than basing their decisions on the employee's talents and worth, managers who lack first-hand knowledge of the staff and the experience or training to mitigate the influence of gender prejudice may rely mainly on perceptions that emerge from stereotypical impressions (Fisher, 2020).

The Concept of Meritocracy

Organizations tend to place emphasis on and concentrate on performance. The paradox of meritocracy suggests that individuals who possess pre-existing advantages may be the ones to reap the benefits of exceptional performance (Block & Nourmair, 2017). When women experience social or cultural disadvantages, a performance appraisal system that solely relies on merit may perpetuate and strengthen those inequities (Ye et al., 2018). In addition, it is possible that managers exhibit overconfidence in their ability to render unbiased judgments and may lack awareness of their own gender biases. In situations where meritocracy is emphasized, it is necessary to implement measures that reduce the discretion given to managers and guarantee that they are held responsible for their actions (Fisher, 2020). It is recommended that compensation and promotions committees consider the potential for unconscious bias in instances where the performance management policy and procedure affords managers a significant degree of discretion, as this may have adverse effects on female employees (Gul & Lynn, 2021).

Leadership Development Programs

Gender disparities persist in leadership development programs, with men and women often experiencing unequal opportunities for participation (Dovido & Gaertner, 2004). This issue is of significant concern, especially considering the pivotal function these programs fulfil in enabling vertical progression within organizational structures (Fiske et al., 2002). The programs cater to senior leaders or individuals with considerable potential. There is an unequal distribution of opportunities among employees. Female employees have reported a significantly lower number of interactions with senior leaders compared to their male counterparts. Furthermore, this disparity becomes more pronounced as women progress in their careers.

Women in the Workplace, a 2016 report by McKinsey & Company more than 34,000 workers from companies all over North America were in the poll group. Each business that took part sent information about its talent pipeline, policies, and programs related to gender diversity by December 31, 2015. Pipeline data included the current gender balance (overall and by race or ethnicity), the number of hires, promotions, and workers who left the company by gender, as well as the number of line and staff roles. A survey of 39 businesses is used to report on how employees feel about their jobs. There were 83 questions in the poll. The data reveals that women's interaction with company leaders is comparatively lower at the senior management level than men's. Specifically, only 51% of women reported interacting. It is advisable to have a weekly meeting with a company executive, while 62% of men said the same about the frequency of interaction.

The Standards and Norms

The established conventions within a workplace may impede the professional advancement of women. The perpetuation of the "manager-think-male" perspective is observed when men predominantly occupy senior leadership positions (Gul & Lynn, 2021). Corporations must consider the prominence of minority groups and their potential implications for perpetuating societal stereotypes (Brescoll et al., 2010). In addition, policies such as quotas may give rise to the perception that the mere presence of women in small numbers indicates significant progress toward achieving gender equality, thereby obviating the need to persist in addressing the underlying problem of gender bias (Dovido & Gaertner, 2004).

Evaluating Implicit Gender Bias in the Workplace

To surmount the challenges delineated in the preceding section, organizations must evaluate their operations to identify latent gender bias and quantify its effects on personnel. Organizations have a range of techniques to assess their performance, such as perception surveys, linguistic analysis, examination of gender disparities in compensation and professional growth, and experimental studies. The following section outlines each of the techniques above.

Perception Surveys

Perception surveys are a research tool to gather data on individuals' subjective views and opinions regarding a particular topic or issue. One general approach for evaluating implicit gender bias in the workplace involves collecting experiential data from individuals. The methodology in the query was employed in the worldwide study on women in corporate and managerial roles and documented locally. Organizations were requested to enumerate impediments hindering women's progress in attaining leadership positions. Seventy percent of the participants in a recent survey of female professionals in science, technology, engineering, and mathematics (STEM) in the kingdom of Bahrain agreed or strongly agreed that unconscious bias had negatively impacted their career progression (Ayari, 2022). Additionally, 60% of the respondents strongly agreed or agreed that unconscious bias harmed their earnings. According to the findings, men identified unconscious bias as the primary obstacle impeding the advancement of women's careers.

The Analysis of Language

In contemporary times, there is a decrease in the prevalence of job descriptions that explicitly state the preferred gender of the optimal candidate, although such instances still occur in some areas of the globe (Dovido & Gaertner, 2004). Notwithstanding the absence of explicit gender bias in a job description, it is plausible that it may perpetuate and strengthen gender-based preconceptions in inconspicuous manners (Glick & Fiske, 1996). As an illustration, specific lexicons are linked to prevalent gender stereotypes, and such lexicons may indicate an inadvertent gender partiality. Different studies identified a correlation between gender and specific adjectives (Ye et al., 2018). Women were found to be associated with adjectives such as "emotional," "mild," "pleasant," "sensitive," "warm," "affective," and "friendly," while men were associated with adjectives such as "dominant," "achievement-oriented," "ambitious," "self-confident," "rational," "tough," and "aggressive." If an organization describes its leaders and job descriptions for leadership positions using language typically associated with male gender traits, such as "dominant" and "ambitious," then male candidates may receive an advantage due to an implicit bias in their favor. Men are often perceived as more suitable candidates, whereas women may face unconscious bias (Bohnet, 2016; Ayari, 2022).

The language utilized in job advertisements posted on prominent job search websites in all countries describe occupations that men predominantly hold compared to women, which revealed a significant association between the utilization of gender-biased language in job advertisements and the ratio of male and female representation in a given occupation (Bohnet, 2016). The job advertisements for professions with a higher proportion of male workers, such as plumbers, contained more words associated with male stereotypes. Conversely, job ads for computer programmers featured a lower frequency of such language (Koc et al., 2021). Similarly, a more substantial proportion of the lexicon related to female gender stereotypes was observed in job postings for administrative assistants compared to those for human resources professionals. Moreover, different researches indicated that women are less inclined to find employment attractive if they perceive it as male-dominated (Dovido & Gaertner, 2004).

An Examination of Disparities Between Genders

The gender disparities in professional settings can be attributed, at least partially, to gender-based prejudice (Dobbin & Kalev, 2018). Gender disparities are prevalent in various domains, encompassing career progression and remuneration, along with discrepancies in recruitment, mentorship, and avenues for career growth (Valian, 1998). A thorough examination of these discrepancies may reveal the influence of implicit gender prejudice. An observable gender disparity has been noted in corporate occupations that are prerequisites for leadership roles and executive management, including line functions that entail profit-and-loss responsibility or a concentration on core operations (Ayari, 2022). There is a correlation between an employee's gender and their specific job function, according to McKinsey and Company's analysis of data from 132 companies. At advanced career stages, female professionals tend to transition from line functions to staff positions, such as those in human resources and public relations (Fisher, 2020). This phenomenon leads to a limited number of women continuing on the trajectory toward the uppermost echelons of management. The observed pattern of women occupying staff positions and men occupying sales and general management positions implies the existence of an implicit gender bias that segregates individuals based on their gender (Ye et al., 2018).

According to research conducted on the workforce of a sizable service entity, it was observed that despite the absence of any gender-based disparities in performance evaluations, a higher proportion of male employees were promoted as compared to their female counterparts. This phenomenon persisted even though the organization explicitly tied incentives to individual performance. Bohnet (2016) posited that the inclination to reward men based on their performance might stem from the societal stereotype that women are less likely to assert themselves and negotiate for a promotion (Moss-Racusin et al., 2012). An investigation was conducted on a sample comprising more than 8,000 financial sector employees to explore the compensation gender disparity. The findings revealed that bonuses and variable pay exhibited a more significant gender gap than base salaries or merit raises after controlling for performance. According to Bohnet (2016), the absence of established regulations for allocating bonuses and variable compensation, in contrast to the formal rules governing base salaries, accounts for this phenomenon (Gul & Lynn, 2021). The phenomenon of unconscious gender bias seems to exert a more pronounced adverse effect on women when decisions are made without established regulations (Block & Noumair, 2017). The phenomenon of unconscious bias can also influence employers' perceptions toward potential employees who are parents (Koc et al., 2021). A comparative analysis was conducted on candidates with similar qualifications, revealing that mothers were notably less likely to receive recommendations for employment. In cases where they were recommended, they were presented with initial salaries that were, on average, US$11,000 less than those offered to childless women with comparable qualifications (Ayari, 2022). In contrast to childless men, fathers were not subject to penalties but received notably high salaries. The observed discrepancy implies the presence of a predisposition that imposes a disadvantage on females, specifically those who are employed and have children. Providing employees with feedback on their work is crucial to facilitating their efforts to enhance their performance (Smith et al., 2021). According to McKinsey's research (2016), there exists a gender disparity in the amount of feedback received by women compared to their male counterparts, despite both genders requesting informal feedback at similar frequencies.

Experiments

This approach is based on the self-reported gender perceptions of participants in response to a given scenario or factual information. The case study titled 'Howard vs. Heidi' delved into the trade-off between competency and likeability that women leaders face. The study's participants were tasked with assessing the aptitude and efficacy of a candidate, who was presented in a rotating fashion as either Howard or Heidi. They were then requested to provide a performance evaluation and competency rating. All other pertinent information remained unchanged. The individual was introduced as a venture capitalist with prior experience as an entrepreneur and exceptional skills in networking. The individual in question was a co-founder of a highly prosperous technology enterprise, subsequently assumed an executive role at Apple, and transitioned to venture capitalism. The candidate has recently been appointed to the board of directors of various esteemed organizations[3].

Upon encountering the individual referred to as 'Howard,' the participants evaluated him as possessing a significant degree of competence and efficacy. Additionally, he was perceived as amiable, and his employability or potential for collaboration was positively regarded. Nonetheless, upon being provided with identical information concerning a candidate identified as 'Heidi,' the participants distinctly evaluated her. Even though her peers thought Heidi was capable and effective, there needed to be more inclination or willingness to work with her. Considering that gender was the sole variable examined in the case study, it is a plausible deduction to make that there exists a gender bias wherein high-achieving women are perceived as less amiable than their high-achieving male counterparts. According to Bohnet (2016), there is a tendency in society to praise male entrepreneurship, self-assurance, and foresight, while females frequently interpret these qualities as conceit and excessive self-promotion. Balancing achievement and affability becomes more pronounced when females occupy positions traditionally associated with masculinity[4].

THE PROCESS OF REDUCING THE IMPACT OF UNCONSCIOUS BIAS

The gender bias that is not consciously recognized can exist in individuals and institutions. This section examines measures organizations can implement to mitigate the impact of unconscious gender biases on an individual's decision-making process.

Approaches to Making Impartial Personnel Determinations and Effectively Managing Talent

Companies must guarantee that their hiring and promotion procedures provide both male and female candidates with equitable opportunities (Kennedy & Jain-Link, 2021). Numerous organizations have reported the existence of policies aimed at facilitating impartial recruitment, evaluation of performance, and promotion (Heilman & Haynes, 2005). However, these policies may not always be all-encompassing or executed optimally. This section outlines strategies organizations can implement to mitigate the effects of unintentional gender bias in crucial workforce management procedures.

Blind Evaluation

Blind evaluation refers to assessing or reviewing a piece of work without knowledge of the identity of the author or creator. Concealing the physical characteristics of job candidates can mitigate the impact of implicit bias on the recruitment and selection process. Despite its relative simplicity, the adoption of this practice has been limited to a minority of companies. Numerous web-based recruitment platforms incorporate software that facilitates the ability of companies to transcend physical attributes and enhance their hiring and evaluation processes. Gap Jumpers mandates that every job applicant complete skill-based assessments indicative of their potential job performance (Moss-Racusin & Johnson, 2016).

Their performance on the challenges solely determines their advancement to the following evaluation stage. This methodology does not entirely preclude the possibility of inadvertent partiality from impeding subsequent phases of the application procedure, but it does eradicate partiality from the preliminary phase (Johnson et al., 2011). As per the findings of Gap Jumpers, after the blind testing phase, a majority of approximately 58 percent of the candidates who were shortlisted for an interview were identified as women. Furthermore, out of the candidates who were ultimately recruited, a significant proportion—approximately 68 percent—were women. Blind testing has resulted in an average 60% increase in job placement for diverse candidates at Gap Jumpers (Rudman & Glick, 2001).

Structured Recruitment and Performance Evaluation

A systematic recruitment procedure can mitigate unconscious biases based on gender. Candidates are assessed using relevant and predetermined criteria related to work performance through structured interviews. To eliminate discrimination based on a candidate's gender, comparing their responses to specific questions using objective measures is helpful (Moss-Racusin & Rudman, 2010).

Unconscious bias can plague a business if employees aren't evaluated consistently. Some companies have instituted a ranking system to ensure managers always consider employees (Madva & Brownstein, 2018). However, there needs to be more research on the influence of rating and ranking systems in performance management on male and female employees, and the evidence needs to be more conclusive (Koc et al., 2021). Training for those in charge of reviewing performance and implementing processes and procedures that enhance judgments, such as having a few evaluators do independent assessments before coming together and listing each metric, could help mitigate the influence of unconscious bias on intuitive decisions. Reviewers may be asked to justify their weightings for certain factors (Kim, 1999). Human resources might monitor any instances of unconscious sexism in the workplace.

Accountability and Openness to Inspection

Companies should encourage employees to evaluate their performance and determine what training and education opportunities will best prepare them for future promotions (Gutek & Morasch, 1982). This method and others were implemented to ensure that a diverse group of people is considered for promotions and judged fairly (Moss-Racusin et al., 2012). Scotiabank is an example of a company that established a Human Investment Committee to facilitate communication between the President and CEO and their direct reports. Scotiabank found the Senior Vice President of Top Talent role and recruited a woman to serve as a role model for the bank's most promising employees (Rudman et al., 2012). The percentage of women in upper-level management rose dramatically, from 18.9% in 2003 to 31% in 2006. The rate of women serving as executive vice presidents or corporate officers increased from 26.7% in 2003 to 36.8% in 2006.

Using Data

The analysis of data trends and the detection of gender gaps can reveal hidden biases. These voids can be evaluated for their suitability as targets for change. It can be challenging to assess results objectively due to preconceived notions and personal prejudices. Two of the significant stock brokerage businesses in the United States pay their female employees roughly 60% of what they pay their male employees (Dasgupta & Asgari, 2004). Women stockbrokers were assumed to make less money than their male counterparts due to the commission structure under which they worked.

However, the data showed that, compared to their male counterparts, female brokers were offered fewer lucrative accounts and fewer sales chances (Brescoll et al., 2010; Rudman et al., 2012). There has been a recent uptick in the use of data analytics by large organizations to address gender disparities in the workplace. For instance, Google's data analysis showed that female employees quit at twice the rate of their male counterparts. Google aimed to lower the turnover rate because it had financial implications. A data study showed that while women, in general, were twice as likely to quit their jobs, young moms were twice as likely to quit their jobs specifically. Google's new parental leave policy came about because the company realized the importance of this factor. Thanks to the strategy, new mothers at Google are no more likely to leave than any other employee. Google has since zeroed in on the five most telling signs of employee turnover and adjusted its retention efforts appropriately (Ye et al., 2018).

Training Employees

Companies have begun investing in diversity training to alter employee mindsets and practices. However, there needs to be more detail on how practical training is. "Best Practices or Best Guesses?" is one such question. According to a study titled "Evaluating the Impact of Corporate Affirmative Action and Diversity Policies," (Dobbin & Kalev, 2018) 800 medium- to large-sized American businesses were evaluated between 1971 and 2002. Diversity training was linked to a lower probability that some under-represented groups would progress to managerial positions in some situations. Unconscious bias may be the missing ingredient in the success of diversity training courses. Instead, deliberate, conscious thought was emphasized in diversity training. While the vast majority of firms provide anti-harassment and discrimination training, just 67% of employers and 56% of managers provide training to eliminate bias in recruiting and performance reviews, respectively (McKinsey & Company, 2016). Workers are less likely to recognize their preferences and make objective judgments when they lack knowledge of how bias operates (Ye et al., 2018). They are less inclined to speak out against prejudice when confronted with it. Unconscious bias training may exist, but it must be implemented more effectively. According to the research and observations of specialists in the field, education about the existence of unconscious prejudice in general, cannot be eliminated in companies (Valian, 1998). Capacity building is an essential adjunct to training to help participants learn to manage the adverse effects of their biases. It should also encourage people to work to overcome their implicit biases (Williams & Dempsey, 2014).

OVERCOMING UNCONSCIOUS GENDER BIAS

This section explains how businesses and individuals can get help to lessen the effects of gender bias at work (Stout et al., 2011). Risk factors, specific dangers, and mitigation strategies can all be discussed and learned about with the assistance of employer organizations. Offering training that addresses implicit biases based on gender is another possibility (Williams & Dempsey, 2014).

Analysis

Unconscious sexism has no cookie-cutter answer. Interventions that work best consider the specific situation and difficulties at hand (Rudman et al., 2012). For instance, Catalyst provides the Stereotypes Diagnostic Instrument to its member companies so that they may evaluate their vulnerability and decide where to focus their efforts. It considers the institutional conditions that socio-psychological studies have shown to play a crucial role in forming and maintaining gender stereotypes (Smith et al., 2021; Ayari, 2022). The Stereotypes Diagnostic Instrument takes into account the following variables:

- ***Organizational size and industry*:** Although the number of employees does not directly increase risk, the number of workers in an organization may alter how other risk factors overlap and the efficacy of human resource practices in encouraging change. Similarly, research shows that women face more obstacles to climbing the corporate ladder in male-dominated industries (Ye et al., 2018).
- ***Gender parity across the company, by department, and at various managerial tiers*:** Stereotypical bias is more likely to arise when there is an imbalance between women and men in the workforce or when a small number of people from underrepresented groups are given prominent positions. When one gender dominates in positions of power, and the other dominates in support roles, broad assumptions can be made regarding the significance of gender in occupational selection (Williams & Dempsey, 2014).
- ***Human resource practices:*** Ongoing efforts to be more inclusive, such as implementing human resource programs to improve hiring and promotion practices and performance evaluation practices (for instance, whether there are objective and unambiguous evaluation criteria), are relevant factors (Stout et al., 2011). Personnel, the ratio of women to men on boards, and staff development are other factors to consider (Williams & Dempsey, 2014). Researchers will need access to the participating organizations' performance management documentation to analyse human resource practices accurately.

- ***The climate in the workplace:*** Primarily, assumptions about what makes an "ideal worker" and how managers should act to foster such a culture (Swim & Sanna, 1996).

Companies can gauge their progress toward gender diversity targets with evaluation tools that help them establish priorities and keep tabs on qualitative and quantitative indicators. Multinational corporations and their affiliates have reaped the benefits of these tools thus far, but many other businesses still need to be included. Employer groups can fill the gap that companies of all sizes face in their communities to lessen the harmful effects of unconscious sexism in the workplace (Williams & Dempsey, 2014). Existing technologies can be localized and adapted to the needs of employers' organizations' members through collaboration with local think tanks, human resources corporations, and academia.

Training

Companies can receive training on addressing and preventing unconscious prejudices linked to gender and other issues from employer advocacy groups. Training programs often consist of three parts:

- Identifying implicit and structural prejudices in the workplace,
- Showing how the bias manifests itself,
- Training participants to recognize and overcome their prejudices by providing them with the necessary information and skills.

For instance, in February 2016, the National Women's Council of Ireland released an unconscious bias training pack that details the drawbacks of ignoring gender bias in hiring, promoting, and retaining employees, as well as the advantages to businesses of having more women in positions of authority (Smith et al., 2021). The training pack is free to businesses and includes everything needed to conduct a half-day seminar on unconscious gender bias. Training participants can learn to recognize and address unconscious prejudice in their workplace by examining real-life examples presented in case studies. Notes for trainers on how to approach the sessions and successfully deliver the training program are also included in the box (Scott et al., 2017).

CONCLUSION

This chapter finds that most research on gender prejudice in the workplace has been conducted in the United States and Europe. However, there is a need for more research to gather data on the impact of unconscious gender bias in many different nations, such as Arabic countries, as previous studies have primarily focused on global corporations. Organizations representing national businesses can help bridge the knowledge divide. They can discuss gender bias in the workplace with their members and the wider business community. In addition, they can offer services to their constituents to lessen the effects of implicit bias in the workplace.

REFERENCES

Ayari. A., (2018). "Women and Careers: The Issues of the Glass Ceiling". *Arab Women and Their Evolving Roles in the Global Business Landscape*. 74-86.

Ayari, A. (2022). *Bahraini Women in the STEM Fields: Sticky Floor, Broken Ladder, and Glass Ceiling*. EDAS.

Block, C. J., & Noumair, D. A. (2017). Understanding Diversity Dynamics in Systems: Social Equality as an Organization Change Issue. *The Journal of Applied Behavioral Science*, *53*(2), 150–155. doi:10.1177/0021886317703250

Bohnet. I. (2016). *What works: Gender Equality by Design*. Harvard University Press.

Brescoll, V. L., Dawson, E., & Uhlmann, E. L. (2010). Hard won and easily lost: The fragile status of leaders in gender-stereotype-incongruent occupations. *Psychological Science*, *21*(11), 1640–1642. doi:10.1177/0956797610384744 PMID:20876882

Cooper, M. J., Kriegel, D. T., & Brownell, M. T. (2018). Implicit bias in schools: A primer. *The Journal of Special Education*, *51*(3), 166–177.

Dasgupta, N., & Asgari, S. (2004). Seeing is believing: Exposure to counter stereotypic women leaders and its effect on the malleability of automatic gender stereotyping. *Journal of Experimental Social Psychology*, *40*(5), 642–658. doi:10.1016/j.jesp.2004.02.003

Dobbin, F., & Kalev, A. (2018). Why does not diversity training work? The challenge for industry and academia. *Anthropology Now*, *10*(2), 48–55. doi:10.1080/19428200.2018.1493182

Dovidio, J. F., & Gaertner, S. L. (2004). Aversive racism. In M. P. Zanna (Ed.), Vol. 36, pp. 1–52). Advances in Experimental Social Psychology. Academic Press.

Eagly, A. H., & Karau, S. J. (2002). Role congruity theory of prejudice toward female leaders. *Psychological Review, 109*(3), 573–598. doi:10.1037/0033-295X.109.3.573 PMID:12088246

Ely, R. J., & Thomas, D. A. (2020, November–December). Getting Serious About Diversity. *Harvard Business Review.*

Fisher, D. R. (2020). *The diversity of the recent Black Lives Matter protests is a good sign for racial equity.*

Fiske, S. T., Cuddy, A. J., Glick, P., & Xu, J. (2002). A model of (often mixed) stereotype content: Competence and warmth, respectively, follow from perceived status and competition. *Journal of Personality and Social Psychology, 82*(6), 878–902. doi:10.1037/0022-3514.82.6.878 PMID:12051578

Gaucher, D., Friesen, J., & Kay, A. C. (2011). There is evidence that gendered wording in job advertisements exists and sustains gender inequality. *Journal of Personality and Social Psychology, 101*(1), 109–128. doi:10.1037/a0022530 PMID:21381851

Glick, P., & Fiske, S. T. (1996). The Ambivalent Sexism Inventory. *Journal of Personality and Social Psychology, 70*(3), 491–512. doi:10.1037/0022-3514.70.3.491

Gul, P., & Lynn, M. (2021). Unconscious Gender Bias. *An Exploratory Study of the Implicit Association Test Journal of Business and Psychology, 36*(2), 303–319. doi:10.100710869-020-09695-y

Gutek, B. A., & Morasch, B. (1982). Sex ratios, sex-role spillover, and sexual harassment of women at Work. *Journal of Social Issues, 38*(4), 55–74

Heilman, M. E., & Haynes, M. C. (2005). No credit where credit is due: An attributional rationalization of women's success in male-female teams. *The Journal of Applied Psychology, 90*(5), 905–916. doi:10.1037/0021-9010.90.5.905 PMID:16162063

Johnson, K. L., Richeson, J. A., & Finkel, E. J. (2011). Middle-class African Americans' perceptions of discrimination, race, and class: A rational analysis. *Journal of Personality and Social Psychology, 101*(6), 1178–1195.

Kennedy, J. T., & Jain-Link, P. (2021, June). What does it take to build a culture of belonging? *Harvard Business Review.*

Kim, D. H. (1999). *Introduction to Systems Thinking* (Vol. 16). Pegasus Communications.

Koc, Y., Hekim, H., & Buyukgoze Kavas, A. (2021). Unconscious Bias and Gender Differences in Language: A Comparative Analysis. *Journal of Gender Studies, 30*(3), 381–396. doi:10.1080/09589236.2020.1773646

Madva, A., & Brownstein, M. (2018). Embodied social cognition. *Ergo, an Open Access Journal of Philosophy, 5*(9), 237–280

Moss-Racusin, C. A., Dovidio, J. F., Brescoll, V. L., Graham, M. J., & Handelsman, J. (2012). The science faculty's subtle gender biases favor male students. *Proceedings of the National Academy of Sciences of the United States of America, 109*(41), 16474–16479. doi:10.1073/pnas.1211286109 PMID:22988126

Moss-Racusin, C. A., & Johnson, K. L. (2016). Implicit bias and women in academia: How do we move forward? *The Journal of Research in Gender Studies, 6*(1), 8–22.

Moss-Racusin, C. A., & Rudman, L. A. (2010). Disruptions in women's self-promotion: The backlash avoidance model. *Psychology of Women Quarterly, 34*(2), 186–202. doi:10.1111/j.1471-6402.2010.01561.x

Rudman, L. A., & Glick, P. (2001). Prescriptive gender stereotypes and backlash toward agentic women. *The Journal of Social Issues, 57*(4), 743–762. doi:10.1111/0022-4537.00239

Rudman, L. A., Moss-Racusin, C. A., Phelan, J. E., & Nauts, S. (2012). Status incongruity and backlash effects: Defending the gender hierarchy motivates prejudice against female leaders. *Journal of Experimental Social Psychology, 48*(1), 165–179. doi:10.1016/j.jesp.2011.10.008

Scott, A., Klein, F. K., & Onovakpuri, U. (2017). *Tech Leavers Study: A First of its Kind Analysis of Why People Voluntarily Left Jobs in Tech.* Kapor Center for Social Impact.

Smith, J. D., Johnson, L. K., & Brown, K. L. (2021). Unconscious bias in the workplace. *Journal of Business and Psychology, 36*(2), 123–135.

Stout, J. G., Dasgupta, N., Hunsinger, M., & McManus, M. A. (2011). Stemming the tide: Using in-group experts to inoculate women's self-concept in science, technology, engineering, and mathematics (STEM). *Journal of Personality and Social Psychology, 100*(2), 255–270. doi:10.1037/a0021385 PMID:21142376

Swim, J. K., & Sanna, L. J. (1996). He is skilled; she is lucky. A meta-analysis of observers' attributions for women's and men's successes and failures. *Personality and Social Psychology Bulletin, 22*(5), 507–519. doi:10.1177/0146167296225008

Valian, V. (1998). *Why so slow? The advancement of women.* MIT Press.

Williams, J. C., & Dempsey, R. (2014). *What works for women at work: four patterns working women need to know New York*. NYU Press.

Ye, S., Cai, S., Chen, C., Wan, Q., & Qian, X. (2018). How have males and females been described over the past two centuries? An analysis of Big-Five personality-related adjectives in the Google English Books. *Journal of Research in Personality*, *76*, 6–16. doi:10.1016/j.jrp.2018.06.007

ENDNOTES

1. ILO ACT/EMP: Women in business and management: Gaining momentum, Global report, 2015.
2. McKinsey & Company Report: women Matter: Ten years of insights on gender diversity. October 4, 2017. Women Matter: Ten years of insights on gender diversity | McKinsey
3. National Center for Women and Information Technology (2016), "Women in IT: The Facts Infographic." https://ncwit.org/women-in-it-the-facts-infographic-2016-update.
4. McKinsey & Company: Women in the workplace, 2016.

Chapter 7
Diversity, Equality, and Inclusion in Education:
A Cultural Analysis of TALIS 2018

Mehmet Tufan Yalçin
Institute of Social Sciences, Çankırı Karatekin University, Turkey

Ramazan Atasoy
https://orcid.org/0000-0002-9198-074X
Faculty of Education, Harran University, Turkey

ABSTRACT

Researchers and policymakers have increasingly recognized the importance of studying diversity, equality, and inclusion in education. These studies can help identify how cultural values influence the learning outcomes of immigrants and inform evidence-based policymaking. This book chapter aims to scrutinize the diversity, equality, and inclusion practices in schools within the scope of Hofstede's cultural values in the sample of the countries participating in the TALIS 2018 survey. The sample consisted of 13,730 schools from 44 countries participating in both studies. The study found that only the masculinity dimension was negatively associated with teachers' diversity beliefs. The study found that DEI beliefs were in many points unrelated to Hofstede's cultural dimensions. Future research could explore multilevel models that include cultural dimensions and diversity and equality beliefs, as well as results from international assessments.

INTRODUCTION

Due to the rapid technological changes, the development of transportation vehicles, pandemic problems and wars in the last half-century, the migration transitivity of

DOI: 10.4018/978-1-6684-9013-6.ch007

individuals between countries has increased considerably in the globalizing world. In a rapidly changing world, the interaction of people from different cultures is increasing, and "cultural diversity" - which can actually be counted as wealth - is sometimes seen as a barrier to be overcome at the personal and organizational level by some individuals and institutions.

Especially in developed countries, due to the high living standards, it has triggered the immigration mobility of individuals who desire social and economic welfare. This mobility which can be seen as humanitarian, can negatively affect the existing systems of the countries exposed to immigration and cause social conflicts and incompatibilities. On the other hand, it is seen that the policies and social approaches of some countries towards immigrants are more egalitarian and respectful of cultural diversity. In the background of these social moulds or prejudices and dominant mental structures of individuals, it is a current field of study developed by Hofstede in order to compare the cultural elements of the countries and how it relates to the widely used cultural dimensions. In the context of Hoftsede's study, previous determinations of collectivist, feminine, high-power distance, uncertainty avoidance and high tolerance tendencies indicate that cultural diversity in education which is discussed in the TALIS study may be important in the perception and preference of equality and inclusion mechanisms.

To cope with social inequality and procure social inclusion towards cultural diversity, many educational systems attempt to develop and perform initiatives to improve the status of disadvantaged groups (e.g., immigrants, gender, and racial/ethnic minority groups). Such diversity, equity, and inclusion (DEI) policies are controversial because people disagree about whether they are necessary and what extent impacts could be. However, research evidence has revealed that people who are in advantaged groups that are fueled by the cultural status quo and mental structures have the potential to be opposite to DEI policies and practices. The dissenters of DEI can consider that the success of the national education policies, corporate psychology and organizational image may undermine the ineffectiveness of human and substance resources. In fact, if the mentioned cultural diversity is managed well, it can be said that the most important power of states to benefit from the advantages of DEI is education. Therefore, the issue of intercultural diversity issue has always been the focus of attention of researchers.

School leaders have a critical role in the practices of DEI policies at the school level. On the other hand, school leadership practices vary among cultures and although these practices contain many similarities, the duties and responsibilities of principals can differ from each other. The authority of school leaders may, in one context, be based primarily on legitimate, referent, or expert power, while in others, it may be based on reward and coercive power. Therefore, school principals' authority stills are unlikely to be the same in all cultural contexts. Accordingly, it is interesting to explore school principals' and teachers' beliefs and practices about diversity, equality, and inclusion by making a general comparison with other TALIS 2018 participating countries under consideration with Hofstede's cultural dimension. In this context, it will be easier/occasion to improve the basis of authority that the countries will give to school principals by clustering the similarities and differences referencing the behavior of school principals towards foreign students according to cultural characteristics.

The Purpose of the Study

This study focuses specifically on how diversity, equity, and inclusion (DEI) beliefs, attitudes and practices are linked with Hofstede's cultural values such as individualist/ collectivist, power distance, uncertainty avoidance, and masculinity/femininity of the countries. In this section, first of all, the definition, theoretical framework and importance of the concepts of diversity, equality and inclusion in education have been mentioned. In the second part, Hofstede's determinations on cultural studies and its dimensions have been presented. In the third part, according to the TALIS 2018 study, the relationship between teachers' beliefs and practices regarding diversity and equality and Hofstede's cultural dimensions have been examined. In the last part of the section, a general evaluation has been explored in the context of Türkiye which hosts the highest number of immigrants among the countries participating in the TALIS 2018 study.

Diversity in Education

In the 21st century, modern differentiated societies are started to be characterized by social transformations. In two decades, school demographics have changed rapidly due to various global challenges, transnationalisation of social environments, and sociocultural contexts such as gender, age, race, income, disability, faith, educational status, socioeconomic status, transnationalities and hybridization, trends in immigration status, sexual identity, political conviction, and literacy (Arsel et al., 2022; Gill et al., 2018). Diversity, equity, and inclusion are mostly linked with educational policy within the many educational systems traced back to deep cultural roots and the (inter)national educational tradition. Even though this diversity serves up potential opportunities for positive transformation, it can present administrative and instructional challenges for school leaders and teachers regarding school experiences/outcomes.

Diversity means actual and/or perceived physical differences in social and cultural identities that could change depending on the cultural context and awareness of difference (Arsel et al., 2022). Cultural experiences, cultural practices, institutions, and social structures can shape human behavior by forcing an impact on his/her goals, values, beliefs, stimuli, emotions, and expectations (Neblett Jr., 2019). Hofmann (2012) has handled the term diversity as a debate field linked with the proper economic, social, political, legal, and educational diversity as contexted by specific theories rather than a unified concept.

Diversity in education is crucial and salient because it exhibits students to various social and cultural teams, groups, and networks, fitting individuals to become better citizens, protecting civil rights and promoting tolerance and indulgence amid increasing racial, ethnic, and cultural diversity. Diversity indulgence can also help teachers who structure lessons to reflect differences and assist their students to identify with each other. Structural inequalities such as age, gender, disability, language, religious differetiation or socio-economic differences and more deeper diversity such as national-ethno-cultural affiliations, social diversity contexts, different cultural backgrounds, caste systems, and cultural relations, have been continuing to affect educational outcomes and individual quality of life. Historically, research labelled diversity has prioritized opportunities and access for excluded and disadvantaged groups at schools. In recent years, educational administration researchers have focused on groups that are under-represented, disadvantaged or vulnerable such as women who are under-represented in academic and leadership positions. However, with the advent of Industry 4.0 in the 21st century, diversity in education is inseparably associated with equality (Volckmar, 2019). So, researchers have addressed to investigate in more detailed styles how diversity could be maintained providing educational fairness and diversity opportunities to all students at the same time. As a result of these changes to the workforce demographics, diversity researchers have taken a closer look at diversity composition from a different perspective and more broadly (Ballard et al., 2020) focused on an inclusive approach, value-in-diversity (Cox & Blake, 1991), cultural sensitivity (Yesufu, 2013), diversity, equity, and global interconnectedness (Merryfield, 2000), multiculturalism and education (McKinney, 2012), integrating education (McGlynn, 2009), and socioeconomic status (Cross, 2004) at schools.

Equity, Equality, and Inclusion Phenomenon in Education

Equity in education is one of the complex touchstones of education policy that aims to provide equal opportunity to all students in the provision of education services. Taking individual circumstances into consideration, it aims to improve valuable knowledge, skills, and competencies to assist them lifelong. Equity associated mostly with utilitarian considerations and fair competition is linked with human capital. It refers to the principle of fairness in providing students with what they need to achieve their educational goals regardless of their family, school and or national background, socioeconomic profile, gender, language, race, learning capability, or disability. To obtain this goal last decades' years, education policy makers have more prioritized equity policies and reforms in school systems of learning.

Researchers set out that there consisted of widespread and strong confusion about equity and equality concepts. Both have interchangeably been used involving in terms of goals and results in educational settings (Espinoza, 2007; Lazenby, 2016). Equity in education is different from equality which means applying, allocating, or distributing the same resources or opportunities to all students (Rawls, 2005). Equity refers to struggling with discrimination against specific groups, especially those discriminated by race and gender. On the other hand, equality refers to providing every student with the same experience. Equality continues to remain on every occasion as an inclusive basis. Therefore, it is essential to keep in mind that equality and equity in education are not mutually exclusive, but complementary and interdependent concepts, and finding the right balance between them is crucial. For example, it is unrealistic to expect that all students will achieve the same academic outcomes because there are many factors that influence their learning.

Equity in education is linked to the support of student' real, expected, or perceived needs. The worldwide reactions and negative perspectives towards multiculturalism (Banting & Kymlicka, 2013) gives to a greater or lesser extent a new debate area for reflection on diversity and equality. It has often been ignored in many times that immigrants, disabled students or students from diverse cultural backgrounds face various challenges in some segments of society (Bosniak, 2006) when it comes to their school experiences, such as their access to education, their acceptance by others, their limitations, and their support needs.

Equity is one of the main focal subjects of Hofstede's cultural values theory. It refers to how people in a culture treat each other fairly and equally. While Hofstede's cultural values theory ensures a helpful framework for understanding how culture affects behavior, it is important to recognize that equity is just one of several dimensions that can influence social interactions and to acknowledge that different cultures may have different definitions of what constitutes 'fairness' or 'equality'. This possible different perception or interpretation of the concept among cultures can complicate efforts to promote greater equity across societies. In cultures with high equity, people are expected to be treated fairly and equally regardless of their social status or background. In societies/schools with high levels of equity, individuals are more likely to trust each other and collaborate effectively, which can lead to greater student achievement, student well-being, and social stability. On the other hand, in cultures with low equity, people are expected to be treated differently based on their social status or background.

Considering that equality is a multidimensional, complex and relevant concept that depends on many factors, one might think that understanding horizontal and vertical inequalities in school settings requires only a cross-cultural assessment at first glance. However, research evidence indicated that even within the same culture, people may have different ways of defining and categorizing themselves and others, and different ways of including or excluding others based on their differences. Moreover, (Solomon, 2013) have pointed out the exploration of the complex and diverse world of families where a child has a horizontal and vertical identity that is very different from that of the parents. People are influenced by various factors to engage in activities that include or exclude others and to create and refine cultural categories. What is even more important for DEI in schools is to acknowledge that identities are not fixed or predetermined entities that people simply adopt and that they can be shaped by certain historical, environmental and political conditions. Inclusive education practices and transformative leadership approaches that view diversity as a source of richness and opportunity can help develop this understanding and improve the school's equality and respect for diversity in education.

Evidence suggests that the highest performing education systems are those that ensure more equity, provide more access, and combine more higher-level skills and knowledge (OECD, 2012). Access to pre-school education at an earlier age is a huge window of opportunity for each education system. Many students may not have the same opportunities to benefit from educational opportunities due to individual, social and economic conditions, or due to inequalities arising from cultural contexts and traditional prejudices. In this reason, disadvantaged students are at greater risk of being negatively impacted on academic achievement, employment and earnings, and civic engagement, and are much more likely than others to experience early learning opportunities. Studies show that the potential cognitive learning gap and socio-emotional skills gap can be up to eight to twenty months (OECD, 2012). If disadvantaged children are to have a chance to be as successful as their advantaged peers, this education gap must be bridged and rapidly evaluated by schools and education policy makers. At this point, preschool education can help bridge the gap by providing a strong foundation for learning and academic and emotional well-being of students.

Inclusion in education is seen as a key strategy to achieve education for all and a more just and equal society. Some researchers suggest that diversity means valuing and managing differences in the workforce for business benefit, while inclusion means integrating differences into business practices to realize their value (Roberson, 2006; Stoermer et al., 2016). UNESCO defines inclusion in education as a principle and a process that aims to ensure that all learners, no matter regardless of their backgrounds, abilities, or needs, can study together in the same classrooms and schools (UNICEF, 2016). It means that the education system must adjust to the diverse needs of students and protect their human rights. It also means that students should have the opportunity to access, participate in, and progress through learning opportunities that are meaningful, relevant, and accessible. Previous research has shown that cultural context is very important (Joshi & Roh, 2009; Oswick & Noon, 2014; Stoermer et al., 2016), managing diversity and inclusion well can improve the inclusion climate, and foster organizational innovation, which is essential for organizational success (Stoermer et al., 2016; West & Sacramento, 2006).

Inclusion in education seems to be related to the implementation of a range of equality and diversity policies. In this context, UNESCO policies and sustainable development goals can guide for all. UNESCO aims to achieve by 2030 free, equitable and quality education for all girls and boys, with relevant and effective learning outcomes. It also strives to promote global citizenship, cultural diversity and sustainable development, as well as safe, non-violent, inclusive and effective learning environments committing to eliminating gender disparities in education (UNICEF, 2016). The vision of education for all is to transform the lives of individuals and the societies they live in, ensuring that everyone has access to quality learning opportunities throughout their lives. This vision requires a comprehensive, holistic, ambitious, aspirational and universal approach to education that is inspired by human rights and dignity, social justice, peace, inclusion and protection. To reach this goal, it is expected that education policymakers and school leaders need to renew their commitment to this inclusive and universal agenda by developing and implementing policies and practices that respond to the diverse needs and aspirations of all learners. However, in the context of cultural dimensions of Hofstede such as masculinity, power of distance, and indulgence, it is wondered to what extent the practices of societies and the deep prejudices and pre-acceptances rooted in the deep layers of culture are effective in achieving these critical and inclusive goals.

Policy implementations and school improvement efforts to provide students with greater capacity and flexibility to provide educational opportunities according to their evolving and changing contexts, interests, abilities and needs, and to give them the best chance to reach their potential are important criteria for equality in education. Nevertheless, most education systems or schools do not it. The achievement gap is not only a matter of comparing different countries or regions. When the student characteristics and backgrounds are taken into account, the achievement gap reveals a more complex and persistent problem. Students who face challenges such as being at-risk, belonging to a minority group, or living in a high-poverty area still lag behind their peers who do not have such disadvantages, even though many education systems around the world have tried to address this issue (OECD, 2019a). Measuring the quality of education in educational organizations often requires international or cross-cultural research design and analysis. Due to the nature and inclusiveness of the school organization, the educational/instructional processes involve not only local or nationally inclusive but also require an ongoing and increasing engagement with students from different national or cultural backgrounds. It is wondered whether these diversity, equity, and inclusion practices in the background cause cultural and contextual differences in a range of school leadership and strategic leadership behaviors as well as managerial decisions. What kind of cultural and social values can clarify our concern with equality of opportunity in education? and this, to what extent can impact on educational practices of school leaders? Is it possible to explain the fact that schools or education systems exhibit rapid, slow or insensitive behavior patterns to overcome this gap in the context of Hofstede's cultural values? Lazenby (2016) claimed that there might be different thoughts of equality of opportunity that individuals have a duty to realize depending on their role at a particular time. This mean that the relative concept 'equality of opportunity' may be perceived by people in different conceptions. In this context, the chapter investigates whether there is a relationship between the cultural values scores of the countries underlying the diversity, equity, and inclusion behaviors of school leaders.

Hofstede's Cultural Dimensions

Hofstede's cultural dimension theory is founded on the impacts of a society's culture on the values of its constituents, and how these values link to behavior. It has been widely resounded for cross-cultural research, particularly in psychology, international management, and cross-cultural communication. Every person develops certain patterns of thinking, feeling and potential acting that define who they are and how they interact with others. These patterns are shaped by shared norms or preferences that differ among various cultures and backgrounds. Hofstede's cultural dimension theory present a useful tool to understand the patterns of cultural values that influence how we communicate and relate to others, as well as how we assess and judge their behaviors and actions.

Culture can have a significant impact on equity in education and it can affect education equity in several ways. For example, cultural differences can lead to different expectations for students, which can be triggered different levels of support from teachers and parents. Additionally, cultural differences can also affect how students learn and how they interact with their peers. In order to promote equity in education, it is important to recognize and address these cultural differences. In this point, schools can work to create a more inclusive environment by promoting cultural awareness and understanding among students. This can be done by providing training for teachers and other education professionals on how to work with students from diverse backgrounds.

Equity is one of the main focal subjects of Hofstede's cultural values theory. It refers to how people in a culture treat each other fairly and equally. While Hofstede's cultural values theory ensures a helpful framework for understanding how culture affects behavior, it is important to recognize that equity is just one of several dimensions that can influence social interactions and to acknowledge that different cultures may have different definitions of what constitutes 'fairness' or 'equality'. This possible different perception or interpretation of the concept among cultures can complicate efforts to promote greater equity across societies. In cultures with high equity, people are expected to be treated fairly and equally regardless of their social status or background. In societies/schools with high levels of equity, individuals are more likely to trust each other and collaborate effectively, which can lead to greater student achievement, student well-being, and social stability. On the other hand, in cultures with low equity, people are expected to be treated differently based on their social status or background.

The communication styles of diverse societies can negatively affect relationships through several factors at schools. The intercultural conversations differing from low to high context with respect to contextualizing the verbal and/or non-verbal message coded by the sender and decoded by the receiver can be interpreted by Hofstede's cultural values including how power and authority are shared in the culture, values of individualism and collectivism, avoidance of uncertainty, indulgence degree, and the role of context in communication. For this reason, it is expected that school leaders and teachers are imperative to be cognizant of all intercultural communication and values possible as well as one's own closely.

Research evidence has shown an inextricable relationship between racial diversity and problems with communication and problem-solving approaches. This means that the interpretation, correct understanding, or distortion of discourses or actions can vary with cultures' degrees of context, indulgence, power distance and masculinity of society as well as perceptions and prejudices of racial diversity. Thus, some studies revealed that low-context cultures accentuate the discourse with less emphasis on context such as who says it and how it is said, whereas in high-context societies, the context of the discourse content is just as crucial as the words used (Hall, 1959). For example, Hall (1959) stated that in American culture, which is a high-context culture, it is essential for children to understand what they have learned. Research has also revealed that many topics that could be easily understood without any embellishments are made harder by the complicated and often inaccurate explanations that accompany them. However, this obsession with explaining and reasoning as a method does not seem to affect the Arab or Japanese culture as much (Hall, 1959). In this point, school principals can provide a positive school climate integrated with diversity, equity, and inclusion school policies by paying attention to intercultural communication between low (such as Canadian) and high-context cultures (such as Asian cultures) the spectrum. Hofstede et al. (2010) proposed a six-dimensional framework of national culture (power distance, individualism, masculinity, uncertainty avoidance, long-term orientation and indulgence) to explain the cultural differences among societies and countries. Cultural dimensions are critical to inform us how people behave, think and adopt technology in different ways.

Power Distance

Power distance is a cultural dimension that describes how much people in a country expect and accept unequal power distribution in different institutions and organizations. It reflects the degree of hierarchy and dependence in various role pairs, such as parent-child, teacher-student, boss-subordinate, and authority-citizen. Power distance indicates how people communicate, negotiate, make decisions and resolve conflicts. In cultures with low power distance, people value equality and interdependence between the powerful and the less powerful. Teachers encourage students to take initiative in class, and parents treat children as equals. Quality of learning depends on two-way communication and student excellence. According to Stoermer and friends (2016) revealed that low power distance cultures serve as a fertile context for creating an inclusion climate. Contrary to this, in cultures with high power distance, people expect and accept unequal power distribution in different institutions and organizations. The less powerful people are either dependent on the more powerful ones or show resistance and opposition to them. Teachers have the authority and responsibility to direct the class activities, and the quality of learning depends on how well they perform their roles. In cultures with high power distance, subordinates tend to follow particularly their superiors' expectations closely. For example, (Nishii & Mayer, 2009) showed that a leadership style that values diversity can create an inclusion climate in organizations. In addition to this, parents have the right to demand obedience from their children, and children have the duty to support their parents in their old age.

Individualism or Collectivism

Individualism is a cultural dimension that describes how much people in a society value independence and personal responsibility. People in individualistic cultures are loosely connected and care for themselves and their immediate family members. They emphasize their personal rights and achievements. Collectivism is the opposite of individualism. It describes how much people in a society value interdependence and group loyalty. People in collectivistic cultures are strongly bonded and belong to groups that protect them and expect their loyalty. They emphasize their group obligations and harmony (Hofstede et al., 2010). In individualistic cultures, students are expected to speak up in class individually and express their opinions and ideas. The purpose of education is to teach them how to learn independently and creatively. They have more freedom and flexibility to change jobs according to their personal interests and goals. Managers are trained to share their feelings honestly and openly with their subordinates and peers. They value direct feedback and constructive criticism. In collectivistic cultures, students are expected to speak up in class as a group and follow the group consensus. The purpose of education is to teach them how to do things according to established norms and rules. They have more stability and security in staying in the same job for a long time. Managers are trained to avoid direct criticism and confrontation with their subordinates and peers. They value harmony and cooperation.

Masculinity or Femininity

Masculinity and femininity indicate how much a culture differentiates between gender roles and values. Masculinity-femininity reflects a society's preference for traits. A society is masculine when men and women have different emotional roles: Men are expected to be assertive, tough, and material success oriented, while women are encouraged to be modest, tender, empathetic, and quality-oriented (Hofstede et al., 2010). Men seek achievement and competition, and women care for the home and the people (p.120). Masculine and feminine cultures have different roles and views on education and life. In masculine societies, education is based on excellence and competition; students who perform well are praised. School failure is a big problem. Women are the main teachers of young children. Couples have separate cars. Status symbols are popular. In feminine societies, education is based on equality, support, and cooperation; students who struggle are praised. Failing in school is a minor issue. Women and men are both teachers of young children. Couples share a car. Home products are popular. Stoermer and friends (2016) argued that cultures that have low power distance are more likely to foster a climate of inclusion and it is harder to create inclusion climates in cultures that are high in masculinity and/or power distance than in cultures that are low in these dimensions.

Uncertainty Avoidance

Some cultures are more anxious than others. uncertainty avoidance is linked with the extent to which societies dislike or cope with unpredictability and ambiguity. According to Hofstede and friends (2010) anxious cultures tend to express their emotions and aggression. Contrary to this, in cultures with low uncertainty avoidance, people are less anxious and more reserved (p.171). In societies with high uncertainty avoidance, people are less happy. Teachers are expected to know everything. However, in societies with low uncertainty avoidance, people are happier. Teachers can say they don't know clearly and people are more agreeable in personality tests. They are curious about differences. In literature, research evidence showed that high uncertainty avoidance societies reveal clear and understandable rules to avoid uncertain situations, while low uncertainty avoidance societies do not endeavor to remove uncertainty and attribute positive value (Smith, 1992). For instant, Stoermer and friends (2016) indicated that this cultural preference of societies for coping with uncertainty is likely to impact their perceptions of diversity. They argued that encountering diversity might stimulate uncertainty, because of their different background and dissimilar assumptions from the majority.

Long Term vs. Short Term Orientation

Hofstede added a fifth dimension to his original model after working with Michael Bond. He called it Confucian work dynamism at first, but later changed it to long-term versus short-term orientation (Bukowski & Rudnicki, 2019; Hofstede et al., 2010). This dimension shows how a culture values future rewards or past and present values. Long-term orientation (LTO) means valuing virtues like perseverance and thrift that lead to future benefits. Societies with a long-term orientation value the virtues that lead to future benefits, such as perseverance and thrift. People who have a high long-term orientation are persistent and adaptable. They respect the hierarchy and status of their relationships. They care about their reputation and image, but they may also see it as a weakness. People in high LTO cultures think practically, plan for the future, and value education.

Short-term orientation means valuing the virtues like respect for tradition and saving face that honor the past and present. Societies with a short-term orientation value the virtues that honor the past and present, such as respect for tradition, and meeting social expectations (Hofstede et al., 2010). People who have a short-term orientation are focused on immediate outcomes. They value personal consistency and stability. They enjoy leisure time. They judge good or evil based on the situation. People in short-term oriented countries have a narrow view of the impact of events. They do not see how the past affects the present or their own lives. They may spend a lot when they have enough, and blame fate when they face problems. They want quick results and instant satisfaction. They do not like to give up anything now for a better future (G. H. Hofstede & Hofstede, 2001; Park, 2012).

Indulgence

Indulgence is the newest cultural dimension in Hofstede's model of culture, introduced by Minkov based on the World Values Survey data. It reflects how much a society values and encourages the gratification of human desires, such as enjoying life and having fun. In contrast, restraint cultures regulate and limit such gratification through strict social norms (Hofstede et al., 2010; Park, 2012; Stoermer et al.,

2016). Indulgence cultures, such as Sweden and the Netherlands, are characterized by extroversion and open-mindedness (Hofstede et al., 2010). These personality traits have been linked to positive attitudes toward diversity (Sawyerr et al., 2005; Strauss & Connerley, 2003). Indulgence cultures also tend to be optimistic, which may help them cope with the changes brought by organizational inclusion efforts. Moreover, indulgence cultures have flexible gender roles and weak heteronormative norms. They also value freedom of speech as a societal asset. In contrast, restraint cultures, such as China and Italy, are more rigid and conservative. Restraint cultures are less receptive to foreign influences, such as movies or music. They also tend to have more neurotic personalities, which may affect their attitudes toward immigrants negatively (Gallego & Pardos-Prado, 2014). Therefore, some researchers argue that indulgence cultures are more conducive to diversity and inclusion management practices and an inclusion climate. Some scholars expect that organizations in indulgence cultures will foster cooperation and appreciation of differences, due to their openness and flexibility. Moreover, they will have less rigid gender roles, which will promote gender equality.

METHODOLOGY

We use literature review method. In addition, the data file has been obtained by combining the secondary data analysis using the TALIS 2018 data and the scores of the countries from Hofstede's cultural dimensions. The TALIS 2018 study, led by the OECD, aims to provide relevant and robust international indicators and analysis on the conditions and practices of teachers and teaching. The study supports countries in reviewing and developing policies that foster effective learning and teaching (Ainley & Carstens, 2018, p. 13). TALIS surveyed the principals and teachers of the same school at primary, lower secondary and upper secondary education levels using clustered sampling. This research used the school-level data set collected from school leaders by TALIS. The data consisted of 13,730 schools from 44 countries (excluding Cyprus and Israel due to missing data from Hofstede's research and combining data from two Chinese regions into one country). This chapter presents the results of the correlational/comparative analysis using these data. It also reviews the related literature and provide various suggestions based on the purpose of this chapter. The school principals who participated in the research had the following characteristics: 48.7% (257,474) were female, 51% (269,905) were male, and 0.3% (1,574) had missing data on gender. Regarding education, 3% (23,375) had associate degrees or lower, 48.4% (260,202) had undergraduate degrees, 40.1% (212,180) had master's degrees and 2.8% (14,833) had doctorate degrees. On average, these principals had 8.37 years of managerial experience.

Data Analysis

The TALIS 2018 study used a "complex survey design" approach, where it randomly selected about 200 schools in each participating country and then sampled 20 teachers from each school using a two-stage cluster sampling method (B. Muthén & Satorra, 1995). Assuming simple random sampling procedures in this type of research design can cause variance and standard errors to be underestimated, which can increase the risk of Type I errors (Raudenbush & Bryk, 2002). This study aims to reduce the errors by using a model-based technique that accounts for the non-independence of observations. To apply this technique, variables at each level are defined and multilevel analysis models are created. It is also important to include sampling weights for data analysis, since the sampling probability and response rates vary across schools. The school-level sampling weights for this study were based on the SCHWGT variable, which the OECD rescaled using multiple steps to adjust for unequal selection probability, different response rates and other specific factors. This ensured that each sample had an equal impact on the parameter estimate. The data analysis used IBM SPSS 25 programs for basic statistics and correlations, and Mplus 8.3 programs for latent variable structures and structural equation modeling.

Variables

The study considers various contextual variables at the school and country levels. The school level variable is the T3PDIVB variable, which reflects the school principal's beliefs about equality and diversity among teachers. This scale asked the school principal to indicate how many of the teachers in his school agreed with 4 items. The answers range from "None or almost none" (1), "Some" (2), "Many" (3), "All or almost all" (4). Example item can be given as "It is important to be responsive to differences in students' cultural backgrounds- TC3G40A". In addition, the scale also had acceptable levels of reliability coefficients, model fit and measurement invariance at all ISCED levels (OECD, 2019b, p. 422).

The country-level independent variables were the scores of the countries on Hofstede's cultural dimensions (power distance, individualism, masculinity, uncertainly avoidance, long term orientation, indulgence). As a principal in the country scores were obtained from https://www.hofstede-insights.com/product/compare-countries/. The control variables were the school principal's gender (1= Female, 2= Male), education level and total years of work experience as a principal. All school-level variables were taken from the TALIS 2018 principal questionnaire. total).

In this study, ICC1 (inter-country variability) was calculated as .088 and ICC2 (inter-country reliability) was calculated as .972 for the T3PDIVB variable and it was observed that the ICC1 value was above .05 and the ICC (2) value was above

Figure 1. Level one and two

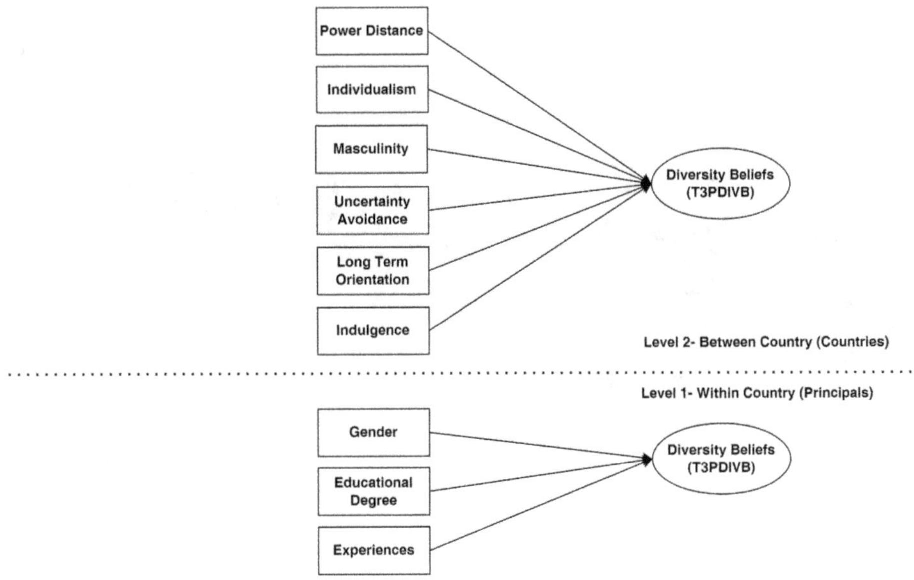

.70 (Bliese, 2000). These results show that the data structure and reliability are suitable for a multilevel analysis.

RESULTS

Preliminary Analyses

Our study investigated how school principals rated the teachers' beliefs about diversity and equality in the TALIS 2018 data. Figure 2 shows the distribution of the average scores for these beliefs. According to Figure 2, the average scores for diversity, equality and inclusion varied from 11.40 to 14.38 among the countries that participated in TALIS 2018. Türkiye's average score (12.51) was close to the overall average. Figure 3 reveals that Singapore (14.24) and United Kingdom (14.38) had the highest scores for diversity and equality beliefs, while Saudi Arabia (11.40) and Belgium (11.67) had the lowest scores.

This study also examined how the countries with different T3PDIVB scores scored on Hofstede's cultural dimensions. Figure 4 displays the results of this analysis.

Figure 4 shows that Saudi Arabia had high scores for power distance and uncertainly avoidance, but low score for indulgence and long term orientation, while United

Figure 2. Distribution of diversity scores by country (TALIS 2018)

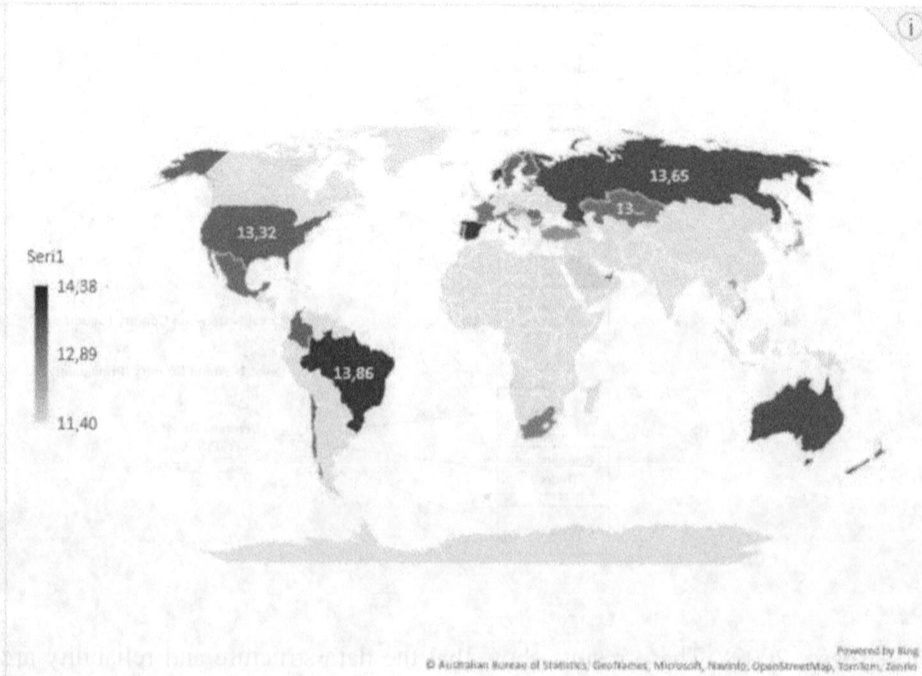

Figure 3. Countries with the highest and lowest diversity belief scores according to TALIS 2018

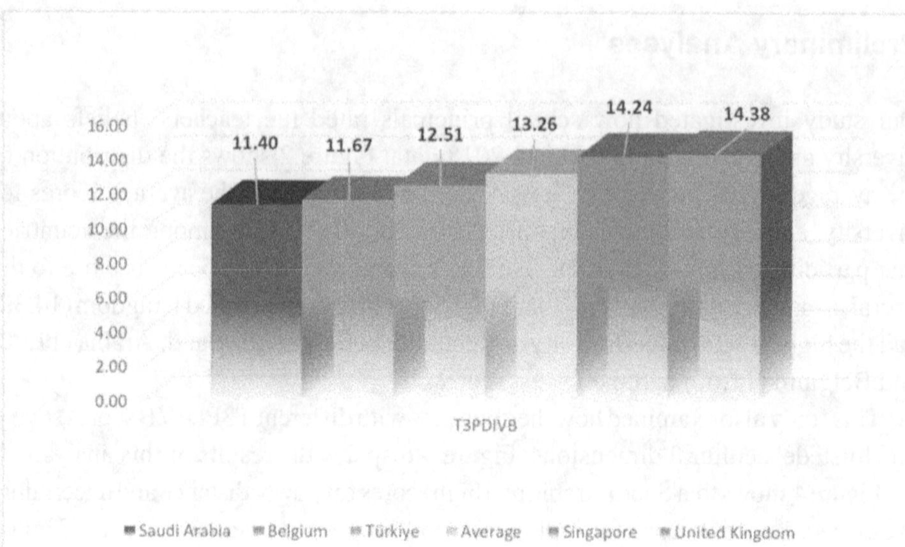

Figure 4. Hofstede cultural values scores of countries

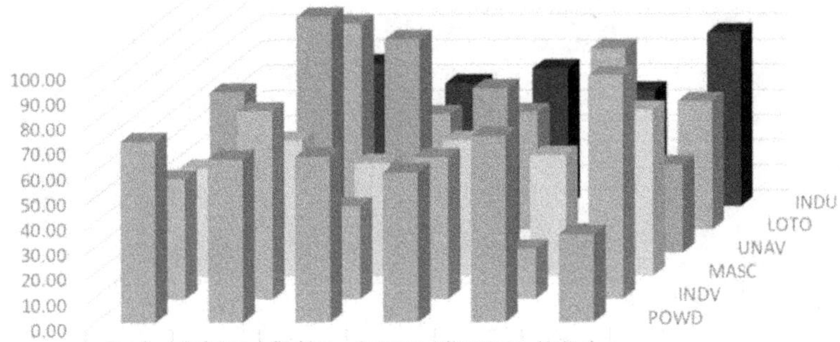

	Saudi Arabia	Belgium	Türkiye	Average	Singapore	United Kingdom
POWD	72.00	65.00	66.00	59.75	74.00	35.00
INDV	48.00	75.00	37.00	56.40	20.00	89.00
MASC	43.00	54.00	45.00	54.07	48.00	66.00
UNAV	64.00	94.00	85.00	65.49	8.00	35.00
LOTO	27.00	82.00	46.00	46.75	72.00	51.00
INDU	14.00	57.00	49.00	54.86	46.00	69.00

Kingdom had low scores for power distance and uncertainty avoidance, but high scores for individualism, masculinity and indulgence. Türkiye and Belgium had high scores for uncertainty avoidance and power distance. Singapore and Türkiye had the lowest scores for individualism. Singapore also had the lowest score for uncertainty avoidance. Türkiye's scores for cultural values were close to the overall average.

To explore the relationships between the variables in the study, we performed a Pearson correlation analysis as the final preliminary analysis. Table 1 shows the means and Pearson correlations of the variables.

Table 1 shows that the mean of the study's dependent variable, T3PDIVB, is 13.113. It also shows that the T3PDIVB variable has a low level of association with other control variables at the school level. There is a moderate and significant relationship between the T3PDIVB variable and country-level variables. To test the contextual model and examine the direct influences on teachers' diversity beliefs, we applied MSEM in the second phase of the study. The model fit statistics indicated a very good fit. The result showed a good fit to the data: RMSEA = .000; CFI = 1.000; TLI = 1.000; $SRMR_{Within}$ = .000; $SRMR_{Between}$ = .000. Table 2 presents the model's results.

Table 1. Descriptive statistics and Pearson correlations among variables

Variable	Mean	1	2	3	4	5	6	7
School level (n=13.730)								
1. T3PDIVB	13.113	1	.066**	.023**	-.007**			
2. Gender	-		1	-.003	-.087			
3. Educational Degree	5.496			1	.028			
4. Experiences	8.828				1			
Country-level (n=44)								
1. T3PDIVB	13.113	1	-.285**	.085**	. -.299**	-.220**	-.357**	.412**
2. POWD	56.884		1	-.656**	.214**	.418**	.209**	-.422**
3. INDV	52.651			1	-.026**	-.285**	-.067**	.310**
4. MASC	47.442				1	.088**	.038**	.066**
5. UNAV	68.000					1	.245**	-.296**
6. LOTO	53.047						1	-.531**
7. INDU	46.605							1

Note(s): T3PDIVB = Equity and diversity: Diversity beliefs, POWD = Power Distance, INDV=Individualism, MASC = Masculinity, UNAV= Uncertainly Avoidance, LOTO= Long Term Orientation, INDU= Indulgence, ** p <. 01. Gender (reference group is female)

Table 2 shows that "Masculinity" is the only dimension from Hofstede's cultural dimensions that significantly affects teachers' equality and diversity beliefs (β = -.288, p < 0.01). Other dimensions are not significant. At the school level, however, the gender of the school principal has a low but notable effect on teachers' diversity beliefs (β = -.066, p < 0.001). In addition, the study's school-level variables explain approximately 1% (R^2=.005, p<.01), of the total variance in diversity beliefs, while country-level variables explain 30% (R^2=.304, p<.001).

CONCLUSION

This study focuses specifically on how diversity, equity, and inclusion beliefs, attitudes and practices are linked with Hofstede's cultural values such as individualist/ collectivist, power distance, uncertainty avoidance, and masculinity/femininity of the countries. According to the TALIS 2018 study on diversity and equality beliefs, Singapore and United Kingdom had the highest scores among the participating

Table 2. MSEM estimates, standard errors and confidence intervals for the model

Construct	Coefficient		95% Confidence Interval		
	Estimate	SE	Lower Bound	Upper Bound	*p*
Direct effects *(Country level)*					
POWD → T3PDIVB	-.098	.175	-.440	.245	.576
INDV→ T3PDIVB	-.097	.188	-.466	.272	.607
MASC → T3PDIVB	-.288	.113	-.509	-.066	.011**
UNAV → T3PDIVB	-.048	.120	-.284	.188	.689
LOTO → T3PDIVB	-.147	.197	-.532	.239	.456
INDU→ T3PDIVB	.327	.197	-.058	.713	.096
Direct effects *(School level)*					
GENDER→ T3PDIVB	.066	.013	.040	.092	.000***
EDUCATIONAL DEGREE → T3PDIVB	.023	.022	- .020	.065	.299
EXPERIENCES → T3PDIVB	.002	.028	-.057	.053	.945

Note(s): T3PDIVB = Equity and diversity: Diversity beliefs, POWD = Power Distance, INDV=Individualism, MASC = Masculinity, UNAV= Uncertainly Avoidance, LOTO= Long Term Orientation, INDU= Indulgence, ** $p < .01$. Gender (reference group is female)

countries, while Saudi Arabia and Belgium had the lowest scores. This study revealed that Türkiye's values are close to the TALIS 2018 average among the participating countries, and it has relatively high levels of uncertainty avoidance and power distance. Saudi Arabia's low score on the Indulgence dimension suggests a lack of diversity, equality and inclusion.

The study found that DEI beliefs were in many points unrelated to Hofstede's cultural dimensions. Teachers' diversity beliefs did not vary much across intercultural or east-west cultures. This means that the study found that teachers' diversity beliefs were not influenced by the power distance, individualism, uncertainty avoidance, long term orientation and indulgence dimensions of Hofstede's model. The only exception was the masculinity dimension, which had a negative relationship with teachers' diversity beliefs. The study suggested that societies with high masculinity scores had low diversity beliefs. This is consistent with the view that creating inclusive climates in cultures with high masculinity is more difficult than in cultures with low dimensions (Stoermer et al., 2016). According to Hofstede's theory of cultural values, societies that are more masculine and value an "always on, always available" culture may have higher levels of gender inequality and associate success with work. In this context, individuals who are displaced for various reasons may face many challenges in accessing and participating in education. Türkiye, which has received the most refugees in recent years, may have relatively lower masculinity cultural characteristics that enable it to provide inclusive education services to diverse cultures. The study also suggested that the educational philosophies and diversity views of societies were related to the equality, support and cooperation values of feminine societies. This suggests that societies with high masculinity values may be more likely to ignore or neglect inclusion practices that promote diversity. This insight could provide researchers with different ways of examining how societies' degrees of masculinity influence their approaches to diversity, equality and inclusive education in various contexts. This study is also crucial to identify the cultural value dimensions that influence the education of immigrants and to provide evidence-based insights for policy development processes. Future research could explore multi-level models that include cultural dimensions and diversity and equality beliefs, as well as results from international assessments such as PISA, TIMSS.

REFERENCES

Ainley, J., & Carstens, R. (2018). *Teaching and learning international survey (TALIS) 2018 conceptual framework*. OECD. doi:10.1787/799337c2-

Arsel, Z., Crockett, D., & Scott, M. L. (2022). Diversity, equity, and inclusion (DEI) in the journal of consumer research: A curation and research agenda. *The Journal of Consumer Research, 48*(5), 5. doi:10.1093/jcr/ucab057

Ballard, D., Allen, B., Ashcraft, K., Ganesh, S., McLeod, P., & Zoller, H. (2020). When words do not matter: Identifying actions to effect diversity, equity, and inclusion in the academy. *Management Communication Quarterly, 34*(4), 4. doi:10.1177/0893318920951643

Banting, K., & Kymlicka, W. (2013). Is there really a retreat from multiculturalism policies? New evidence from the multiculturalism policy index. *Comparative European Politics, 11*(5), 577–598. doi:10.1057/cep.2013.12

Bliese, P. D. (2000). Within-group agreement, non-independence, and reliability: Implications for data aggregation and analysis. In *Multilevel theory, research, and methods in organizations: Foundations, extensions, and new directions* (pp. 349–381). Jossey-Bass/Wiley.

Bosniak, L. (2006). *The citizen and the alien: The dilemmas of contemporary membership*. Princeton University Press. doi:10.1515/9781400827510

Bukowski, A., & Rudnicki, S. (2019). Not only individualism: The effects of long-term orientation and other cultural variables on national innovation success. *Cross-Cultural Research, 53*(2), 2. doi:10.1177/1069397118785546

Cox, T. H., & Blake, S. (1991). Managing cultural diversity: Implications for organizational competitiveness. *The Executive, 5*(3), 3.

Cross, M. (2004). Institutionalising campus diversity in South African higher education: Review of diversity scholarship and diversity education. *Higher Education, 47*(4), 387–410. doi:10.1023/B:HIGH.0000020854.04852.80

Espinoza, O. (2007). Solving the equity–equality conceptual dilemma: A new model for analysis of the educational process. *Educational Research, 49*(4), 343–363. doi:10.1080/00131880701717198

Gallego, A., & Pardos-Prado, S. (2014). The big five personality traits and attitudes towards immigrants. *Journal of Ethnic and Migration Studies, 40*(1), 1. doi:10.1080/1369183X.2013.826131 PMID:24563610

Gill, G. K., McNally, M. J., & Berman, V. (2018). Effective diversity, equity, and inclusion practices. *Healthcare Management Forum, 31*(5), 5. doi:10.1177/0840470418773785 PMID:30114938

Hall, E. (1959). *The Silent Language*. Doubleday and Company.

Hofmann. (2012). Gesellschaftstheoretische Grundlagen für einen reflexiven und inklusiven Umgang mit Diversitäten in Organisationen [Social theoretical foundations for a reflexive and inclusive approach to diversity in organizations]. In *Diversität und Diversitätsmanagement, In R. Bendl, E. Hanappi-Egger, & R. Hofmann,* (pp. 23–60). University of Vienna.

Hofstede, G., Hofstede, G., & Mirkov, M. (2010). *Cultures and organizations: Software of the mind* (3rd ed.). McGraw-Hill Professional.

Hofstede, G. H., & Hofstede, G. (2001). Culture's consequences: Comparing values, behaviors, institutions and organizations across nations. *Sage (Atlanta, Ga.).*

Joshi, A., & Roh, H. (2009). The role of context in work team diversity research: A meta-analytic review. *Academy of Management Journal, 52*(3), 3. doi:10.5465/amj.2009.41331491

Lazenby, H. (2016). What is equality of opportunity in education? *Theory and Research in Education, 14*(1), 65–76. doi:10.1177/1477878515619788

McGlynn, C. (2009). Integrating education: Parekhian multiculturalism and good practice. *Intercultural Education, 20*(4), 299–310. doi:10.1080/14675980903351938

McKinney, S. (2012). Multiculturalism and education. *Journal of Education Policy, 28*(1), 154–156. doi:10.1080/02680939.2012.688539

Merryfield, M. M. (2000). Why aren't teachers being prepared to teach for diversity, equity, and global interconnectedness? A study of lived experiences in the making of multicultural and global educators. *Teaching and Teacher Education*, *16*(4), 429–443. doi:10.1016/S0742-051X(00)00004-4

Neblett, E. W. Jr. (2019). Diversity (psychological) science training: Challenges, tensions, and a call to action. *The Journal of Social Issues*, *75*(4), 4. doi:10.1111/josi.12357

Nishii, L. H., & Mayer, D. M. (2009). Do inclusive leaders help to reduce turnover in diverse groups? The moderating role of leader–member exchange in the diversity to turnover relationship. *The Journal of Applied Psychology*, *94*(6), 1412–1426. doi:10.1037/a0017190 PMID:19916652

OECD. (2012). *Equity and quality in education: Supporting disadvantaged students and schools*. OECD. doi:10.1787/9789264130852-

OECD. (2019a). *PISA 2018 results (volume I): What students know and can do?* OECD. . doi:10.1787/5f07c754-en

OECD. (2019b). *TALIS 2018 technical report* (p. 494) [Research Report]. OECD. https://www.oecd.org/education/talis/TALIS_2018_Technical_Report.pdf

Oswick, C., & Noon, M. (2014). Discourses of diversity, equality and inclusion: Trenchant formulations or transient fashions? *British Journal of Management*, *25*(1), 1. doi:10.1111/j.1467-8551.2012.00830.x

Park, J.-H. (2012). The effects of principal's leadership style on support for innovation: Evidence from Korean vocational high school change. *Asia Pacific Education Review*, *13*(1), 89–102. doi:10.100712564-011-9182-9

Rawls, J. (2005). *A theory of justice: Original edition*. Belknap Press. http://gen.lib.rus.ec/book/index.php?md5=d2eec200ebed5373c6e2c58c7d645b5f

Roberson, Q. M. (2006). Disentangling the meanings of diversity and inclusion in organizations. *Group & Organization Management*, *31*(2), 2. doi:10.1177/1059601104273064

Sawyerr, O. O., Strauss, J., & Yan, J. (2005). Individual value structure and diversity attitudes: The moderating effects of age, gender, race, and religiosity. *Journal of Managerial Psychology*, *20*(6), 498–521. doi:10.1108/02683940510615442

Smith, P. B. (1992). Organizational behaviour and national cultures. *British Journal of Management*, *3*(1), 1. Advance online publication. doi:10.1111/j.1467-8551.1992.tb00034.x

Solomon, A. (2013). *Far from the tree: A dozen kinds of love*. Chatto and Windus.

Stoermer, S., Hildisch, A. K., & Froese, F. J. (2016). Culture matters: The influence of national culture on inclusion climate. *Cross Cultural & Strategic Management, 23*(2). doi:10.1108/CCSM-11-2014-0135

Strauss, J. P., & Connerley, M. L. (2003). Demographics, personality, contact, and universal-diverse orientation: An exploratory examination. *Human Resource Management, 42*(2), 159–174. doi:10.1002/hrm.10074

UNICEF. (2016). *Education 2030: Incheon declaration and framework for action: Towards inclusive and equitable quality education and lifelong learning for all* (Research Report ED-2016/WS/2). UNESCO. https://unesdoc.unesco.org/ark:/48223/pf0000245745

Volckmar, N. (2019). The Enduring Quest for Equity in Education: Comparing Norway and Australia. *Scandinavian Journal of Educational Research, 63*(4), 617–631. doi:10.1080/00313831.2017.1415967

West, M. A., & Sacramento, C. A. (2006). Flourishing in teams: Developing creativity and innovation. In J. Henry, Creative Management and Development (pp. 25–44). SAGE Publications Ltd. doi:10.4135/9781446213704.n3

Yesufu, A. (2013). Challenges of the visible minority families: Cultural sensitivity to the rescue. *Canadian Journal of Family and Youth / Le Journal Canadien de Famille et de La Jeunesse, 5*(1), Article 1. doi:10.29173/cjfy18950

Chapter 8
Creating the Climate for Workplace Diversity

Simon Cleveland
https://orcid.org/0000-0001-9293-3905
Purdue University Global, USA

Marisa Cleveland
Northeastern University, USA

ABSTRACT

The advancement of the digital landscape has caused organizations to scrutinize their actions and practices through constant re-evaluation of its practices and this has yielded some valuable implications for society. This chapter proposes that effective leadership arises from an individual's capacity to engage in cross-cultural interactions. The study revealed that reward systems, communication processes, and diversity opportunities were three patterns that emerged within the institution under review. Implications for how diversity has the power to impact personal and professional lives in positive ways are examined and recommendations for leadership on embracing diversity initiatives are proposed.

INTRODUCTION

The purpose of this chapter is to examine the perspectives of the workplace at a midsize higher educational institution located in the Pacific Northwest, the institution's organizational culture and its cultural aspects of diversity (Cleveland, 2021). In this chapter, workplace diversity adopts the definition from the Office of Personnel Management (2011) as "characteristics such as national origin, language, race,

DOI: 10.4018/978-1-6684-9013-6.ch008

color, disability, ethnicity, gender, age, religion, sexual orientation, gender identity, socioeconomic status, veteran status, and family structures" (p. 5). Schein and Schein (2017) argued that organizational culture represents the identity of the organization, its beliefs, assumptions, values and employees' shared understandings through adaptation and integration processes (Cleveland, 2021). The interviews conducted for this chapter focused on two aspects of the selected institution, specifically the general organizational culture from the perspective of those within a given work environment and the cultural aspects from the perspective of diversity.

This chapter proposes that effective leadership arises from an individual's capacity to engage in cross-cultural interactions. Organizations have their own culture, developed around the unique way each organization does things (Driskill & Brenton, 2011). Alvesson (2011) argued that cultured is rooted in the management of organizations. Therefore, the ability to navigate within one organization while comprehending how its culture is affected by the decisions of its leaders as well as the impact of diversity is complex.

The advancement of the digital landscape has caused organizations to scrutinize their actions and practices through constant re-evaluation of its practices and this has yielded some valuable implications for society. Hatch and Schultz (2002) argued that the increased transparency in the digital environment means that society has greater access to how an organization's identity and culture are formed and evolve. Some organizations may thrive through corporate social responsibility practices and community engagement, yet the same organizations may stumble with their diversity initiatives.

For example, Klein (2016) argued that attention to diversity management in higher education institutions in Europe is a newer phenomenon, while in North America, the National Association of Diversity Officers in Higher Education formed with 30 names representing 30 institutions. The same association expanded within six months to over 120 names and institutions, demonstrating US institutional interest in supporting diversity initiatives.

In the succeeding sections, the results of the interviews are analyzed and three patterns, which emerged from the interviews are examined: reward systems, communication processes and diversity opportunities. In addition, the analysis will focus on how diversity has the power to impact personal and professional lives in positive ways and explore recommendations for leadership on embracing diversity initiatives.

METHODOLOGY

This chapter is based on interviews with leaders from a mid-size higher education institution located in the Pacific Northwest area of the United States. The institution was selected, because its profile represented a large number of higher education institutions in the US, who are accredited by the Northwestern Commission on Colleges and Universities, employee hundreds of faculty and staff, and provide education to thousands of students each year (Cleveland, 2021). This chapter includes interviews from two leaders from the university's School of Management.

The two interview participants are administrators (a dean and an associate dean) were chosen because they took large part in establishing strategy and executing on this strategy for the school, especially with regards to hiring, downsizing, curriculum improvements, execution of rewards systems and communication planning (Cleveland 2021).

REWARDS SYSTEMS THEME

During the interviews with the participants, the theme of pay and sparse reward systems emerged. Strategists use extrinsic motivations by praising their employees, rewarding them when the employees demonstrate commitment to the organizational strategy and punishing them when they veer off course. Rewards systems are considered tools for motivating and retaining employees, for supporting organizational goals and for enhancing employee performance (Petera, 2011; Noor et al., 2020).

The dean reflected on the fact that the university does not pay much and the raises -- tied to the performance reviews -- were meager, at best, in the range of one percent, saying, *"It's hard, because some people measure their raise as to how they're doing, and also conversely they think, you know, no matter what I do, it's not going to matter anyway, my pay is going to be pretty much the same."* Moreover, the dean argued that due to the limited budget, it was difficult to reward deserving employees at a higher rate, but other employees would see a steep decrease in their compensation. Instead, the dean proposed alternative ways to recognize employees as a way to mitigate rewards.

The associate dean provided further insight into the university's reward system by mentioning the Dean's List for faculty members who performed well on the individual department goals such as frequency of communication with students, timeliness of grading, and engagement with students during classwork. These performance markers for the higher education institution indicate the importance of a student-centric model of the university, and the need for faculty to have clear guidance on how to behave in order to best embody this instruction's culture.

Blanding (2018) examined which rewards motivate employees and found that employee perceptions mattered. The performance of the employees changed based on not only who received the reward, but also on who was expecting to receive the reward. If rewards reflect organization's values and incentives provide insight into organization's culture, then it is critical for leaders of all organizations to implement reward programs where employees feel like they are striving to reach a goal, which adds value to their work and to the mission of the organization.

COMMUNICATIONS THEME

Communication is central to an organization's well-being, and organizations would benefit from creating a multichannel communication system allowing for everyone to connect (Schein & Schein, 2017). Paulson et al. (2012) argued that culture is created by members of a society who possess a common collection of attitudes, knowledge about reality, beliefs and experiences. The critical component of this argument is that culture is not created in isolation, but is constructed through communication within this society. When different societies interact, Paulson et al. (2012) proposed that communication is intercultural and employees strive to understand what others are attempting to convey. This occurs through frequent questions and affirmations to ensure the messages are clear and unambiguous. After analyzing the responses from the interviewees regarding the series of questions related to communication, a common theme emerged from the perspective of the organization and how the organizational members communicated officially and unofficially.

The first and unanimous response to the question of how people preferred to communicate was, "Email." The dean noted: *"Email is a big way to communicate around here."* The associate dean also reported: *"We very frequently use email..."* This method of day-to-day communication is not uncommon for any organization. In fact, literature shows that written communication is of significant importance for employees. For example, in a case study conducted by Denison and Mishra (1995), Proctor and Gamble placed a strong emphasis on written communication, and new recruits received lessons on how to write a memo in the proper Proctor and Gamble format. The result of this study demonstrated that such an activity is regarded as of central importance in how new employees socialized by providing them with a common language to efficiently communicate with others within the organization.

However, the interviewees claimed face-to-face interaction was their preferred method when dealing with sensitive issues such as disciplinary action or sensitive student information as evident by the comments for the associate dean: *"Face-to-face, number one. Number two would be as a follow-up email...,"* while the dean noted: *"...it's verbal until it becomes serious... It's mostly verbal."*

Finally, both the interviewees noted that communicating organizational values takes place through a variety of mediums such as websites, social media, and annual meetings with faculty and staff.

COMMITMENT TO DIVERSITY THEME

In order for universities to support diversity, leadership must first comprehend what it means to be diverse. Chen and Hamilton (2015) conducted two studies to investigate how people define and perceive diversity. Their findings correlated with the associate dean's response that diversity is, *"The ability of people from all backgrounds, races, and sexes to be able to work together in a collaborative way without being hampered by any kind of prejudices to accomplish a goal."*

This idea of both representation and social acceptance is ultimately lacking within this university. When asked about the policies in place to promote diversity, the dean said, *"There are boiler plates in place that says we're a diverse organization and we support all that stuff."* However, when pressed for ways the higher education institution recruits for diversity, the dean responded by admitting, *"It's a challenge, because I think we could be more diverse... sometimes we don't have any qualified candidates... we just usually post on higher ed, well, we don't know who's checking higher ed, and if all the responses are fifty-year-old white males... because they're the only ones who read that, then... maybe we should advertise somewhere else to."*

Inclusion and diversity are words that the interviewees used with familiarity, and they both acknowledged the need for more inclusion and a wider breadth of diversity, but even as the associate dean pointed out, *"We have European, Asian, and African-American staff within our different schools,"* the dean admitted it can be difficult to fill a position, and if a qualified marginalized individual doesn't apply, then that person can't be hired. This ties back to the need for the university to implement real efforts in recruiting more diverse candidates.

LIMITED STRUCTURAL DIVERSITY THEME

Within the higher education institution, there is a predominate population of international students. During the interview, the dean said the diversity of the university did not match the population they served, because the population *"is sort of bifurcated in that we have tons of young international students... I don't think we would fit exactly mostly because we have tons and tons of Asian students."*

Even though the associate dean exampled the number of international students working in the organization as teaching assistants and student assistants, when asked about being a privileged member of the university, the answer was positive. The likelihood that someone else of the same group would be available as a mentor was, *"Very likely."* This includes the dean, as well as the university's provost, the chief financial officer, and the president. All five share the same components within the default group when considering diversity: they are all white, educated men.

This leads to another theme within the realm of diversity: structural diversity. Though mixed evidence exists linking increased representation of marginalized individuals leading to more frequent interactions among students from different racial and ethnic groups (Bowman, 2012), this university is lacking in diversity, where structural diversity is characterized as the proportional representation of the surrounding community or larger society (Wolniak, 2017).

With a predominantly white male administration and an international — predominantly Asian — student population, it is critical that faculty understand best practices in teaching international students. When the leadership and faculty are not representative of the community they serve, those minority students may become disempowered in the American higher education setting (Hsieh, 2007). Therefore, regardless of the best intentions of the university's leadership, faculty and staff must also recognize disconnect among international students, marginalized groups, and the default group at the university.

RECOMMENDATIONS

Rewards System

Based on the analysis from the interviews, it is proposed that incentives for preferred employee behavior should be aligned with employees' perceived value of the award. If the award is not perceived as acceptable by an employee, the effect would be negative and may lead to loss of trust in the capabilities of leadership to recognize and encourage behavior that aligns with the organizational culture (Noe, Hollenbeck, Gerhart &Wright, 2021). This in turn may lead to either the filing of grievances, or potential loss off talent as employees may leave to pursue other opportunities in organizations whether the culture regards their perceived value.

As a result, the rewards system at this university should be re-envisioned to one that supports the mission and values of the university. The new system should incentivize employees who strive to promote knowledge increase and educational advancement of the students.

Communications System

Even in this digital age, where the interviewees communicate predominantly via email, formal and informal channels of communication exist for them to share ideas, follow-up on a previous email, or discuss sensitive information. The ways employees communicate reflect facets of their organization's culture (Tierney, 1988). While organizational cultures are broad and ambiguous (Hartnell & Walumbwa, 2011), the use of email is not sufficient to facilitate robust communication practices at this university. As a result, it is proposed that a more robust communications system should be enacted, which supports both formal and informal communication channels in order to allow for employees to connect with other employees and build trust through interaction. This new system will allow employees to gain greater understanding of acceptable ways to behave within the organization. Furthermore, such behaviors should be spotlighted within the employee's performance review and rewards system.

Hire a Chief Diversity Officer

A chief diversity officer is the individual who spearheads the plan, implementation and monitoring of diversity initiatives in institutions (Thompson et al., 2017). Organizations with more diverse cultural resources are better able to handle unpredicted events (Schein & Schein, 2017). Yet, within the higher education institutions in the United States, Chubin and Malcom (2006) proposed that diversity initiatives are usually avoided as a result of faculty bias and legal actions. The underrepresentation of marginalized groups comprises on race, ethnicity, sex, and disability among students and faculty. In opposition to this friction, there has been a rise in universities hiring diversity officers to helm the efforts of diversity, equity, and inclusion (Valbrun, 2018).

By hiring a chief diversity officer, one who could educate members of the university and create initiatives promoting diversity and inclusion, the institution will signal the commitment to create a well-educated and willing community that values diversity. The chief diversity officer would be charged with developing best practices for capitalizing on the diverse perspectives and student backgrounds, providing an environment for faculty and students to share different points of views and build relationships (Gurin et al., 2002). Additionally, the chief diversity officer would be the symbolic bridge in how the organization and its employees could align their personal and professional cultures and well-being by educating the community on healthy ethnic foods, access to healthcare for marginalized groups, and new trends or initiatives as societal shifts create new marginalized groups.

Campaign for More Structural Diversity

Driskill and Brenton (2011) propose that an organizational culture captures the norms and values of a group and learning to use cultural data in order to become a more effective leader. Aligning the values of the organization with the recruitment, training, and diversity policies will provide a positive environment in the workplace regardless of race, ethnicity, sexual orientation, gender, and religion. Meyerson (1994) studied social workers to understand the way organizations address the behaviors of their social workers and one finding from the study could be applicable in this institution: "an acceptance of multiple notions of 'normality'" (p. 637). When higher education administrators allow for the acceptance of marginalized groups as a different version of normal, then diversity becomes less about a numeric representation of diverse faculty, staff, and students and more about creating a culture that cultivates, through meaningful engagement, constructive exchanges (Wolniak, 2017).

In order for the university to embrace multiculturalism in recruitment efforts of faculty, staff, and students, the leaders must examine the organization's goals and values. Higher education administrators committed to increasing structural diversity can build diversity into comprehensive strategies that make other leaders accountable for increasing and supporting diversity within the organization. As the dean recalled advice given to him from another person in charge of diversity for a big company, *"... she said the way to solve it is to go out to places where candidates of diverse backgrounds are either virtually or electronically or actually going to organizations saying you're looking to recruit black engineers and there are black engineer societies and so you can go there..."*

As noted by Burrell and Morgan (2001), there is a relationship between human beings and their environment. With this higher education institution hosting a high percent of international students, administrators, faculty, and staff should be aware of the distinct challenges those international students face, regardless of how academically prepared they are (Macgregor & Folinazzo, 2018). For a higher education institution where the business school caters to many international students, the associate dean does demonstrate awareness of the need to diversify by saying, *"We have European, Asian, and African-American staff within our different schools... I have a European, a South Asian, and an American based staff."* However, this is only one piece to an entire organization, a subculture of the larger university.

If the university leaders are interested in synthesizing their taken-for-granted assumptions and spotlighting underlying values to align them with a more comprehensive and inclusive organizational culture then they should take responsibility for multicultural employees through policy (Smircich, 1983; Torres & Tarozzi, 2020). If they engage diverse groups to achieve common goals, then they will create opportunities for faculty, staff, and students to identify with groups outside of the traditionally associated group formation, and marginalized newcomers unsure about their role and how to act within the organization (Ashforth & Mael, 1989). This will result in a higher chance to identify with someone from the organization with increased structural diversity.

CONCLUSION

This chapter investigated the organizational culture and diversity initiatives at a midsize higher education institution. The analysis of the data yielded three important themes that permeated through the messages from the participants: 1) Rewards systems are important and necessary tool to recognize and encourage employee behaviors that align with the overall organizational culture. Monetary awards are not always available and necessary to recognize behaviors. Instead, leadership leverages other techniques to recognize employees and inspire further alignment of desired behavior; 2) Communication practices are often centered around technology, with email recognized as the preferred medium to facilitate inter and intra-personal communication; however, the face-to-face method of communication is the preferred method when having to address behavior issues that should remain on the record. This signifies that leadership recognizes that need to interact personally with those employees whose behavior does not align with the organizational values and norms; 3) Diversity is an important factor in the organizational culture and leadership recognizes that more needs to be done to embrace and integrate diversity into the organization. If organizational culture portrays a set of artifacts, espoused beliefs and values, then organizational leaders must look closely at the message their organizational culture is sending. Given the population of the international students and the default white male administration for the school, even with measures in place, other challenges will arise, and the university's leadership should be prepared to handle cross-cultural perspectives. While organizational cultures might be too broad and ambiguous to give clear direction for how employees ought to behave, the organizational culture is embodied in the norms, beliefs and values of the employees' collective mind (Hartnell & Walumbwa, 2011).

The two recommendations based upon the analysis of two interviews would be the first steps in creating a climate where workplace diversity really means how relationships are built beyond an employee's race and gender. By hiring a chief diversity officer, someone who understands the rich dimensions to diversity — disabilities, ethnic cultures, religion, etc. — and supporting that individual with resources and staff to promote empowerment and inclusion, the university will be so much closer to operating as a post-racial institution.

REFERENCES

Alvesson, M. (2011). Organizational culture. In N. M. Ashkanasy, C. P. Wilderom, & M. F. Peterson (Eds.), *The handbook of organizational culture and climate* (pp. 600–613). Sage.

Ashforth, B. E., & Mael, F. (1989). Social identity theory and the organization. *Academy of Management Review, 14*(1), 20–39. doi:10.2307/258189

Blanding, M. (2018, March 26). *To motivate employees, give an unexpected bonus (or penalty)*. HBS. https://hbswk.hbs.edu/item/to-motivate-employees-give-an-unexpected-bonus-or-penalty

Bowman, N. A. (2012). Structural diversity and close interracial relationships in college. *Educational Researcher, 41*(4), 133–135. doi:10.3102/0013189X12439934

Burrell, G., & Morgan, G. (2001). *Sociological paradigms and organisational analysis: elements of the sociology of corporate life*. Ashgate.

Chen, J. M., & Hamilton, D. L. (2015). Understanding diversity: The importance of social acceptance. *Personality and Social Psychology Bulletin, 41*(4), 586–598. doi:10.1177/0146167215573495 PMID:25713169

Chubin, D. E., & Malcom, S. M. (2006). The new backlash on campus. *College and University, 81*(4), 65.

Cleveland, S. (2021). *Interview Based Proposal*. Submitted as assignment in partial fulfillment for the requirement of EDU 7272: Organizational Culture and Change course.

Denison, D. R., & Mishra, A. K. (1995). Toward a theory of organizational culture and effectiveness. *Organization Science, 6*(2), 204–223. doi:10.1287/orsc.6.2.204

Driskill, G. W., & Brenton, A. L. (2011). *Organizational culture in action: A cultural analysis workbook* (2nd ed.). Sage. doi:10.4135/9781483349282

Gurin, P., Dey, E., Hurtado, S., & Gurin, G. (2002). Diversity and higher education: Theory and impact on educational outcomes. *Harvard Educational Review, 72*(3), 330–367. doi:10.17763/haer.72.3.01151786u134n051

Hartnell, C., & Walumbwa, F. (2011). Transformational leadership and organizational culture. In N. M. Ashkanasy, C. P. Wilderom, & M. F. Peterson (Eds.), *The handbook of organizational culture and climate* (pp. 600–613). Sage.

Hatch, M. J., & Schultz, M. (2002). The dynamics of organizational identity. *Human Relations, 55*(8), 989–1018. doi:10.1177/0018726702055008181

Hsieh, M. H. (2007). Challenges for international students in higher education: One student's narrated story of invisibility and struggle. *College Student Journal, 41*(2).

Klein, U. (2016, January). Gender equality and diversity politics in higher education: Conflicts, challenges and requirements for collaboration. [). Pergamon.]. *Women's Studies International Forum*, *54*, 147–156. doi:10.1016/j.wsif.2015.06.017

Macgregor, A., & Folinazzo, G. (2018). Best practices in teaching international students in higher education: Issues and strategies. *TESOL Journal*, *9*(2), 299–329. doi:10.1002/tesj.324

Meyerson, D. E. (1994). Interpretations of stress in institutions: The cultural production of ambiguity and burnout. *Administrative Science Quarterly*, *39*(4), 628–653. doi:10.2307/2393774 PMID:10144744

Noe, R., Hollenbeck, J., Gerhart, B., & Wright, P. (2021). *Human Resource Management: Gaining a Competitive Advantage* (12th ed.). McGraw Hill.

Noor, Z., Nayaz, N., Solanki, V., Manoj, A., & Sharma, A. (2020). Impact of Rewards System on Employee Motivation: A Study of a Manufacturing Firm in Oman. *International Journal of Business and Management Future*, *4*(2), 6–16. doi:10.46281/ijbmf.v4i2.692

Office of Personnel Management. (2011). Government-wide diversity and inclusion strategic plan. Energy.gov. www.energy.gov/diversity/downloads/government-wide-diversityand-inclusion-strategic-plan-2011-office-personnel

Paulston, C. B., Kiesling, S. F., & Rangel, E. S. (2012). *The handbook of intercultural discourse and communication*. Wiley-Blackwell. doi:10.1002/9781118247273

Petera, P. (2011). Evaluating the quality of rewards systems. *European Financial and Accounting Journal*, *6*(3), 66–91. doi:10.18267/j.efaj.26

Schein, E. H., & Schein, P. (2017). *Organizational culture and leadership* (5th ed.). Routledge.

Smircich, L. (1983). Concepts of culture and organizational analysis. *Administrative Science Quarterly*, *28*(3), 339–358. doi:10.2307/2392246

Thompson, S., Forde, T., & Otieno, T. (2017). A sustainable, culturally competent approach to academic leadership. In *Global and culturally diverse leaders and leadership* (pp. 279–305). Emerald Publishing Limited. doi:10.1108/S2058-880120170000003014

Tierney, W. G. (1988). Organizational culture in higher education: Defining the essentials. *The Journal of Higher Education*, *59*(1), 2–21. doi:10.1080/00221546.1988.11778301

Torres, C. A., & Tarozzi, M. (2020). Multiculturalism in the world system: Towards a social justice model of inter/multicultural education. *Globalisation, Societies and Education, 18*(1), 7–18. doi:10.1080/14767724.2019.1690729

Valbrun, M. (2018, May 7). From diversity chief to college president. *Inside Higher Ed.* https://www.insidehighered.com/news/2018/05/07/chief-diversity-officer-position-new-path-presidency

Wolniak, G. (2017, January 31). *What diversity on the american campus can teach us: an interview with gregory wolniak.* NYU. https://steinhardt.nyu.edu/site/ataglance/2017/01/what-diversity-on-the-american-campus-can-teach-us-an-interview-with-gregory-wolniak.html

Chapter 9
Ethnopsychology in the Digital Era:
Culturally Diverse Psychology

Anjali Daisy
St. Joseph's Institute of Management, Trichy, India

ABSTRACT

A determination of current and probably future issues is tendered to in four segments. The first area manages the inescapable discussion among relativistic and universalistic introductions. In the second area, the authors talk about how the idea of culture is utilized in experimental investigations, attracting regard for, in addition to other things, the low accentuation on culturally diverse likenesses that rise up out of numerous informational indexes. The third segment addresses three topics that may well turn out to be progressively vital later on, to be specific inquiries concerning the level of soundness in culturally diverse information crossing bigger scopes of conduct, the coordination of discoveries from non-western social orders, and expansion in look into on human improvement in a social setting. The fourth segment stresses the duty of culturally diverse clinicians to apply their ability, particularly to issues of monetary and social imbalance, to add to human prosperity.

INTRODUCTION

A choice of current and future issues are classified into four segments. The first segment manages the inescapable discussion among relativistic and universalistic introductions. In the second area, the creators talk about how the idea of culture is utilized in experimental investigations, attracting consideration regarding, in addition

DOI: 10.4018/978-1-6684-9013-6.ch009

to other things, the low accentuation onIndeedculturally diverse likenesses that rise out of numerous informational collections. The third segment addresses three subjects that may well turn out to be progressively essential later on, to be specific inquiries concerning the level of lucidness in multifaceted information traversing bigger scopes of conduct, the incorporation of discoveries from non-Western social orders, and expansion in inquiring about on human advancement in social setting. The fourth segment underlines the obligation of multifaceted analysts to apply their aptitude, particularly to issues of financial and social disparity, to add to human prosperity. A determination of current and probable future issues is tendered in four segments. The first area manages the inescapable discussion among relativistic and universalistic introductions. In the second area, the creators talk about how the idea of culture is utilized in experimental investigations, attracting regard for, in addition to other things, the low accentuation on culturally diverse likenesses that rise out of numerous informational indexes. The third segment addresses three topics that may well turn out to be progressively vital later on, to be specific inquiries concerning the level of soundness in culturally diverse information crossing bigger scopes of conduct, the coordination of discoveries from non-western social orders, and expansion in look into on human improvement in social setting. The fourth segment stresses the duty of culturally diverse clinicians to apply their ability, particularly to issues of monetary and social imbalance, to add to human prosperity.

CULTURALLY DIVERSE PSYCHOLOGY

Issues And Overarching Themes

A choice of current and probable future issues are tended to in four segments. The principal area manages the unavoidable debate among relativistic and universalistic introductions. In the second area, the creators talk about how the thought of culture is utilized in exact investigations, attracting thoughtfulness regarding, in addition to other things, the low accentuation on culturally diverse likenesses that rise out of numerous informational collections. The third segment tends to three topics that may well turn out to be increasingly critical later on, to be specific questions concerning the level of soundness in diverse information crossing bigger scopes of conduct, the coordination of discoveries from non-Western social orders, and an expansion in research on human improvement in social setting. The fourth segment stresses the obligation of culturally diverse therapists to apply their aptitude, particularly to issues of financial and social disparity, to add to human prosperity. In this last commitment to the uncommon issue, we attract consideration regarding some more significant subjects. The writers of every one of the past articles in were requested to address one space or angle from the comprehensive exhibit that comprises the field of culturally diverse brain science. This article will go for a few coordination just as mirror our perspectives on some important current issues and patterns in multifaceted brain science. Our composition, just as this entire unique issue, is necessarily specific, restricted all things considered by our very own insight, viewpoints, and interests. The main area manages the difference between relativistic and universalistic points of view. With most of alternate creators, we concur that ways are expected to connect the celebration and to figure positions that take into account both social collection and social contrasts. The issue will most likely be seen more and more as an unproductive division, yet, to some degree not at all like others, we feel that the issue, one might say, will remain since it cannot generally be settled. The second segment manages the topic of how the thought of culture is managed in ordinary diverse investigations. We center around three points, specifically the relatively low accentuation on several likenesses when contrasted with contrasts, the utilization of culture as an informative name, and the dubious issue of how we characterize culture as particular from different societies. In the third segment, we address three patterns that are probably going to shape the fate of multifaceted brain research in real ways, to be specific diverse perspectives on the mental intelligibility of societies, an increment in commitments from the lion's share world and a conceivable move in consideration from social-mental subjects to ontogenetic improvement. The fourth segment is about the ethical and social avocation of the multifaceted undertaking, to be specific the scope for application. Increasingly more science is considered responsible to society. It might be guaranteed that as science concentrated on the human reality, brain science and exceptionally multifaceted brain science conveys a significantly more prominent social duty. We talk about the degree to which this duty is figured out.

Characterizing Behavior-Culture Relationships

The fundamental hypothetical and methodological issue in multifaceted brain science is how the relationship between conduct and culture ought to be characterized. Normally, two noteworthy positions are recognized, relativism and universalism. The refinement harmonizes with the continuing and sensible strains and introduction in brain science that can be followed through its whole history (Jahoda and Krewer, 1997). It is similarly reflected in the refinement between nomothetic and idiographic methodologies in brain science, distinguished by (Allport,1937) who, thus, alluded to prior sources in logic. There are further parallels in the subjective and hermeneutic versus the quantitative and positivistic methodologies in humanism and human social studies (Tadros, E., & Owens, D. 2021). What is normal in the idiographic (hermeneutic, emic, indigenous, relativist, social, and so on.) approaches is ah accentuation on the uniqueness of wonders, as they get their implications from specific settings. The remarkable singular case must be examined from inside and in its very own right, resisting correlation. On the other hand, the nomothetic (positivist, etic, universalist, culture-near, and so forth.) approaches examine what is normal furthermore, can be looked at, not the extraordinary. The qualification rises in the meaning of the object of logical inquiry, strictness of hypotheses, reliability of techniques and methods, and ideas of observational testing (O'Keefe, V. M., Cwik, M. F., Haroz, E. E., & Barlow, A., 2021). Brain science can be said to have a place with both of the two noteworthy domains. However our history demonstrates that the greater part of us are in one of the two camps concerning how we characterize our ideas, what we see as promising techniques, and how important we think about specific discoveries. The distinctions in the substance of the Diary of Cross-Cultural Psychology and Culture and Psychology frame an important precedent. One's decision of position has essential ramifications for strategy. Seeing that there is nonidentity of mental procedures diversely (Neubern, M. S.,2022). there is noncomparability of information. Emphasis on the uniqueness of wonders opposes examination and makes the utilization of conventional techniques and instruments wrong. Subsequently, the whole venture of culture-similar research breakdown if the suspicion of clairvoyant solidarity of humanity is rejected (Broere, S., 2019). Many culturally diverse analysts do not feel quiet with such a perspective. In any case, considerably more are awkward with an absolutist position in which the connections among conduct and hidden procedures are thought to be the equivalent all over the place (Shala. M.,etal., 2020). For precedent, no cross-culturist today would translate a low contrast in scores on a knowledge battery between tests drawn from two social populaces as an impression of a comparing contrast in scholarly limit. The two meta-theoretical points of view will, in general, show up as fundamentally unrelated and which one is bought into involves scholarly (even close to home) decision (Heim, E., & Kohrt, B. A., 2019). All things considered, as brain science dares to incorporate culture into its examinations, there is an expanding need to address and manage the essential clash between what (Lightfood & Valsiner,1992) called "the need to conceptualize 'setting reliance' of mental marvels and the 'setting disposing of' hypothetical customs of brain research. There have been different endeavors to connect relativistic and universalistic methodologies.

The way culture is handled in empirical research raises several issues that may not be as prominent in theoretical discussions but affect cross-cultural psychology's practical application. One such issue is the tendency to focus only on differences in behavior across cultures while ignoring the similarities in emotions, cognition, and social-structural mechanisms that exist across societies. This tendency stems from the assumption that similarities are biologically determined and, therefore, not relevant to cross-cultural psychology. However, while the primary goal of cross-cultural psychology is to uncover and explain cultural differences, an exclusive emphasis on differences can obscure the significance of cultural commonalities. When conducting cross-cultural research, it is essential to understand and consider the role of culture in shaping human behavior. However, how culture is handled in empirical research can have significant implications for the interpretation of findings and the understanding of cultural differences and similarities.One issue that arises is the tendency to focus solely on differences in behavior across cultures, while neglecting the similarities that exist between them. While there are undoubtedly cultural variations in behavior, it is also important to recognize that many aspects of human behavior are universal across cultures. For instance, emotions and cognition are common to all humans, regardless of cultural background, and societies have similar social-structural mechanisms, such as rules for maintaining group solidarity and socializing children. These commonalities are often attributed to biology and are thus considered outside of the purview of cross-cultural psychology. However, ignoring cultural similarities can lead to a narrow understanding of culture and behavior. An exclusive emphasis on differences can obscure the significance of cultural commonalities and limit the understanding of how culture shapes behavior. By acknowledging both similarities and differences in behavior across cultures, cross-cultural psychology can provide a more nuanced and comprehensive understanding of the role of culture in shaping human behavior. highlighted by (van de Vijver & Leung,2000). In culture-comparative research articles, it is often noted explicitly that both similarities and differences in conduct collection were found between tests drawn from social populaces. Be that as it may, creators at that point will, in general, proceed with the clarification of contrasts and to disregard the similitudes as opposed to asking to what degree and how culture impacts conduct (Aycan, 2020). There are various purposes for this. In any case, culturally diverse brain research as a field of look into has come to fruition as a response against the inclination in brain science to disregard social varieties, furthermore, to think of them as disturbance factors. Honestly, the legitimization for our field lies in the way that multifaceted contrasts exist (Kytina, V., Pochinok, T. V., & Bartosh, D., 2020). A second reason lies in understood presumptions about the uniqueness of each culture, got from human social studies. Portrayals of the Indian self, the Korean mother, or terms, for example, Japanese amae, Greek philotimo, or Mexican noteworthy sociocultural premises are promptly utilized (Heim, E. M etal ., 2020). Be that as it may, similar designs are seen in different nations frequently stay understood. For instance, (Triandis,1989) noted notions comparable to the Greek philotimo in other social gatherings, and (Aycicegi,1993) found the Mexican interesting sociocultural premises (Diaz-Guerrero, 1991) as to give jobs to be essential in Turkey. A third reason has to do with approach, (van de Vijver & Leung, 2000) portray how to examine structure and examination in conventional test approaches are fixated on the testing of the invalid speculation.

Interpretable proof has been discovered when the invalid speculation can be rejected, ideally with an abnormal state of measurable certainty. The accentuation is currently moving toward the extent of change that is clarified (Casadei, F., & Monti, M. C., 2022). This implies we should take a gander at the extent of multifaceted contrasts concerning the variation between people inside common examples. This has two outcomes. In the first place, the utilization of homogeneous examples will turn out to be less adequate in the future. Second, the proportion of between-culture variety and inside culture variety will turn into the fundamental measurement for revealing contrasts (Mutiso, V., 2019).

Culture as an Explanatory Concept

The second issue concerning the translation that we might want to attract thoughtfulness regarding is the free utilization of culture as a name in the clarification of contrasts in conduct collection. When a trademark attribute has been depicted, it will, in general, be summoned all the more unnecessarily by different scientists in consequent examinations, regardless of whether the relationship of the marvels under scrutiny to such quality has never been inspected (cf. Singelis, 2000). Considerably more questionable are references to culture as a worldwide mark (Segall, 1984); if Turkish transients in the Netherlands have a high rate of psychosomatic protestations, it is a direct result of their Turkish (or Mediterranean) culture. Social "clarifications" have turned out to be so well known and promptly accessible that they will in general block more significant investigations. Like this, imperative social-basic factors, for example, social class standing, neediness, and low instruction levels are veiled. This is especially dangerous in those examples in which ethnic minority status covers with low financial status. Characterizing a culture. The third and last issue we might want to refer to in this segment is the topic of how a culture ought to be characterized opposite different societies. In human social studies, there is a progression of as often as possible referenced criteria, including lastingness after some time, land area, dialect, religion, monetary subsistence, self-proclaimed (ethnic) personality, etc. Refinements between social populaces are fundamentally subject to the choice of a standard or a blend of criteria (Consoli, A. J., López, I., & Whaling, K. M., 2022). Going above and beyond, one can address whether these criteria ate still crucial in a period of extensive correspondence and travel furthermore, of expanding trade of data among significant parts of the total populace. It has been contended that social limits are liquid (Hermans and Kempen, 1998). This sort of contention powers specialists to think about which constituent parts of the setting are essential to their examine. It is trusted that this will debilitate the continuous distinguishing proof of "a culture" with "a nation" which is as yet a sign of a significant part of contemporary writing (Paudel, D., 2021). For some parts of conduct, nations comprise a dimension at which the proportion of between-gather variety furthermore, inside gathering variety is high; in different examples different dimensions are progressively significant. One case of an unavoidable variable that indicates provincial variety inside numerous nations is the measure of iodine in the drinking water (Heim, E., Mewes, Knaevelsrud, C., 2021). By differentiating sets of towns, (Bleichrodt, Drenth, & Querido, 1980) demonstrated that iodine lack prompts hindrance of intellectual advancement even in people who do not appear indications of goiter. To put it, clear pointers, for example, "the" Japanese or "the" American culture is inadequate; populaces should be portrayed (and tested) correctly as far as what we need to know. These days, we appropriately demonstrate enthusiasm for the social dimension rather than the individual dimension of examination (Kirvalidze, N.,2020). Be that as it may, maybe an inquiry ought to be included, specifically, which social dimension?

THREE FUTURE TRENDS

Association of Behavior in Cultural Context

The significant inquiry here is to what different degree parts of culture hang together importantly; this is the subject of lucidness of culture as talked about by social anthropologists of the inquiry of speculation of contrasts as talked about by culturally diverse therapists. The origination of culture fundamental a large portion of the anthropological writing is that of a rational entirety in which everything hangs together with everything else (Ellenberger, H. F., 2020). Most ethnographies endeavor to depict intelligibility in the mental presence of the populace contemplated. Be that as it may, this conviction is not very perfect with the relativist rule of some social anthropologists that from their science, no forecasts about the future can be reasonable (Pydiura, O., 2020). In a framework with intelligent association, inner interdependencies just as their outcomes ought to be apparent. However, replication look into in ethnography has appeared, fat, numerous extensive disparities and couple of understandings (Kloos, 1988). At the other extraordinary is the thought that culture is an allot gathering of traditions that ate generally developed and can best be imagined as self-assertive assertions about the proper behavior in specific circumstances, which standards to apply, and what to trust (Girndt, 1997). Such understandings can be unequivocal or understood. Laws and traffic rules ate express. Eating with blade and fork or with chopsticks is ah case of ah verifiable assertion; it has never been liable to interview. As a group of creators, we have our understandings and differences (Inozemtsev, V. A., Sanakoev, I. B., & Bagramyants, N. L., 2021). Let us first notice a point on which we have robust assertion, in particular, the significance of culture as setting for conduct. We ate both persuaded that many multifaceted contrasts in conduct ate a pretty much direct result of the financial and financial conditions under which individuals live. Financial riches or destitution of a country have full results. It decides if there will be top-notch therapeutic consideration for a wiped out baby, regardless of whether you can hazard being terminated for saying something that disappoints your predominant, regardless of whether you approach a courtroom when treated seriously by familiar specialists or the police, thus on. Financial prosperity is a compound variable; specifically, it is exceedingly associated with number of long stretches of school training. In the area of utilization of culturally diverse brain research, we return to the global disparities reflected in the north-south partition. We will, in general, differ among ourselves with regards to the disguise of contrasts in setting (Kagitcibasi, Van lair Heuvel & Poortinga, 1999).

Porting is slanted to contend that the legitimacy of wide speculations has never been shown agreeably. Prior expansive originations -, for example, social development hypothesis, culture and identity ideas as cutting edge by (Mead & Benedict, 1934), the assumed nonappearance of a workforce for unique reasoning in ignorant people - all have been deserted. Also, the lucidness of measurement like independence community can be addressed, both for theoretical and experimental reasons (Fijneman, Willemsen, & Poortinga, 1996). As per mistakes made in the past should encourage us exercises yet ought not dissuade us from hunting down hidden measurements to clarify social results. Hypothesis advancement fundamentally includes speculation. What is critical is that speculations depend on exact soundproof and are available to disconfirmation. Moreover, the empirical record of studies on individualism-collectivism is impressive even though there is room for improvement (Kagitcibasi, 1997). Also, in this series of articles, most authors leave no doubt that in their view, conceptions with significant dimensions are the models of choice for cross-cultural psychology.

THE INTEGRATION OF INDIGENOUS MOVEMENTS

The passage discusses the emergence of indigenous approaches in cross-cultural psychology, which have gained momentum in the past few decades. These approaches emphasize the importance of local concepts and reject the dominant Western theories and methods in psychology. The impetus for this trend towards indigenous psychology has been two-fold: a search for local relevance and a desire to use indigenous psychological knowledge to reach universals. There are different orientations towards indigenization, with one approach focusing on uncovering the diversity in human behavior to enrich psychological theory, and the other aiming to develop psychology for each diverse cultural reality. The former orientation is seen as promising to enrich psychological inquiry, while the latter carries the risk of producing an unwieldy and incomparable body of knowledge. This highlights that indigenous approaches differ widely in their assumptions about the nature and extent of cross-cultural differences. Nevertheless, by taking local concepts as a starting point, indigenous approaches tend to lean towards relativism, at least as an initial position. Finally, the passage notes that while it is not entirely clear how other indigenous bodies of knowledge can be integrated with the currently dominant indigenous psychology of the West, some beginnings can be noted in integrative constructs deriving from indigenous thinking and research. These constructs include nurturant-task leader, socially-oriented achievement motivation, relationship harmony, and autonomous-relational self.

ONTOGENETIC DEVELOPMENT

The Handbook of Cross-Cultural Psychology highlights the importance of studying ontogenetic development, which refers to the interaction between genetic factors and the overall cultural context in human development. However, Keller and Greenfield's complaint that there is a lack of culture-comparative research on developmental issues is still valid. To address this gap, a comparative, cross-cultural approach can provide a better understanding of the organism-context interface and the relative contribution of each to behavioral outcome.

In studying ontogenetic development, it is necessary to consider both cohort and historical period effects as well as age-related maturation. Additionally, a specific social or culturally diverse point of view is needed to supplement the recorded information to avoid dichotomizing the relevant and the all-inclusive. A developmental psychology that is relevant to the historical and social context is necessary to be considered scientific enough.Current research in diverse psychology often involves describing or categorizing behavior and mental processes based on culturally defined selves, such as independent or dependent selves. However, to understand how these differences in self come about, it is necessary to examine the context-based developmental processes and socialization that explain the variations in self in different economic and familial settings.

To answer the question of why a specific type of socialization occurs in a particular economic setting and not in another, and when a change in this process of self-improvement may be necessary, we need to understand the functional underpinnings of socialization as the interface of society and family. Family communication patterns and socialization values are influenced by economic and social contexts, and these, in turn, affect child-rearing practices. Any changes in the context would have implications for changes in the chain of relationshipTo address these questions, a model of family change that analyzes the development of different types of self within different family organization patterns can be used. This model takes into account the adaptable relationships between individual, familial, and societal entities and provides answers to the how and why questions about human development in the context. It can also be used to study the economic changes that are occurring globally and their implications for human development.

POTENTIAL FOR APPLICATION

Riches and prosperity are unevenly dispersed inside and between nations. Analysts who need to keep up the excellent high gauges of their calling (American Mental Affiliation, 1992) cannot overlook this shamefulness. This holds even more valid for therapists who pride themselves on having a more extensive, diverse point of view. In this segment, we address the subject of what therapists can and ought to do to improve disparities on the planet, which are regularly demonstrated as a differentiate among north and south. We notice three covering focuses: utilizing brain research for modern improvement, bringing society into wellbeing and training, and making commitments to human advancement. Mechanical Improvement In the unpredictable interrelationships of monetary, social, and instructive components, factors identifying with work also, work associations are of incredible significance. Maybe the beginning of types of personal and societal changes that are related to industrialization can be started by Mechanical innovation and the structure of (global) associations are not identified with social factors; even though a result of human culture, they demonstrate couple of contrasts between nations. In any case, the working of associations is from various perspectives reliant on the mental qualities of the individuals included (Drenth and Groenendijk, 1984). Contrasts in customs, work understanding, connections in hierarchical orders, and various other individual and relational variables require a culture-educated methodology. The requirement for modern improvement in the lion's share world nations makes the development of modern and hierarchical brain science to these nations significant (Aycan, 2000). The constrained degree to which this has happened so far recommends that we can talk here of hidden potential.

BRINGING CULTURE INTO EDUCATION AND HEALTH

The advantages of training at both the societal and the individual dimensions are very much recorded. For instance, market analysts point to the importance of interest in instruction, especially fundamental training, for commercial development

(McGranahan, 1995). At the dimension of the individual, much research focuses on the positive commitment of tutoring to psychological capability (Ceci and Williams, 1997; Segall, Dasen, Berry, and Poortinga, 1999). Specifically, number of years in school seems, by all accounts, to be a significantly essential variable in low-salary settings. There is proof indicating a causal connection between tutoring what's more, IQ that cannot be clarified based on higher IQ kids remaining in school longer (Ceci and Williams, 1997; Harnqvist, 1968; Heckman, 1995). There are additionally ability building and enabling impacts of tutoring, particularly for ladies (Min, 1994). Given the unavoidable, positive proof, a solid promotion for expanded tutoring in the dominant part world is required. Clinicians ought to be in the cutting edge of backing endeavors, particularly in the dominant part world, for arrangements to expand interest in "training for every single" (United Nations Children's Fund, 1993), which is not the case. This is another case of the up 'til now undiscovered connected capability of culturally diverse brain research - impacting arrangement. Ir gives the idea that numerous analysts are not exactly mindful of the expansive approach ramifications of their insight and mastery. There is a need to reinforce the voice of backing of analysts concerning the approach ramifications of their discoveries. Moving in the direction of expanded tutoring for all does not mean support of low-quality tutoring. Formal training in once in the past colonized, low-pay nations regularly will, in general, be of low quality and socially insignificant (Serpell, 1993). Culturally diverse analysts should assume a job both in rendering school instruction socially significant and in advancing proficiency as an attractive all-around arrangement of aptitudes. Multifaceted brain science can likewise add to wellbeing applications all around, as worried by Harkness also, (Keefer,2000). With ongoing movements from absolutely therapeutic to more extensive, natural social-conduct conceptualizations of wellbeing, the notability of wellbeing conduct has incredibly expanded. While brain science's pertinence for wellbeing was recently perceived chiefly in the territory of psychological well-being, a lot more extensive interface is being perceived today, enveloping diverse parts of wellbeing. This is much more the case with the move in center from treatment of illness to anticipation of infection and advancement of wellbeing. Hence, there is a developing requirement for mental conceptualizations, evaluations, what is more, markers of wellbeing that are additionally socially substantial. Multifaceted points of view are in this manner more important than at any other time. Applications make wide progress, from expanding the effect of wellbeing training on changing (Levinger, 1996). Brain science lingers behind, especially concerning strategy situated research in the lion's share world, where the requirements are increasingly genuine. In societal advancement, human perspectives ate going to the fore, reflected in dimensions of proficiency and tutoring, sexual orientation value, wellbeing, business, etc, together comprising what is called human improvement at a large scale level (Joined

Countries Advancement Program, 1997). There is a requirement for the aptitude of culturally diverse clinicians, for instance, to evaluate the mental parts of human advancement, to some degree as the personal satisfaction develop. Also, there is an incredible need to set up age-related formative standards to parallel the current (physical) development standards for kids. These would be of critical significance in screening formative dangers in settings of financial drawback.

A noteworthy test is coordinating all-inclusive markers with a socially delicate introduction (cf. Harkness and Keefer, 2000). Appraisal, including the development, interpretation, and adjustment of tests, surveys, and perception plans are ah region where culturally diverse brain research has gathered applied and methodological learning (van de Vijver & Leung, 2000). There are numerous different zones with potential for application. A volume of the ongoing Handbook of Diverse Brain science (Berry, Segall, and Kagitcibasi, 1997) gives audits of utilization territories counting intergroup relations, wrongdoing and fighting, and cultural assimilation. Lamentably, we have not been ready to incorporate these into this uncommon issue. Among them, issues of cultural assimilation and minority status go to the fore. Multiculturalism will have significant issues as long as social class and power contrasts cover with ethnic contrasts and insofar as preference proceeds even though moving from unmistakable to "unpretentious partiality" (Pettigrew, 1998) in social orders where obvious segregation is politically off base. Once more, culturally diverse brain science can and ought to contribute. With huge inward and global relocation, numerous earlier unicultural social orders have turned out to be multicultural. Surely,

practically all social orders today are multicultural; in (Harkness and Keefer's, 2000) words, "multifaceted inconstancy has turned out to be nearby inconstancy." Maybe the most immediate type of use as a commitment to human prosperity is through mediation programs. Such projects can address differing issue regions including early training, wellbeing, nourishment, child-rearing, education. They can target distinctive gatherings (kids, grown-ups, families, ladies) and can be coordinated toward objectives, for example, new improvement for youthful youngsters, building capability, changing practices and dispositions, etc. Analysts cannot change existing imbalances in the public arena. In any case, they can enhance the proximal human condition to advance human prosperity, especially of youngsters experiencing childhood in neediness, and to balance some of the weakening impacts of social and financial hindrance. In all occurrences, the exceptional commitment of a diverse methodology is the combination of universalist and culture-delicate points of view. Mediations more often than not begin at a little scale, however they can impact social arrangements and create toward extensive scale usage. For instance, in Israel, coordinated endeavors are put into mediation projects to advance the social joining and ability of ongoing universal foreigners from burdened foundations just as to impact approaches (Feuerstein, 1991; Tzuriel and Kaufman, 1999). In India, a lot of pertinent approach research is led to consider the living conditions and advance the prosperity of ladies and youngsters (Borooah et al., 1994; Saraswathi and Kaur, 1993). (Kagitcibasi's, 1996b) intercession work with low-pay ladies and kids in Istanbul has forme need to legitimize their contribution. There are contrasts of conclusion concerning the accomplishments of (diverse) brain research, running from rather positive ones, for example, those held by (Harkness and Keefer, 2000) to first ones (Poortinga and Lunt, 1997). Here, we are unequivocally focusing on the potential for applications and are asking the accompanying inquiry: Is this potential sufficiently acknowledged? As for expert morals, analysts should act in a socially and logically mindful way and know about the confinements of their aggregated learning. Mental clarifications of conduct have their breaking points; they may now and again be intermediaries for, and cover with, monetary and social-basic variety. The north-south partition is genuine and ground-breaking. Regularly, monetary components are solid indicators of social varieties among populaces, as found as to "the pace of life" in 31 nations (Levine and Norenzayan, 1999). Brain research has a task to carry out what's more, has collected free information, however the learning has regularly not been definitive. What is imperative is that we reasonably survey our qualities and shortcomings and, in the meantime, be conscious of various dimensions of examination and the requirement for coordinated effort with other social researchers what's more, approach creators. Concerning the moral inquiry of whether analysts have the privilege to force their insight and values on others, there is no simple answer. Esteem based applications going from the inconvenience of absolutist gauges to relativistic free enterprise can shape unsuitable practices for the sake of culture. What is more, genuinely challenge connected multifaceted research. Two commonsense insurances can help. The first is to include both neighborhood specialists who are educated by indigenous learning and outcasts with skill. The second is to include the objective people of intercession or the exploration subjects as members partaking in the basic leadership. These measures will undoubtedly help. However we ought to likewise acknowledge the reality that connected research cannot be without esteem, make our qualities or suppositions unequivocal, and be available to challenge by those with opposite suppositions.

CONCLUSION

The significance of culture for brain science, at last, rests with the amount of the conduct collection can be better comprehended with the thought of culture than without it. In this sense, the status of culture shows up as an observational issue. The present arrangement of articles clarifies that such a situation without anyone else does not reveal to us how we can best approach the investigation of conduct in social settings. There are numerous contrasts of assessment on theoretical and methodological issues, demonstrating that our comprehension of the branch of knowledge of conduct and culture is restricted. In the meantime, the significance of social setting these days has all the earmarks of being past discussion in brain science, both as a science and as a calling. This gives a firm premise of what is to come. How this future will be formed stays to be seen. Our undertaking today, what's more, tomorrow is to enhance what we have, to advance our theoretical and methodological instruments to build up a superior comprehension of human wonders, and to go for contributing all around to human prosperity

REFERENCES

Adair, J. G. (1999). Indigenisation of psychology: The concept and its practical implementation. *Applied Psychology, 48*(4), 403–418. doi:10.1111/j.1464-0597.1999.tb00062.x

Allport, G. W. (1937). *Personality: A psychological interpretation.* APA.

Aycan, Z. (2000). Cross-cultural industrial and organizational psychology: Contributions, past developments, and future directions. *Journal of Cross-Cultural Psychology, 31*(1), 110–128. doi:10.1177/0022022100031001009

Berry, J. W. (1969). On cross-cultural comparability. *International Journal of Psychology, 4*(2), 119–128. doi:10.1080/00207596908247261

Berry, J. W., Berry, J. W., Poortinga, Y. H., Segall, M. H., & Dasen, P. R. (2002). *Cross-cultural psychology: Research and applications.* Cambridge University Press.

Bleichrodt, N., Drenth, P. J., & Querido, A. (1980). Effects of iodine deficiency on mental and psychomotor abilities. *American Journal of Physical Anthropology, 53*(1), 55–67. doi:10.1002/ajpa.1330530110 PMID:7416250

Consoli, A. J., López, I., & Whaling, K. M. (2022). Alternate cultural paradigms in Latinx psychology: An empirical, collaborative exploration. *Journal of Humanistic Psychology, 62*(4), 516–539. doi:10.1177/00221678211051797

Diaz-Guerrero, R. (1991). Historic-sociocultural premises (HSCPs) and global change. *International Journal of Psychology, 26*(5), 665–673. doi:10.1080/00207599108247152

Díaz-Loving, R., & Díaz-Loving, R. (2019). Ethnopsychology: Inserting Socio-cultural Components into a Bio-psychological Discipline. *Ethnopsychology: Pieces from the Mexican Research Gallery*, 13-55.

Ellenberger, H. F. (2020). *Ethnopsychiatry* (Vol. 56). McGill-Queen's Press-MQUP.

Fjneman, Y. A., Willemsen, M. E., Poortinga, Y. H., Erelcin, F. G., Georgas, J., Hui, C. H., Leung, K., & Malpass, R. S. (1996). Individualism-collectivism: An empirical study of a conceptual issue. *Journal of Cross-Cultural Psychology*, *27*(4), 381–402. doi:10.1177/0022022196274001

Girndt, T. (1997). An intervention strategy to managing diversity: Discerning conventions. *European Journal of Work and Organizational Psychology*, *6*(2), 227–240. doi:10.1080/135943297399213

Heim, E. M., Burchert, S., Shala, M., Cerga, A., Morina, N., Schaub, M., & Maercker, A. (2020). *Effect of cultural adaptation of a smartphone-based self-help programme on its acceptability and efficacy: Study protocol for a randomized controlled trial.* Psych Archives.

Inozemtsev, V. A., Sanakoev, I. B., & Bagramyants, N. L. (2021, September). Actualization of Ethnic Identity in the Digital Age. In *6th International Conference on Contemporary Education, Social Sciences and Humanities.(Philosophy of Being Human as the Core of Interdisciplinary Research)(ICCESSH 2021)* (pp. 54-60). Atlantis Press. 10.2991/assehr.k.210902.009

Jahoda, G., & Krewer, B. (1997). *History of cross-cultural and cultural psychology* (Vol. 1). Handbook of cross-cultural psychology.

Jahoda, G., & Krewer, B. (1997). *History of cross-cultural and cultural psychology* (Vol. 1). Handbook of cross-cultural psychology.

Kağitçibasi, Ç. (1996). The autonomous-relational self: A new synthesis. *European Psychologist*, *1*(3), 180–186. doi:10.1027/1016-9040.1.3.180

Kashima, Y. (2000). Conceptions of culture and person for psychology. *Journal of Cross-Cultural Psychology*, *31*(1), 14–32. doi:10.1177/0022022100031001003

Keith, K. D. (Ed.). (2019). *Cross-cultural psychology: Contemporary themes and perspectives*. John Wiley & Sons. doi:10.1002/9781119519348

Kirvalidze, N. (2020). Developing Higher School Students' cross-Cultural Awareness And Communicative Competence Through Phraseology. In *INTED2020 Proceedings* (pp. 5141-5150). IATED.

Kloos, B., Hill, J., Thomas, E., Wandersman, A., Elias, M. J., & Dalton, J. H. (2012). *Community psychology*. Cengage Learning.

Klotz, J. (2004). Sociocultural study of intellectual disability: Moving beyond labelling and social constructionist perspectives. *British Journal of Learning Disabilities, 32*(2), 93–104. doi:10.1111/j.1468-3156.2004.00285.x

Lightfoot, C., & Valsiner, J. (1992). *Parental belief systems under the influence: Social guidance of the construction of personal cultures.* APA.

Mendenhall, E., Rinehart, R., Musyimi, C., Bosire, E., Ndetei, D., & Mutiso, V. (2019). An ethnopsychology of idioms of distress in urban Kenya. *Transcultural Psychiatry, 56*(4), 620–642. doi:10.1177/1363461518824431 PMID:30672722

Pydiura, O. (2020). Use of Virtual Reality and Digital Technologies for Studying Folklore in Ukraine's Educational Institutions. *Journal «ScienceRise. Pedagogical Education, 1*(34), 4–7.

Segall, A. H. (1984). More than we need to know about culture, but are afraid not to ask. *Journal of Cross-Cultural Psychology, 15*(2), 153–162. doi:10.1177/0022002184015002004

Shala, M., Morina, N., Burchert, S., Cerga-Pashoja, A., Knaevelsrud, C., Maercker, A., & Heim, E. (2020). Cultural adaptation of Hap-pas-Hapi, an internet and mobile-based intervention for the treatment of psychological distress among Albanian migrants in Switzerland and Germany. *Internet Interventions : the Application of Information Technology in Mental and Behavioural Health, 21*, 100339. doi:10.1016/j.invent.2020.100339 PMID:32983906

Singelis, T. M. (2000). Some thoughts on the future of cross-cultural social psychology. *Journal of Cross-Cultural Psychology, 31*(1), 76–91. doi:10.1177/0022022100031001007

Stigler, J. W., Shweder, R. A., & Herdt, G. E. (1990). Cultural psychology: Essays on comparative human development. In *All but three of the chapters in this book are revised versions of presentations from two symposia held by the University of Chicago Committee on Human Development: " Culture and Human Development"(Oct 23-25, 1986) and" Children's Lives in Cultural Context"(Nov 5-7, 1987).* Cambridge University Press.

Van de Vijver, F. J., & Leung, K. (2000). Methodological issues in psychological research on culture. *Journal of Cross-Cultural Psychology, 31*(1), 33–51. doi:10.1177/0022022100031001004

Van de Vijver, F. J., & Poortinga, Y. H. (1992). Testing in culturally heterogeneous populations: When are cultural loadings undesirable? *European Journal of Psychological Assessment.*

Compilation of References

Abtar, D., & Moustafa, H. (2017). *In pursuit of Smart Learning Environments for the 21st Century*. IBE-UNESCO.

Adair, J. G. (1999). Indigenisation of psychology: The concept and its practical implementation. *Applied Psychology*, *48*(4), 403–418. doi:10.1111/j.1464-0597.1999.tb00062.x

Agarwal, P. (2019). *How Microaggressions Can Affect Wellbeing in the Workplace*. Forbes. https://www.forbes.com/sites/pragyaagarwaleurope/2019/03/29/howmicroaggressions -can-affect-wellbeing-in-the-workplace/#18fc6a1973cb

Aguinis, H., Jensen, S. H., & Kraus, S. (2022). Policy Implications of Organizational Behavior and Human Resource Management Research. *The Academy of Management Perspectives*, *36*(3), 857–878. doi:10.5465/amp.2020.0093

Ainley, J., & Carstens, R. (2018). *Teaching and learning international survey (TALIS) 2018 conceptual framework*. OECD. doi:10.1787/799337c2-

Ainscow, M. (2016) Collaboration as a strategy for promoting equity in education possibilities and barriers. *CSC JES*. https://www.cscjes-cronfa.co.uk/api/storage/2a6d51d2-92c2-45e3-97a8-2567619e7fb6/Ainscow-paper-for-JPCC-February-2016.pdf

Ainscow, M., & Messiou, K. (2017). *Engaging with the views of students to promote inclusion in education*. Springer.

Aiscow, M. (2016). *Diversity and Equity: A Global Education Challenge*. Springer.

Al A'ali, E. (2022). Human Behaviour in Organizations: An Enhancement perspective. In. E. Al A'ali & M. Masmoudi (Eds), Religion and Its Impact on Organizational Behavior. IGI Global. doi:10.4018/978-1-7998-9319-6.ch001

Al A'ali, E., & Alazali, R. (2018). Gender Differences in Relation to Organization Sources of Power. In E. Al-A'ali, M.M. Al—Shammari & H. Masri (Eds) Arab Wimen and their Evolving Roles in Global Business Landscape. IGI Global. doi:10.4018/978-1-5225-3710-6.ch001

Al A'ali, E., & Al-Sarraf, A. R. (2016), Ethical Consumerism: Contextual Issues Of Ethical Decision-making Processes: An Exploratory Study. In Ethical and Social Perspectives on Global Business interaction in Emerging Markets (pp.133-149). IGI Global

Al A'ali, E. (2009). Women Leadership Styles. In *Scientific Journal for Business and Finance. Vol. No. 1*. Tanta University press.

Al A'Ali, E. (2020). The Role of Auditing Firms in Promoting Ethical Consumerism. In E. A. Al-A'Ali & M. Masmoudi (Eds.), *Ethical Consumerism and Comparative Studies Across Different Cultures* (pp. 39–52). IGI GLOBAL. doi:10.4018/978-1-7998-0272-3.ch004

Al-A'ali, E. (1991). *The Phenomenon of women in Management: An alternative Perspective and its Implications in the Case of Bahrain*, [Unpublished PhD thesis, University of Lancaster].

Al-Alawi, A., & El Naggar, N. F. (2018). Factors Affecting Women Leadership to Reach Top Management and Its Impact on the Economy: The Case of the Kingdom of Bahrain. In E. Al-A'ali, M. M. Al-Shammari & H. Masri (Eds), Arab Women and Their Evolving Roles in the Global Business Landscape. IGI Global. doi:10.4018/978-1-5225-3710-6.ch005

Al-Alawi, A. I. (2016). Status of Bahraini Women in the Banking and Financial Sector: Challenges and Opportunities. *Journal of International Women's Studies, 17*(4), 210–228. https://vc.bridgew.edu/jiws/Vol17/iss4/15

Allport, G. W. (1937). *Personality: A psychological interpretation*. APA.

AlSaffar, G., & Al A'ali, E. (2021). Psychiatry in the midst of the Pandemic:A Narrative Perspective. In E. Al A'Ali & M. Masmoudi (Ed's), Global perspectives on change Management and Leadership in the post -Covid 19 Era. IGI Global. doi:10.4018/978-1-7998-6948-1.ch002

Alvesson, M. (2011). Organizational culture. In N. M. Ashkanasy, C. P. Wilderom, & M. F. Peterson (Eds.), *The handbook of organizational culture and climate* (pp. 600–613). Sage.

Arsel, Z., Crockett, D., & Scott, M. L. (2022). Diversity, equity, and inclusion (DEI) in the journal of consumer research: A curation and research agenda. *The Journal of Consumer Research, 48*(5), 5. doi:10.1093/jcr/ucab057

Ashforth, B. E., & Mael, F. (1989). Social identity theory and the organization. *Academy of Management Review, 14*(1), 20–39. doi:10.2307/258189

Ayari. A., (2018). "Women and Careers: The Issues of the Glass Ceiling". *Arab Women and Their Evolving Roles in the Global Business Landscape*. 74-86.

Ayari, A. (2022). *Bahraini Women in the STEM Fields: Sticky Floor, Broken Ladder, and Glass Ceiling*. EDAS.

Aycan, Z. (2000). Cross-cultural industrial and organizational psychology: Contributions, past developments, and future directions. *Journal of Cross-Cultural Psychology, 31*(1), 110–128. doi:10.1177/0022022100031001009

Bachmann, R., Gillespie, N., & Priem, R. (2015). Repairing Trust in Organizations and Institutions: Toward a Conceptual Framework. *Organization Studies, 36*(9), 1123–1142. doi:10.1177/0170840615599334

Baker College. (2021). *Examples of workplace microaggressions and how to reduce them.* Baker College. https://www.baker.edu/about/get-to-know-us/blog/examples-of-workplace-microaggressions-and-how-to-reduce-them

Ballard, D., Allen, B., Ashcraft, K., Ganesh, S., McLeod, P., & Zoller, H. (2020). When words do not matter: Identifying actions to effect diversity, equity, and inclusion in the academy. *Management Communication Quarterly*, *34*(4), 4. doi:10.1177/0893318920951643

Banting, K., & Kymlicka, W. (2013). Is there really a retreat from multiculturalism policies? New evidence from the multiculturalism policy index. *Comparative European Politics*, *11*(5), 577–598. doi:10.1057/cep.2013.12

Berry, J. W. (1969). On cross-cultural comparability. *International Journal of Psychology*, *4*(2), 119–128. doi:10.1080/00207596908247261

Berry, J. W., Berry, J. W., Poortinga, Y. H., Segall, M. H., & Dasen, P. R. (2002). *Cross-cultural psychology: Research and applications*. Cambridge University Press.

BetterUp. (n.d.). The impact of microaggressions in everyday life. *BetterUp*. https://www.betterup.com/en-us/resources/microaggressions

Blanding, M. (2018, March 26). *To motivate employees, give an unexpected bonus (or penalty)*. HBS. https://hbswk.hbs.edu/item/to-motivate-employees-give-an-unexpected-bonus-or-penalty

Bleichrodt, N., Drenth, P. J., & Querido, A. (1980). Effects of iodine deficiency on mental and psychomotor abilities. *American Journal of Physical Anthropology*, *53*(1), 55–67. doi:10.1002/ajpa.1330530110 PMID:7416250

Bliese, P. D. (2000). Within-group agreement, non-independence, and reliability: Implications for data aggregation and analysis. In *Multilevel theory, research, and methods in organizations: Foundations, extensions, and new directions* (pp. 349–381). Jossey-Bass/Wiley.

Block, C. J., & Noumair, D. A. (2017). Understanding Diversity Dynamics in Systems: Social Equality as an Organization Change Issue. *The Journal of Applied Behavioral Science*, *53*(2), 150–155. doi:10.1177/0021886317703250

Bohnet. I. (2016). *What works: Gender Equality by Design*. Harvard University Press.

Bosniak, L. (2006). *The citizen and the alien: The dilemmas of contemporary membership.* Princeton University Press. doi:10.1515/9781400827510

Bowman, N. A. (2012). Structural diversity and close interracial relationships in college. *Educational Researcher*, *41*(4), 133–135. doi:10.3102/0013189X12439934

Brescoll, V. L., Dawson, E., & Uhlmann, E. L. (2010). Hard won and easily lost: The fragile status of leaders in gender-stereotype-incongruent occupations. *Psychological Science*, *21*(11), 1640–1642. doi:10.1177/0956797610384744 PMID:20876882

Brondolo, E., Brady ver Halen, N., Pencille, M., Beatty, D., & Contrada, R. J. (2009). Coping with racism: A selective review of the literature and a theoretical and methodological critique. *Journal of Behavioral Medicine*, *32*(1), 64–88. doi:10.100710865-008-9193-0 PMID:19127420

Brown, M. E., Treviño, L. K., & Harrison, D. A. (2005). Ethical leadership: A social learning perspective for construct development and testing. *Organizational Behavior and Human Decision Processes*, *97*(2), 117–134. doi:10.1016/j.obhdp.2005.03.002

Brown, S. P. (1996). A meta-analysis and review of organizational research on job involvement. *Psychological Bulletin*, *120*(2), 235–255. doi:10.1037/0033-2909.120.2.235

Bukowski, A., & Rudnicki, S. (2019). Not only individualism: The effects of long-term orientation and other cultural variables on national innovation success. *Cross-Cultural Research*, *53*(2), 2. doi:10.1177/1069397118785546

Bullough, A., De Luque, M.S., Abdelzaher, D., & Heim, W. (2015) . Developing women leaders through entrepreneurship education and training. *Academy of Management Perspectives, 29*(2) 250-270.

Burrell, G., & Morgan, G. (2001). *Sociological paradigms and organisational analysis: elements of the sociology of corporate life*. Ashgate.

California University. (2021). *El ser biopsicosocial y espiritual.* California University. www.socialwelfare.Berkeley.edu

Capodilupo, C. M., Nadal, K. L., Corman, L., Hamit, S., Lyons, O. B., & Weinberg, A. (2010). *The manifestation of gender microaggressions. Microaggressions and marginality: manifestation, dynamics, and impact.* Wiley.

Cassell, C., Watson, K., Ford, J., & Kele, J. (2022). Understanding inclusion in the retail industry: Incorporating the majority perspective. *Personnel Review*, *51*(1), 230–250. doi:10.1108/PR-02-2020-0083

CEC. (2012). *Co-Teaching and Collaboration. A collection of Articles*. CEC.

Chen, J. M., & Hamilton, D. L. (2015). Understanding diversity: The importance of social acceptance. *Personality and Social Psychology Bulletin*, *41*(4), 586–598. doi:10.1177/0146167215573495 PMID:25713169

Chubin, D. E., & Malcom, S. M. (2006). The new backlash on campus. *College and University*, *81*(4), 65.

Cleveland, S. (2021). *Interview Based Proposal.* Submitted as assignment in partial fulfillment for the requirement of EDU 7272: Organizational Culture and Change course.

Collet, J., & Grinberg, S. (2021). hacia una escuela para lo común. Debates, luchas y propuestas en América Latina y España. Madrid: Morata.

Consoli, A. J., López, I., & Whaling, K. M. (2022). Alternate cultural paradigms in Latinx psychology: An empirical, collaborative exploration. *Journal of Humanistic Psychology, 62*(4), 516–539. doi:10.1177/00221678211051797

Cooper, D. R., & Schindler, P. S. (2008). *Business Research Methods* (10th ed.). McGraw Hill.

Cooper, M. J., Kriegel, D. T., & Brownell, M. T. (2018). Implicit bias in schools: A primer. *The Journal of Special Education, 51*(3), 166–177.

Cox, T. H., & Blake, S. (1991). Managing cultural diversity: Implications for organizational competitiveness. *The Executive, 5*(3), 3.

Creto, S. C., & Creto, S. T. (2019). *Modern Management: Concepts and Skills (global edition).* Pearson Education Limited.

Cross, M. (2004). Institutionalising campus diversity in South African higher education: Review of diversity scholarship and diversity education. *Higher Education, 47*(4), 387–410. doi:10.1023/B:HIGH.0000020854.04852.80

Darling-Hammond, L. (2020). *Implications for educational practice of the sciences of learning and development.* Taylor and Francis. doi:10.10.1080/10888691.2018.1537791

Dasgupta, N., & Asgari, S. (2004). Seeing is believing: Exposure to counter stereotypic women leaders and its effect on the malleability of automatic gender stereotyping. *Journal of Experimental Social Psychology, 40*(5), 642–658. doi:10.1016/j.jesp.2004.02.003

DeAngelis, T. (2009). Unmasking racial microaggressions. *Monitor on Psychology, 40*(2), 42.

Denison, D. R., & Mishra, A. K. (1995). Toward a theory of organizational culture and effectiveness. *Organization Science, 6*(2), 204–223. doi:10.1287/orsc.6.2.204

Denzin, N. K., & Lincoln, T. S. (2011). *The SAGE handbook of Qualitative research*. Sage.

Dewidar, O., Elmestekaway, N., & Welch, V. (2022). Improving equity, diversity, and inclusion in academia in Research Integrity and Peer Review. *2020 International Conference on Data Analytics*.

Diaz-Guerrero, R. (1991). Historic-sociocultural premises (HSCPs) and global change. *International Journal of Psychology, 26*(5), 665–673. doi:10.1080/00207599108247152

Díaz-Loving, R., & Díaz-Loving, R. (2019). Ethnopsychology: Inserting Socio-cultural Components into a Bio-psychological Discipline. *Ethnopsychology: Pieces from the Mexican Research Gallery*, 13-55.

Dobbin, F., & Kalev, A. (2018). Why does not diversity training work? The challenge for industry and academia. *Anthropology Now, 10*(2), 48–55. doi:10.1080/19428200.2018.1493182

Dong, X. T., & Chung, Y. W. (2021). The Mediating Effect of Perceived Stress and Moderating Effect of Trust for the Relationship Between Employee Silence and Behavioral Outcomes. *Psychological Reports, 124*(4), 1715–1737. doi:10.1177/0033294120942914 PMID:32674670

Dover, A. M. (2016). The moment of microaggression: The experience of acts of oppression, dehumanization, and exploitation. *Journal of Human Behavior in the Social Environment, 26*(7-8), 7–8, 575–586. doi:10.1080/10911359.2016.1237920

Dovidio, J. F., & Gaertner, S. L. (2004). Aversive racism. In M. P. Zanna (Ed.), Vol. 36, pp. 1–52). Advances in Experimental Social Psychology. Academic Press.

Driskill, G. W., & Brenton, A. L. (2011). *Organizational culture in action: A cultural analysis workbook* (2nd ed.). Sage. doi:10.4135/9781483349282

Dufour, L., Maoret, M., & Montani, F. (2020). Coupling High Self-Perceived Creativity and Successful Newcomer Adjustment in Organizations: The Role of Supervisor Trust and Support for Authentic Self-Expression. *Journal of Management Studies, 57*(8), 8. doi:10.1111/joms.12547

Eagly, A. H., & Karau, S. J. (2002). Role congruity theory of prejudice toward female leaders. *Psychological Review, 109*(3), 573–598. doi:10.1037/0033-295X.109.3.573 PMID:12088246

Ebert, R. J., & Griffin, R. W. (2019) Business essential. New York: Pearson (12ed.)

Ebert, R. J., & Griffin, R. W. (2019) Business essential., New York: Pearson (12ed.)

Einarsen, S., Hoel, H., Zapf, D., & Cooper, C. L. (2003). The concept of bullying at work. In S. Einarsen, H. Hoel, D. Zapf, & C. L. Cooper (Eds.), *Bullying and emotional abuse in the workplace: International perspectives in research and practice* (pp. 3–30). Taylor & Francis.

Ellenberger, H. F. (2020). *Ethnopsychiatry* (Vol. 56). McGill-Queen's Press-MQUP.

Ely, R. J., & Thomas, D. A. (2020, November–December). Getting Serious About Diversity. *Harvard Business Review.*

Espinoza, O. (2007). Solving the equity–equality conceptual dilemma: A new model for analysis of the educational process. *Educational Research, 49*(4), 343–363. doi:10.1080/00131880701717198

Etling, A. (2005) Liderazgo efectivo, técnicas, recursos y actividades didácticas en la dinámica de grupos. *The inclusive leadership handbook..* Association. https://inclusiveleadership.eu/

Fattoracci, J., Kwon, P., & Kwon, J. (2021). Intersectional microaggressions and mental health among sexual and gender minority people of colour. *Journal of Counseling Psychology, 68*(2), 179–191. doi:10.1037/cou0000539

Fichman, M. (2003). Straining towards trust: Some constraints on studying trust in organizations. *Journal of Organizational Behavior, 24*(2), 133–157. doi:10.1002/job.189

Fisher, D. R. (2020). *The diversity of the recent Black Lives Matter protests is a good sign for racial equity.*

Fiske, S. T., Cuddy, A. J., Glick, P., & Xu, J. (2002). A model of (often mixed) stereotype content: Competence and warmth, respectively, follow from perceived status and competition. *Journal of Personality and Social Psychology, 82*(6), 878–902. doi:10.1037/0022-3514.82.6.878 PMID:12051578

Fjneman, Y. A., Willemsen, M. E., Poortinga, Y. H., Erelcin, F. G., Georgas, J., Hui, C. H., Leung, K., & Malpass, R. S. (1996). Individualism-collectivism: An empirical study of a conceptual issue. *Journal of Cross-Cultural Psychology*, *27*(4), 381–402. doi:10.1177/0022022196274001

Flecha, R. (2010). *Aprendizaje dialógico en la sociedad de la información*. Hipatia.

Florian, L., & Camedda, D. (2020). Enhancing teacher education for inclusion. *European Journal of Teacher Education*, *43*(1), 4–8. doi:10.1080/02619768.2020.1707579

Forlin, Ch. (2012). *Future Directions for Inclusive Teacher Education*. Routledge. doi:10.4324/9780203113585

Forrest-Bank, S. S., Jenson, J. M., & Trecartin, S. (2015). The revised 28-item racial and ethnic microaggressions scale (r28rems): Examining the factorial structure for black, Latino/Hispanic, and Asian young adults. *Journal of Social Service Research*, *41*(3), 326–344. doi:10.1080/01488376.2014.987944

Forrest-Bank, S., Jenson, J. M., & Trecartin, R. (2015). Microaggressions and the clinical supervision process. *Journal of Counseling and Development*, *93*(4), 427–436. doi:10.1002/jcad.12054

Fuglsang, L., & Jagd, S. (2015). Making sense of institutional trust in organizations: Bridging institutional context and trust. *Organization*, *22*(1), 23–39. doi:10.1177/1350508413496577

Furst, S. A., & Cable, D. M. (2008). Employee resistance to organizational change: Managerial influence tactics and leadermember exchange. *The Journal of Applied Psychology*, *93*(2), 453–462. doi:10.1037/0021-9010.93.2.453 PMID:18361644

Galkienė, O. M (eds). (2021) Improving Inclusive Education through Universal Design for Learning. inclusive learning and Educational Equity 5. doi:10.1007/978-3-030-80658-3_1

Gallego, A., & Pardos-Prado, S. (2014). The big five personality traits and attitudes towards immigrants. *Journal of Ethnic and Migration Studies*, *40*(1), 1. doi:10.1080/1369183X.2013.826131 PMID:24563610

Garcia- Huidobro, J. (2001) Conflictos y alianzas en las reformas educativas: siete tesis basadas en la experiencia chilena. Santiago: PREL/CIDE

Gaucher, D., Friesen, J., & Kay, A. C. (2011). There is evidence that gendered wording in job advertisements exists and sustains gender inequality. *Journal of Personality and Social Psychology*, *101*(1), 109–128. doi:10.1037/a0022530 PMID:21381851

Gigliotti, R. A., Dwyer, B., & Ruiz-Mesa, K. (2018). Campus Unrest in American Higher Education: Challenges and Opportunities for Strategic Diversity Leadership in J. L. Chin; J. E. Trimble & J. E. Garcia (Eds) Global and Culturally Diverse Leaders and Leadership: New Dimensions and Challenges for Businesses, Education and Society. (pp.211-229), UK: Emerald Publishing Limited

Gill, G. K., McNally, M. J., & Berman, V. (2018). Effective diversity, equity, and inclusion practices. *Healthcare Management Forum, 31*(5), 5. doi:10.1177/0840470418773785 PMID:30114938

Girndt, T. (1997). An intervention strategy to managing diversity: Discerning conventions. *European Journal of Work and Organizational Psychology, 6*(2), 227–240. doi:10.1080/135943297399213

Giroux, H. (1990). *Los profesores como intelectuales*. Paidós.

Glick, P., & Fiske, S. T. (1996). The Ambivalent Sexism Inventory. *Journal of Personality and Social Psychology, 70*(3), 491–512. doi:10.1037/0022-3514.70.3.491

Goodman, R. (2005). Risks in process control. Graphic Arts Monthly. *Arts & Humani-ties, 77*(8), 32–36.

Gul, P., & Lynn, M. (2021). Unconscious Gender Bias. *An Exploratory Study of the Implicit Association Test Journal of Business and Psychology, 36*(2), 303–319. doi:10.100710869-020-09695-y

Gultekin, S. (2009). Citizen Involvement and Law Enforcement: Does Oproduction Affect Organizational Efficiency and Organizational Effectiveness? Dissertation Doctor of Philosophy, University of North Texas, Denton.

Gurin, P., Dey, E., Hurtado, S., & Gurin, G. (2002). Diversity and higher education: Theory and impact on educational outcomes. *Harvard Educational Review, 72*(3), 330–367. doi:10.17763/haer.72.3.01151786u134n051

Gustafsson, S., Gillespie, N., Searle, R., Hope Hailey, V., & Dietz, G. (2021). Preserving Organizational Trust During Disruption. *Organization Studies, 42*(9), 1409–1433. doi:10.1177/0170840620912705

Gutek, B. A., & Morasch, B. (1982). Sex ratios, sex-role spillover, and sexual harassment of women at Work. *Journal of Social Issues, 38*(4), 55–74

Hall, E. (1959). *The Silent Language*. Doubleday and Company.

Harriman, A. (1985). *Women/Men/Management*. Praeger Publications.

Harris, A. (2012). *Liderazgo y desarrollo de capacidades en la escuela*. Fundación Chile.

Hartnell, C., & Walumbwa, F. (2011). Transformational leadership and organizational culture. In N. M. Ashkanasy, C. P. Wilderom, & M. F. Peterson (Eds.), *The handbook of organizational culture and climate* (pp. 600–613). Sage.

Hatch, M. J., & Schultz, M. (2002). The dynamics of organizational identity. *Human Relations, 55*(8), 989–1018. doi:10.1177/0018726702055008181

Heilman, M. E., & Haynes, M. C. (2005). No credit where credit is due: An attributional rationalization of women's success in male-female teams. *The Journal of Applied Psychology, 90*(5), 905–916. doi:10.1037/0021-9010.90.5.905 PMID:16162063

Heim, E. M., Burchert, S., Shala, M., Cerga, A., Morina, N., Schaub, M., & Maercker, A. (2020). *Effect of cultural adaptation of a smartphone-based self-help programme on its acceptability and efficacy: Study protocol for a randomized controlled trial*. Psych Archives.

Higgins, C., Judge, T. A., & Ferris, G. R. (2003). Influence tactics and work outcomes: A meta-analysis. *Journal of Organizational Behavior*, *24*(1), 89–106. doi:10.1002/job.181

Hofmann. (2012). Gesellschaftstheoretische Grundlagen für einen reflexiven und inklusiven Umgang mit Diversitäten in Organisationen [Social theoretical foundations for a reflexive and inclusive approach to diversity in organizations]. In *Diversität und Diversitätsmanagement, In R. Bendl, E. Hanappi-Egger, & R. Hofmann,* (pp. 23–60). University of Vienna.

Hofstede, G. H., & Hofstede, G. (2001). Culture's consequences: Comparing values, behaviors, institutions and organizations across nations. *Sage (Atlanta, Ga.)*.

Hofstede, G., Hofstede, G., & Mirkov, M. (2010). *Cultures and organizations: Software of the mind* (3rd ed.). McGraw-Hill Professional.

Howard, G., & Laskin, E. (1998). *Mentes líderes. Una dicotomía del liderazgo*. Paidós.

Hsieh, M. H. (2007). Challenges for international students in higher education: One student's narrated story of invisibility and struggle. *College Student Journal*, *41*(2).

Human Resource Standards Institute (HRCI). (2022). *Combating microaggressions in the workplace*. HRCI. https://www.hrci.org/community/blogs-and-announcements/hr-leads-business-blog/hr-leads-business/2022/02/14/combating-microaggressions-in-the-workplace

Hunter, R. L. (2011). *An examination of workplace racial microaggressions and their effect on employee performance (Order No. 1503508)*. Available from ProQuest Dissertations & Theses Global. (915679506). https://lavasalibrary.remotexs.in/docview/915679506?accountid=38885

Inozemtsev, V. A., Sanakoev, I. B., & Bagramyants, N. L. (2021, September). Actualization of Ethnic Identity in the Digital Age. In *6th International Conference on Contemporary Education, Social Sciences and Humanities.(Philosophy of Being Human as the Core of Interdisciplinary Research)(ICCESSH 2021)* (pp. 54-60). Atlantis Press. 10.2991/assehr.k.210902.009

Jahoda, G., & Krewer, B. (1997). *History of cross-cultural and cultural psychology* (Vol. 1). Handbook of cross-cultural psychology.

Johnson, K. L., Richeson, J. A., & Finkel, E. J. (2011). Middle-class African Americans' perceptions of discrimination, race, and class: A rational analysis. *Journal of Personality and Social Psychology*, *101*(6), 1178–1195.

Jones, G. R., & George, J. M. (2003). *Contemporary Management* (3rd ed.). McGraw-Hill.

Joshi, A., & Roh, H. (2009). The role of context in work team diversity research: A meta-analytic review. *Academy of Management Journal*, *52*(3), 3. doi:10.5465/amj.2009.41331491

Kağitçibasi, Ç. (1996). The autonomous-relational self: A new synthesis. *European Psychologist*, *1*(3), 180–186. doi:10.1027/1016-9040.1.3.180

Kanungo, R. (1982a). Measurement of job and work involvement. *The Journal of Applied Psychology*, *67*(3), 341–349. doi:10.1037/0021-9010.67.3.341

Kashima, Y. (2000). Conceptions of culture and person for psychology. *Journal of Cross-Cultural Psychology*, *31*(1), 14–32. doi:10.1177/0022022100031001003

Keith, K. D. (Ed.). (2019). *Cross-cultural psychology: Contemporary themes and perspectives*. John Wiley & Sons. doi:10.1002/9781119519348

Kennedy, J. T., & Jain-Link, P. (2021, June). What does it take to build a culture of belonging? *Harvard Business Review*.

Kim Nguyen, H., & Block, C. J. (2018). The impact of microaggressions on mental health: Intersectionality and clinical implications. *Journal of Counseling and Development*, *96*(4), 390–400. doi:10.1002/jcad.12222

Kim, D. H. (1999). *Introduction to Systems Thinking* (Vol. 16). Pegasus Communications.

Kim, J., Nguyen, D., & Block, C. (2018). *The 360-degree experience of workplace microaggressions: who commits them? How do individuals respond? What Are the Consequences?* Influence and Implications., doi:10.1002/9781119466642.ch10

Kim, S. L. (2019). Enticing high performers to stay and share their knowledge: The im-portance of trust in leader. *Human Resource Management*, *58*(4), 341–351. doi:10.1002/hrm.21955

Kinicki, A., & Williams, B. K. (2020). Management (ninth edition). New York: McGraw-Hill Education

Kinicki, A., & Williams, B. K. (2020). *Management (ninth edition)*. New York: McGraw-Hill Education https://www.relias.com/blog/how-diversity-equity-inclusion-influence-healthcare https://www.fdic.gov/about/diversity/pdf/dei2021.pdf

Kirvalidze, N. (2020). Developing Higher School Students'cross-Cultural Awareness And Communicative Competence Through Phraseology. In *INTED2020 Proceedings* (pp. 5141-5150). IATED.

Klein, U. (2016, January). Gender equality and diversity politics in higher education: Conflicts, challenges and requirements for collaboration. []. Pergamon.]. *Women's Studies International Forum*, *54*, 147–156. doi:10.1016/j.wsif.2015.06.017

Kloos, B., Hill, J., Thomas, E., Wandersman, A., Elias, M. J., & Dalton, J. H. (2012). *Community psychology*. Cengage Learning.

Klotz, J. (2004). Sociocultural study of intellectual disability: Moving beyond labelling and social constructionist perspectives. *British Journal of Learning Disabilities*, *32*(2), 93–104. doi:10.1111/j.1468-3156.2004.00285.x

Koc, Y., Hekim, H., & Buyukgoze Kavas, A. (2021). Unconscious Bias and Gender Differences in Language: A Comparative Analysis. *Journal of Gender Studies*, *30*(3), 381–396. doi:10.1080/09589236.2020.1773646

Koku, P. S. (2022). *Critical Perspectives on Diversity, Equity, and Incy in Marketing: The case of Business Schools in the United States*. IGI Global. doi:10.4018/9781-1-6684-3590-8-ch008

Kostis, A., Bengtsson, M., & Näsholm, M. H. (2022). Mechanisms and Dynamics in the Interplay of Trust and Distrust: Insights from project-based collaboration. *Organization Studies*, *43*(8), 1173–1196. doi:10.1177/01708406211040215

Kouzes, J., & Posner, B. (2017). *The leadership challenge: How to Make Extraordinary Things Happen in Organizations*. Wiley and Son, Inc.

Kruse, K. (2013) What is Leadership? Cited by the Article: Effective Leadership in the 21st Century. *Open Journal of Social Science, 4*(2).

Lazenby, H. (2016). What is equality of opportunity in education? *Theory and Research in Education, 14*(1), 65–76. doi:10.1177/1477878515619788

Leithwood, et al (2004) *How Leadership Influences Student Learning*. University of Minnesota: Carei.

Lightfoot, C., & Valsiner, J. (1992). *Parental belief systems under the influence: Social guidance of the construction of personal cultures*. APA.

Lipford, W. J., & Rood, S. A. (2020). That's What "Generation We" Said? The Office Enables Active Learning and Improved Retention in the Modern Human Resource Management Classroom. *Journal of Hospitality & Tourism Education*, *32*(3), 178–185. doi:10.1080/10963758.2019.1655435

Liu, G., Tsui, E., & Kianto, A. (2021). Knowledge-friendly organizational culture and performance: A meta-analysis. *Journal of Business Research*, *134*, 738–753. doi:10.1016/j.jbusres.2021.05.048

Lodge, C. (2005). From hearing voices to engaging a dialogue: Problematizing student participation in school improvement. *Journal of Educational Change*, *6*(2), 125–146. doi:10.100710833-005-1299-3

Long, C. P., & Sitkin, S. B. (2018). Control-trust dynamics in organizations: Identifying shared perspectives and charting conceptual fault lines. *The Academy of Management Annals*, *12*(2), 725–751. doi:10.5465/annals.2016.0055

Lorenzo, M. (2005). El liderazgo en las organizaciones educativas: Revisión y perspectivas actuales. *Revista Española de Pedagogía*, *232*, 367–388.

Louis, K. (2010). *How Does Leadership Affect Student Achievement? Results from a National US Survey*. University of Minnesota. doi:10.1080/09243453.2010/486586

Lovell, S. E., Kahn, A. S., Anton, J., Davidson, A., Dowling, E., Post, D., & Mason, C. (1999). Does gender affect the link between organizational citizenship behavior and performance evaluation? *Sex Roles*, *41*(5–6), 469–478. doi:10.1023/A:1018883018719

Lumineau, F., Schilke, O., & Wang, W. (2023). Organizational Trust in the Age of the Fourth Industrial Revolution: Shifts in the Form, Production, and Targets of Trust. *Journal of Management Inquiry*, *32*(1), 21–34. doi:10.1177/10564926221127852

Luna-Scott, C. (2015) The futures of Learning 3. *What kind of pedagogies for the 21st Century?* Working Papers, No 15. Paris. UNESCO.

Lutgen-Sandvik, P. (2006). Take this job, quit, and other forms of resistance to workplace bullying. *Communication Monographs*, *73*(4), 406–433. doi:10.1080/03637750601024156

Macedo, D. (1994). *Literacies of power: what Americans are not allowed to know*. Paradigm.

Macgregor, A., & Folinazzo, G. (2018). Best practices in teaching international students in higher education: Issues and strategies. *TESOL Journal*, *9*(2), 299–329. doi:10.1002/tesj.324

Madva, A., & Brownstein, M. (2018). Embodied social cognition. *Ergo, an Open Access Journal of Philosophy*, *5*(9), 237–280

Martinelli, V. (2020). How to Spot and Shut Down Microaggressions in the Workplace. *FAIRYGODBOSS Blog*. https://fairygodboss.com/articles/microaggressions-in-the-workplace

McGlynn, C. (2009). Integrating education: Parekhian multiculturalism and good practice. *Intercultural Education*, *20*(4), 299–310. doi:10.1080/14675980903351938

McKinney, S. (2012). Multiculturalism and education. *Journal of Education Policy*, *28*(1), 154–156. doi:10.1080/02680939.2012.688539

Meagher, K. J., & Wait, A. (2020). Worker Trust in Management and Delegation in Organizations. *Journal of Law Economics and Organization*, *36*(3), 495–536. Advance online publication. doi:10.1093/jleo/ewaa008

Medical News Today. (2020). Microaggressions in the workplace: examples, responding, and how to help. *Medical News Today*. https://www.ef.com/wwen/blog/language/understanding-microaggressions/

Mendenhall, E., Rinehart, R., Musyimi, C., Bosire, E., Ndetei, D., & Mutiso, V. (2019). An ethnopsychology of idioms of distress in urban Kenya. *Transcultural Psychiatry*, *56*(4), 620–642. doi:10.1177/1363461518824431 PMID:30672722

Men, L. R., & Sung, Y. (2022). Shaping Corporate Character Through Symmetrical Communication: The Effects on Employee-Organization Relationships. *International Journal of Business Communication*, *59*(3), 427–449. doi:10.1177/2329488418824989

Merryfield, M. M. (2000). Why aren't teachers being prepared to teach for diversity, equity, and global interconnectedness? A study of lived experiences in the making of multicultural and global educators. *Teaching and Teacher Education*, *16*(4), 429–443. doi:10.1016/S0742-051X(00)00004-4

Meyerson, D. E. (1994). Interpretations of stress in institutions: The cultural production of ambiguity and burnout. *Administrative Science Quarterly*, *39*(4), 628–653. doi:10.2307/2393774 PMID:10144744

Mohr, D. C., Young, G. J., & Burgess, J. F. Jr. (2012). Employee turnover and operational performance: The moderating effect of group-oriented organizational culture. *Human Resource Management Journal*, *22*(2), 216–233. doi:10.1111/j.1748-8583.2010.00159.x

Moorhead, G., & Griffin, R. S. (2011). *Organizational Behavior* (11th ed.).

Morgan, D. E., & Zeffane, R. (2003). Employee involvement, organizational change and trust in management. *International Journal of Human Resource Management*, *14*(1), 55–75. doi:10.1080/0958519021015851O

Morrison, E. W. (1994). Role definitions and organizational citizenship behavior: The importance of the employee's perspective. *Academy of Management Journal*, *37*(6), 1543–1567. doi:10.2307/256798

Moss-Racusin, C. A., Dovidio, J. F., Brescoll, V. L., Graham, M. J., & Handelsman, J. (2012). The science faculty's subtle gender biases favor male students. *Proceedings of the National Academy of Sciences of the United States of America*, *109*(41), 16474–16479. doi:10.1073/pnas.1211286109 PMID:22988126

Moss-Racusin, C. A., & Johnson, K. L. (2016). Implicit bias and women in academia: How do we move forward? *The Journal of Research in Gender Studies*, *6*(1), 8–22.

Moss-Racusin, C. A., & Rudman, L. A. (2010). Disruptions in women's self-promotion: The backlash avoidance model. *Psychology of Women Quarterly*, *34*(2), 186–202. doi:10.1111/j.1471-6402.2010.01561.x

Mukhuty, S., Upadhyay, A., & Rothwell, H. (2022). Strategic sustainable development of Industry 4.0 through the lens of social responsibility: The role of human resource practices. *Business Strategy and the Environment*, *31*(5), 1–14. doi:10.1002/bse.3008

Nadal, K. L. (2011). The Racial and Ethnic Microaggressions Scale (REMS): Construction, reliability, and validity. *Journal of Counseling Psychology*, *58*(4), 470–480. doi:10.1037/a0025193 PMID:21875180

Nadal, K. L., Davidoff, K. C., Davis, L. S., & Wong, Y. (2015). Emotional and behavioral responses to racial microaggressions: A closer look at Black Americans. *Race and Social Problems*, *7*(1), 17–26. doi:10.100712552-014-9138-5

Nadal, K. L., Griffin, K. E., Wong, Y., Hamit, S., & Rasmus, M. (2014). The impact of racial microaggressions on mental health: Counselling implications for clients of colour. *Journal of Counseling and Development*, *92*(1), 57–66. doi:10.1002/j.1556-6676.2014.00130.x

Nadal, K. L., & Wong, Y. (2017). Microaggressions and social work: A review of the literature. *Journal of Ethnic & Cultural Diversity in Social Work, 26*(1-2), 1–17. doi:10.1080/15313204.2016.1268989

Nadal, K. L., Wong, Y., & Sriken, J. (2019). The impact of racial microaggressions on mental health: A systematic review and meta-analysis. *Journal of Counseling Psychology, 66*(6), 637–655. doi:10.1037/cou0000386

Neblett, E. W. Jr. (2019). Diversity (psychological) science training: Challenges, tensions, and a call to action. *The Journal of Social Issues, 75*(4), 4. doi:10.1111/josi.12357

Negi, P. S., & Dangwal, R. C. (2021) *Identifying the aspects of organizational culture: a study of Indian banking industry*. Emerald Insights. https://www.emerald.com/insight/2399-1747.htm

Ngunjiiri, F. w., & Gardiner, R. A. (2017). Future Strategies for developing women as leaders. In *Handbook of research on gender and leadership* (pp. 423–437). Edward Elgar Publishing. doi:10.4337/9781785363863.00038

Nieto, C. (2004) Modelos de asesoramiento a organizaciones educativas En: Jesús Domingo Segovia (coord.) Asesoramiento al Centro Educativo: colaboración y cambio en la Institución. Barcelona. Octaedro-EUB pp.147-166

Nishii, L. H., & Mayer, D. M. (2009). Do inclusive leaders help to reduce turnover in diverse groups? The moderating role of leader–member exchange in the diversity to turnover relationship. *The Journal of Applied Psychology, 94*(6), 1412–1426. doi:10.1037/a0017190 PMID:19916652

Noble, D. S. (2000). Human Resource Management Strategy: The Dual Pursuit of Employee Involvement and Workforce Adaptability. Dissertation Doctor of Philosophy, Wayne State University, Detroit.

Noe, R., Hollenbeck, J., Gerhart, B., & Wright, P. (2021). *Human Resource Management: Gaining a Competitive Advantage* (12th ed.). McGraw Hill.

Noor, Z., Nayaz, N., Solanki, V., Manoj, A., & Sharma, A. (2020). Impact of Rewards System on Employee Motivation: A Study of a Manufacturing Firm in Oman. *International Journal of Business and Management Future, 4*(2), 6–16. doi:10.46281/ijbmf.v4i2.692

Norton, M. I., Mochon, D., & Ariely, D. The «IKEA Effect»: When Labor Leads to Love. — https://www.hbs.edu/faculty/Publication%20Files/11-091.pdf

OECD. (2012). *Equity and quality in education: Supporting disadvantaged students and schools*. OECD. doi:10.1787/9789264130852-

OECD. (2019). *Skills Strategy 2019. Skills to shape a better future*. OECD. doi:10.1787/9789264313835-

OECD. (2019a). *PISA 2018 results (volume I): What students know and can do?* OECD. . doi:10.1787/5f07c754-en

OECD. (2019b). *TALIS 2018 technical report* (p. 494) [Research Report]. OECD. https://www.oecd.org/education/talis/TALIS_2018_Technical_Report.pdf

Office of Personnel Management. (2011). Government-wide diversity and inclusion strategic plan. Energy.gov. www.energy.gov/diversity/downloads/government-wide-diversity and-inclusion-strategic-plan-2011-office-personnel

Ogbonna, E. (2019). The uneasy alliance of organizational culture and equal opportunities for ethnic minority groups: A British example. *Human Resource Management Journal*, *29*(3), 309–327. doi:10.1111/1748-8583.12227

Opertti, R. (2017). *15 Clues of Analysis Reflecting Upon the Education 2030 Agenda*. IBE-UNESCO.

Oswick, C., & Noon, M. (2014). Discourses of diversity, equality and inclusion: Trenchant formulations or transient fashions? *British Journal of Management*, *25*(1), 1. doi:10.1111/j.1467-8551.2012.00830.x

Owen, G., & Currie, G. (2022). Beyond the Crisis: Trust repair in an interorganizational network. *Organization Studies*, *43*(8), 1273–1295. doi:10.1177/01708406211031732

Ozyilmaz, A., Erdogan, B., & Karaeminogullari, A. (2018). Trust in organization as a moderator of the relationship between self-efficacy and workplace outcomes: A social cognitive theory-based examination. *Journal of Occupational and Organizational Psychology*, *91*(1), 181–204. doi:10.1111/joop.12189

Palmer, C. T., Orabi, J., & Harvey, J. B. (2019). The impact of microaggressions on employees' mental health: The role of resilience. *Journal of Occupational Health Psychology*, *24*(2), 246–258. doi:10.1037/ocp0000129

Park, J.-H. (2012). The effects of principal's leadership style on support for innovation: Evidence from Korean vocational high school change. *Asia Pacific Education Review*, *13*(1), 89–102. doi:10.100712564-011-9182-9

Park, N., Cho, M., & Lee, J. W. (2021). Building a culture of innovation: How do agency leadership and management systems promote innovative activities within the government? *Australian Journal of Public Administration*, *80*(3), 453–473. doi:10.1111/1467-8500.12474

Paulston, C. B., Kiesling, S. F., & Rangel, E. S. (2012). *The handbook of intercultural discourse and communication*. Wiley-Blackwell. doi:10.1002/9781118247273

Pérez Huber, L., & Solorzano, D. G. (2015). Racial microaggressions as a tool for critical race research. *Race, Ethnicity and Education*, *18*(3), 297–320. doi:10.1080/13613324.2014.994173

Pérez-Huber, H. L., & Solorzano, D. G. (2015). *Microaggressions in everyday life: race, gender, and sexual orientation*. John Wiley & Sons, Inc.

Petera, P. (2011). Evaluating the quality of rewards systems. *European Financial and Accounting Journal*, *6*(3), 66–91. doi:10.18267/j.efaj.26

Pierce, C. M. (1970). Offensive mechanisms. In R. K. Merton (Ed.), *Robert K. Merton: Selected Writings* (pp. 289–316). Free Press.

Pont, B. (2020). A Literature Review of School Leadership Policy Reforms. *European Journal of Education, 52*(2), 154–168. doi:10.1111/ejed.12398

Prospects 151. (2009) *Inclusive Education: controversies and debates.* UNESCO-IBE.

PROSPECTS 159. (2011) International Developments in Teacher Education for Inclusive Education: issues and challenges. UNESCO-IBE.

Pydiura, O. (2020). Use of Virtual Reality and Digital Technologies for Studying Folklore in Ukraine's Educational Institutions. *Journal «ScienceRise. Pedagogical Education, 1*(34), 4–7.

Rawls, J. (2005). *A theory of justice: Original edition.* Belknap Press. http://gen.lib.rus.ec/book/index.php?md5=d2eec200ebed5373c6e2c58c7d645b5f

Rizan, M.,, Khan, M.,, & Nadeem, B., & Qalb, A. (2016). The Impacts of Workplace Diversity Towards Employee Performance. *Evidence from Banking Sector of Pakistan in American Journal of Matketing Research, 2*(2), 53–60.

Roberson, Q. M. (2006). Disentangling the meanings of diversity and inclusion in organizations. *Group & Organization Management, 31*(2), 2. doi:10.1177/1059601104273064

Rodríguez, F. (2014) *La co-enseñanza, una estrategia para el mejoramiento educativo y la inclusión.* Educrea. https://educrea.cl/wp-content/uploads/2017/08/DOC- co_enseñanza.pdf

Rudman, L. A., & Glick, P. (2001). Prescriptive gender stereotypes and backlash toward agentic women. *The Journal of Social Issues, 57*(4), 743–762. doi:10.1111/0022-4537.00239

Rudman, L. A., Moss-Racusin, C. A., Phelan, J. E., & Nauts, S. (2012). Status incongruity and backlash effects: Defending the gender hierarchy motivates prejudice against female leaders. *Journal of Experimental Social Psychology, 48*(1), 165–179. doi:10.1016/j.jesp.2011.10.008

Salazar, M. (2009). Weaving promising practices for inclusive excellence into the higher education classroom. In LB. Nilson and J: E Miller (Eds.) to improve the academy.

Samoilovich, D. (2020) *Liderazgo en tiempos de Covid-19.* UNESCO. https://www.iesalc.unesco.org

Savater, F. (1997). el valor de educar. Barcelona. *Ariel.*

Sawyerr, O. O., Strauss, J., & Yan, J. (2005). Individual value structure and diversity attitudes: The moderating effects of age, gender, race, and religiosity. *Journal of Managerial Psychology, 20*(6), 498–521. doi:10.1108/02683940510615442

Schein, E. H., & Schein, P. (2017). *Organizational culture and leadership* (5th ed.). Routledge.

Scott, A., Klein, F. K., & Onovakpuri, U. (2017). *Tech Leavers Study: A First of its Kind Analysis of Why People Voluntarily Left Jobs in Tech.* Kapor Center for Social Impact.

Searle, R., Den Hartog, D. N., Weibel, A., Gillespie, N., Six, F., Hatzakis, T., & Skinner, D. (2011). Trust in the employer: The role of high-involvement work practices and procedural justice in European organizations. *International Journal of Human Resource Management*, *22*(5), 1069–1092. doi:10.1080/09585192.2011.556782

Segall, A. H. (1984). More than we need to know about culture, but are afraid not to ask. *Journal of Cross-Cultural Psychology*, *15*(2), 153–162. doi:10.1177/0022002184015002004

Shala, M., Morina, N., Burchert, S., Cerga-Pashoja, A., Knaevelsrud, C., Maercker, A., & Heim, E. (2020). Cultural adaptation of Hap-pas-Hapi, an internet and mobile-based intervention for the treatment of psychological distress among Albanian migrants in Switzerland and Germany. *Internet Interventions : the Application of Information Technology in Mental and Behavioural Health*, *21*, 100339. doi:10.1016/j.invent.2020.100339 PMID:32983906

Singelis, T. M. (2000). Some thoughts on the future of cross-cultural social psychology. *Journal of Cross-Cultural Psychology*, *31*(1), 76–91. doi:10.1177/0022022100031001007

Singha, S., & Sivarethinamohan, R. (2022). Social Inclusion, Equity, Leadership, and Diversity to Attain Sustainable Development Goal 5 in the Indian Banking Industry. *Journal of International Women's Studies*, *23*(5), 135–142. http://VC.bridgew.edu/jiwa/vol23/iss5/9

Sinha, C. (2020), Women in the Bahraini Financial Sector: Opportunities, Challenges and Strategic Choices. In SAGA Journals. doi:10.1177/0049085719901069

Siri, A., Leone, C., & Bencivenga, R. (2022). Equality, Diversity, and Inclusion Strategies Adopted in European University Alliance to Facilitate the Higher Education-to-Work Transition. *Societies (Basel, Switzerland)*, *12*(5), 140. doi:10.3390oc12050140

Six F., & Sorge A. (2008) Creating a High-Trust Organization: An Exploration into Organizational Policies that Stimulate Interpersonal Trust Building. *Journal of Management Studies 45*(5). doi:. 00763.x doi:10.1111/j.1467-6486.2007

Smircich, L. (1983). Concepts of culture and organizational analysis. *Administrative Science Quarterly*, *28*(3), 339–358. doi:10.2307/2392246

Smith, J. D., Johnson, L. K., & Brown, K. L. (2021). Unconscious bias in the workplace. *Journal of Business and Psychology*, *36*(2), 123–135.

Smith, P. B. (1992). Organizational behaviour and national cultures. *British Journal of Management*, *3*(1), 1. Advance online publication. doi:10.1111/j.1467-8551.1992.tb00034.x

Solomon, A. (2013). *Far from the tree: A dozen kinds of love*. Chatto and Windus.

Spanierman, L. B., Todd, N. R., & Anderson, C. J. (2021). Racial microaggressions: Critical questions, state of the science, and future directions. *Cultural Diversity & Ethnic Minority Psychology*, *27*(3), 357–368. doi:10.1037/cdp0000429

Spillane, J. Paquin, R. y Asmaa Al-Fadala (2019). Educational Leadership: A Multilevel Distributed Perspective. *Wise Qatar.* www.wise-qatar.org/educational-leaderhip-a-multilevel-distributed-perspective

Stigler, J. W., Shweder, R. A., & Herdt, G. E. (1990). Cultural psychology: Essays on comparative human development. In *All but three of the chapters in this book are revised versions of presentations from two symposia held by the University of Chicago Committee on Human Development: " Culture and Human Development"(Oct 23-25, 1986) and" Children's Lives in Cultural Context"(Nov 5-7, 1987).* Cambridge University Press.

Stoermer, S., Hildisch, A. K., & Froese, F. J. (2016). Culture matters: The influence of national culture on inclusion climate. *Cross Cultural & Strategic Management, 23*(2). doi:10.1108/CCSM-11-2014-0135

Stout, J. G., Dasgupta, N., Hunsinger, M., & McManus, M. A. (2011). Stemming the tide: Using in-group experts to inoculate women's self-concept in science, technology, engineering, and mathematics (STEM). *Journal of Personality and Social Psychology, 100*(2), 255–270. doi:10.1037/a0021385 PMID:21142376

Strauss, J. P., & Connerley, M. L. (2003). Demographics, personality, contact, and universal-diverse orientation: An exploratory examination. *Human Resource Management, 42*(2), 159–174. doi:10.1002/hrm.10074

Sue, D. W., Capodilupo, C. M., Torino, G. C., Bucceri, J. M., Holder, A. M. B., Nadal, K. L., & Esquilin, M. (2007). Racial microaggressions in everyday life: Implications for clinical practice. *The American Psychologist, 62*(4), 271–286. doi:10.1037/0003-066X.62.4.271 PMID:17516773

Sumner, E., Scarduzio, J., & Daggett, J. (2016). Drama at Dunder Mifflin: Workplace Bullying Discourses in the Office. *Journal of Interpersonal Violence, 35*(1-2), 127–149. Advance online publication. doi:10.1177/0886260516681158 PMID:27920361

Swim, J. K., & Sanna, L. J. (1996). He is skilled; she is lucky. A meta-analysis of observers' attributions for women's and men's successes and failures. *Personality and Social Psychology Bulletin, 22*(5), 507–519. doi:10.1177/0146167296225008

TED. (2019, December 9). *Eliminating Microaggressions: The Next Level of Inclusion | Tiffany Alvoid.* [Video]. YouTube. https://youtu.be/cPqVit6TJjw

Thanetsunthorn, N., & Wuthisatian, R. (2020). Trust and culture: Applications for organization development. *Organization Development Journal, 38*(1), 33–43.

Thompson, S., Forde, T., & Otieno, T. (2017). A sustainable, culturally competent approach to academic leadership. In *Global and culturally diverse leaders and leadership* (pp. 279–305). Emerald Publishing Limited. doi:10.1108/S2058-880120170000003014

Tierney, W. G. (1988). Organizational culture in higher education: Defining the essentials. *The Journal of Higher Education, 59*(1), 2–21. doi:10.1080/00221546.1988.11778301

Torres, C. A., & Tarozzi, M. (2020). Multiculturalism in the world system: Towards a social justice model of inter/multicultural education. *Globalisation, Societies and Education, 18*(1), 7–18. doi:10.1080/14767724.2019.1690729

Torres-Harding, S. R., Andrade, A. L., Romero Diaz, C. E., & Garcia, C. (2012). Microaggressions and Latina/o Americans: An analysis of nativity, gender, and subjective social status. *Journal of Latina/o Psychology, 1*(1), 37–51. doi:10.1037/a0026469

Tuitt, F. (2016). *Race, Equity, and the learning environment: the global relevance of critical and inclusive pedagogies in higher education.* Stylus Publishing, LLC.

Umeh, C., Cornelius, N., & Wallace, J. (2023). Exploring equality, diversity, and inclusion in multiethnic settings: A context-sensitive approach. *Human Resource Management Journal, 33*(1), 148–169. doi:10.1111/1748-8583.12441

UN (2016). *Observación General No. 4 sobre el derecho a la educación inclusiva.* UN.

UN. (2006) *Convention on the rights of persons with disabilities.* NY: ONU www.social.desa.un.org

UNESCO. (2015). *Rethinking Education. Towards a global common good?* UNESCO.

UNESCO. (2016). *Reaching out to All Learners: A Resource Pack for Supporting Inclusive Education.* UNESCO-IBE.

UNESCO. (2017). *A Guide for Ensuring Inclusion and Equity in Education.* UNESCO.

UNESCO. (2019a). *The UNESCO Salamanca Statement 25 years on. Developing inclusive and equitable education system.* UNESCO.

UNESCO. (2019b). *Final Report of the international forum on inclusion and equity in education Paris.* UNESCO.

UNESCO. (2019c). *Futures of Education Initiative.* UNESCO. **www.es.unesco.org/futuresofeducation/**

UNESCO. (2020). *Education in a post- COVID world: nine ideas for public action. International Commission on the Futures of Education.* Paris: UNESCO. https://en.unesco.org/futuresofeducation

UNESCO. (2021). *Garantizar la enseñanza y el aprendizaje inclusivos para la recuperación educativa: formas prácticas de avanzar.* UNESCO.

UNESCO. (2023). *Global Education Monitoring Report on leadership and education.* UNESCO.

UNESCO-GEM. (2020). *Inclusión y Educación. Mensajes clave y recomendaciones. América Latina y el Caribe.* UNESCO. https://en.unesco.org/gem-report/LAC202

UNESCO-IESALC. (2020). *COVID-19 and Higher Education: Today and Tomorrow. Impact analysis, policy responses, and recommendations. April, No.9 Paris.* UNESCO.

UNESCO-UIS. (2012). *A Place to Learn. Lesson from Research on Learning Environments.* Paris, UNESCO. http://www.uis.unesco.org/

UNICEF. (2016). *Education 2030: Incheon declaration and framework for action: Towards inclusive and equitable quality education and lifelong learning for all* (Research Report ED-2016/WS/2). UNESCO. https://unesdoc.unesco.org/ark:/48223/pf0000245745

UNICEF. (2020). *Averting a lost COVID generation. A six-point plan to protect our children.* UNICEF.

Valbrun, M. (2018, May 7). From diversity chief to college president. *Inside Higher Ed.* https://www.insidehighered.com/news/2018/05/07/chief-diversity-officer-position-new-path-presidency

Valian, V. (1998). *Why so slow? The advancement of women.* MIT Press.

Van de Vijver, F. J., & Leung, K. (2000). Methodological issues in psychological research on culture. *Journal of Cross-Cultural Psychology, 31*(1), 33–51. doi:10.1177/0022022100031001004

Van de Vijver, F. J., & Poortinga, Y. H. (1992). Testing in culturally heterogeneous populations: When are cultural loadings undesirable? *European Journal of Psychological Assessment.*

Volckmar, N. (2019). The Enduring Quest for Equity in Education: Comparing Norway and Australia. *Scandinavian Journal of Educational Research, 63*(4), 617–631. doi:10.1080/00313831.2017.1415967

West, M. A., & Sacramento, C. A. (2006). Flourishing in teams: Developing creativity and innovation. In J. Henry, Creative Management and Development (pp. 25–44). SAGE Publications Ltd. doi:10.4135/9781446213704.n3

Williams, J. C., & Dempsey, R. (2014). *What works for women at work: four patterns working women need to know New York.* NYU Press.

Wing Sue, D., Alsaidi, S., Awad, M. N., Glaeser, E., & Yan, M. C. (2019). Disarming racial microaggressions: Micro-intervention strategies for targets, White allies, and bystanders. *The American Psychologist, 74*(1), 128–142. doi:10.1037/amp0000296 PMID:30652905

Wolniak, G. (2017, January 31). *What diversity on the american campus can teach us: an interview with gregory wolniak.* NYU. https://steinhardt.nyu.edu/site/ataglance/2017/01/what-diversity-on-the-american-campus-can-teach-us-an-interview-with-gregory-wolniak.html

World Bank. (2018). *Learning to Realize Education's Promise.* WBP.

Xu, A. J., Loi, R., & Ngo, H. (2016). Ethical Leadership Behavior and Employee Justice Perceptions: The Mediating Role of Trust in Organization. *Journal of Business Ethics, 134*(3), 493–504. doi:10.100710551-014-2457-4

Ye, S., Cai, S., Chen, C., Wan, Q., & Qian, X. (2018). How have males and females been described over the past two centuries? An analysis of Big-Five personality-related adjectives in the Google English Books. *Journal of Research in Personality, 76*, 6–16. doi:10.1016/j.jrp.2018.06.007

Yesufu, A. (2013). Challenges of the visible minority families: Cultural sensitivity to the rescue. *Canadian Journal of Family and Youth / Le Journal Canadien de Famille et de La Jeunesse*, *5*(1), Article 1. doi:10.29173/cjfy18950

Yukl, G. A. (1989) Leadership in Organizations. New Jersey: Prentice-Hall International.

Yukl, G., & Tracey, J. B. (1992). Consequences of influence tactics used with subordinates' peers, and the boss. *The Journal of Applied Psychology*, *77*(4), 525–535. doi:10.1037/0021-9010.77.4.525

Zhang, S. (2014). Impact of Job Involvement on Organizational Citizenship Behaviors in China. *Journal of Business Ethics*, *120*(2), 165–174. doi:10.100710551-013-1654-x

Related References

To continue our tradition of advancing information science and technology research, we have compiled a list of recommended IGI Global readings. These references will provide additional information and guidance to further enrich your knowledge and assist you with your own research and future publications.

Abdul Razak, R., & Mansor, N. A. (2021). Instagram Influencers in Social Media-Induced Tourism: Rethinking Tourist Trust Towards Tourism Destination. In M. Dinis, L. Bonixe, S. Lamy, & Z. Breda (Eds.), *Impact of New Media in Tourism* (pp. 135-144). IGI Global. https://doi.org/10.4018/978-1-7998-7095-1.ch009

Abir, T., & Khan, M. Y. (2022). Importance of ICT Advancement and Culture of Adaptation in the Tourism and Hospitality Industry for Developing Countries. In C. Ramos, S. Quinteiro, & A. Gonçalves (Eds.), *ICT as Innovator Between Tourism and Culture* (pp. 30–41). IGI Global. https://doi.org/10.4018/978-1-7998-8165-0.ch003

Abir, T., & Khan, M. Y. (2022). Importance of ICT Advancement and Culture of Adaptation in the Tourism and Hospitality Industry for Developing Countries. In C. Ramos, S. Quinteiro, & A. Gonçalves (Eds.), *ICT as Innovator Between Tourism and Culture* (pp. 30–41). IGI Global. https://doi.org/10.4018/978-1-7998-8165-0.ch003

Abtahi, M. S., Behboudi, L., & Hasanabad, H. M. (2017). Factors Affecting Internet Advertising Adoption in Ad Agencies. *International Journal of Innovation in the Digital Economy*, *8*(4), 18–29. doi:10.4018/IJIDE.2017100102

Afenyo-Agbe, E., & Mensah, I. (2022). Principles, Benefits, and Barriers to Community-Based Tourism: Implications for Management. In I. Mensah & E. Afenyo-Agbe (Eds.), *Prospects and Challenges of Community-Based Tourism and Changing Demographics* (pp. 1–29). IGI Global. doi:10.4018/978-1-7998-7335-8.ch001

Agbo, V. M. (2022). Distributive Justice Issues in Community-Based Tourism. In I. Mensah & E. Afenyo-Agbe (Eds.), *Prospects and Challenges of Community-Based Tourism and Changing Demographics* (pp. 107–129). IGI Global. https://doi.org/10.4018/978-1-7998-7335-8.ch005

Agrawal, S. (2017). The Impact of Emerging Technologies and Social Media on Different Business(es): Marketing and Management. In O. Rishi & A. Sharma (Eds.), *Maximizing Business Performance and Efficiency Through Intelligent Systems* (pp. 37–49). Hershey, PA: IGI Global. doi:10.4018/978-1-5225-2234-8.ch002

Ahmad, A., & Johari, S. (2022). Georgetown as a Gastronomy Tourism Destination: Visitor Awareness Towards Revisit Intention of Nasi Kandar Restaurant. In M. Valeri (Ed.), *New Governance and Management in Touristic Destinations* (pp. 71–83). IGI Global. https://doi.org/10.4018/978-1-6684-3889-3.ch005

Alkhatib, G., & Bayouq, S. T. (2021). A TAM-Based Model of Technological Factors Affecting Use of E-Tourism. *International Journal of Tourism and Hospitality Management in the Digital Age*, *5*(2), 50–67. https://doi.org/10.4018/IJTHMDA.20210701.oa1

Altinay Ozdemir, M. (2021). Virtual Reality (VR) and Augmented Reality (AR) Technologies for Accessibility and Marketing in the Tourism Industry. In C. Eusébio, L. Teixeira, & M. Carneiro (Eds.), *ICT Tools and Applications for Accessible Tourism* (pp. 277-301). IGI Global. https://doi.org/10.4018/978-1-7998-6428-8.ch013

Anantharaman, R. N., Rajeswari, K. S., Angusamy, A., & Kuppusamy, J. (2017). Role of Self-Efficacy and Collective Efficacy as Moderators of Occupational Stress Among Software Development Professionals. *International Journal of Human Capital and Information Technology Professionals*, *8*(2), 45–58. doi:10.4018/IJHCITP.2017040103

Aninze, F., El-Gohary, H., & Hussain, J. (2018). The Role of Microfinance to Empower Women: The Case of Developing Countries. *International Journal of Customer Relationship Marketing and Management*, *9*(1), 54–78. doi:10.4018/IJCRMM.2018010104

Antosova, G., Sabogal-Salamanca, M., & Krizova, E. (2021). Human Capital in Tourism: A Practical Model of Endogenous and Exogenous Territorial Tourism Planning in Bahía Solano, Colombia. In V. Costa, A. Moura, & M. Mira (Eds.), *Handbook of Research on Human Capital and People Management in the Tourism Industry* (pp. 282–302). IGI Global. https://doi.org/10.4018/978-1-7998-4318-4.ch014

Arsenijević, O. M., Orčić, D., & Kastratović, E. (2017). Development of an Optimization Tool for Intangibles in SMEs: A Case Study from Serbia with a Pilot Research in the Prestige by Milka Company. In M. Vemić (Ed.), *Optimal Management Strategies in Small and Medium Enterprises* (pp. 320–347). Hershey, PA: IGI Global. doi:10.4018/978-1-5225-1949-2.ch015

Aryanto, V. D., Wismantoro, Y., & Widyatmoko, K. (2018). Implementing Eco-Innovation by Utilizing the Internet to Enhance Firm's Marketing Performance: Study of Green Batik Small and Medium Enterprises in Indonesia. *International Journal of E-Business Research, 14*(1), 21–36. doi:10.4018/IJEBR.2018010102

Asero, V., & Billi, S. (2022). New Perspective of Networking in the DMO Model. In M. Valeri (Ed.), *New Governance and Management in Touristic Destinations* (pp. 105–118). IGI Global. https://doi.org/10.4018/978-1-6684-3889-3.ch007

Atiku, S. O., & Fields, Z. (2017). Multicultural Orientations for 21st Century Global Leadership. In N. Baporikar (Ed.), *Management Education for Global Leadership* (pp. 28–51). Hershey, PA: IGI Global. doi:10.4018/978-1-5225-1013-0.ch002

Atiku, S. O., & Fields, Z. (2018). Organisational Learning Dimensions and Talent Retention Strategies for the Service Industries. In N. Baporikar (Ed.), *Global Practices in Knowledge Management for Societal and Organizational Development* (pp. 358–381). Hershey, PA: IGI Global. doi:10.4018/978-1-5225-3009-1.ch017

Atsa'am, D. D., & Kuset Bodur, E. (2021). Pattern Mining on How Organizational Tenure Affects the Psychological Capital of Employees Within the Hospitality and Tourism Industry: Linking Employees' Organizational Tenure With PsyCap. *International Journal of Tourism and Hospitality Management in the Digital Age, 5*(2), 17–28. https://doi.org/10.4018/IJTHMDA.2021070102

Ávila, L., & Teixeira, L. (2018). The Main Concepts Behind the Dematerialization of Business Processes. In M. Khosrow-Pour, D.B.A. (Ed.), Encyclopedia of Information Science and Technology, Fourth Edition (pp. 888-898). Hershey, PA: IGI Global. https://doi.org/ doi:10.4018/978-1-5225-2255-3.ch076

Ayorekire, J., Mugizi, F., Obua, J., & Ampaire, G. (2022). Community-Based Tourism and Local People's Perceptions Towards Conservation: The Case of Queen Elizabeth Conservation Area, Uganda. In I. Mensah & E. Afenyo-Agbe (Eds.), *Prospects and Challenges of Community-Based Tourism and Changing Demographics* (pp. 56–82). IGI Global. https://doi.org/10.4018/978-1-7998-7335-8.ch003

Baleiro, R. (2022). Tourist Literature and the Architecture of Travel in Olga Tokarczuk and Patti Smith. In R. Baleiro & R. Pereira (Eds.), *Global Perspectives on Literary Tourism and Film-Induced Tourism* (pp. 202-216). IGI Global. https://doi.org/10.4018/978-1-7998-8262-6.ch011

Barat, S. (2021). Looking at the Future of Medical Tourism in Asia. *International Journal of Tourism and Hospitality Management in the Digital Age*, *5*(1), 19–33. https://doi.org/10.4018/IJTHMDA.2021010102

Barbosa, C. A., Magalhães, M., & Nunes, M. R. (2021). Travel Instagramability: A Way of Choosing a Destination? In M. Dinis, L. Bonixe, S. Lamy, & Z. Breda (Eds.), *Impact of New Media in Tourism* (pp. 173-190). IGI Global. https://doi.org/10.4018/978-1-7998-7095-1.ch011

Bari, M. W., & Khan, Q. (2021). Pakistan as a Destination of Religious Tourism. In E. Alaverdov & M. Bari (Eds.), *Global Development of Religious Tourism* (pp. 1-10). IGI Global. https://doi.org/10.4018/978-1-7998-5792-1.ch001

Bartens, Y., Chunpir, H. I., Schulte, F., & Voß, S. (2017). Business/IT Alignment in Two-Sided Markets: A COBIT 5 Analysis for Media Streaming Business Models. In S. De Haes & W. Van Grembergen (Eds.), *Strategic IT Governance and Alignment in Business Settings* (pp. 82–111). Hershey, PA: IGI Global. doi:10.4018/978-1-5225-0861-8.ch004

Bashayreh, A. M. (2018). Organizational Culture and Organizational Performance. In W. Lee & F. Sabetzadeh (Eds.), *Contemporary Knowledge and Systems Science* (pp. 50–69). Hershey, PA: IGI Global. doi:10.4018/978-1-5225-5655-8.ch003

Bechthold, L., Lude, M., & Prügl, R. (2021). Crisis Favors the Prepared Firm: How Organizational Ambidexterity Relates to Perceptions of Organizational Resilience. In A. Zehrer, G. Glowka, K. Schwaiger, & V. Ranacher-Lackner (Eds.), *Resiliency Models and Addressing Future Risks for Family Firms in the Tourism Industry* (pp. 178–205). IGI Global. https://doi.org/10.4018/978-1-7998-7352-5.ch008

Bedford, D. A. (2018). Sustainable Knowledge Management Strategies: Aligning Business Capabilities and Knowledge Management Goals. In N. Baporikar (Ed.), *Global Practices in Knowledge Management for Societal and Organizational Development* (pp. 46–73). Hershey, PA: IGI Global. doi:10.4018/978-1-5225-3009-1.ch003

Bekjanov, D., & Matyusupov, B. (2021). Influence of Innovative Processes in the Competitiveness of Tourist Destination. In J. Soares (Ed.), *Innovation and Entrepreneurial Opportunities in Community Tourism* (pp. 243–263). IGI Global. https://doi.org/10.4018/978-1-7998-4855-4.ch014

Bharwani, S., & Musunuri, D. (2018). Reflection as a Process From Theory to Practice. In M. Khosrow-Pour, D.B.A. (Ed.), Encyclopedia of Information Science and Technology, Fourth Edition (pp. 1529-1539). Hershey, PA: IGI Global. doi:10.4018/978-1-5225-2255-3.ch132

Bhatt, G. D., Wang, Z., & Rodger, J. A. (2017). Information Systems Capabilities and Their Effects on Competitive Advantages: A Study of Chinese Companies. *Information Resources Management Journal, 30*(3), 41–57. doi:10.4018/IRMJ.2017070103

Bhushan, M., & Yadav, A. (2017). Concept of Cloud Computing in ESB. In R. Bhadoria, N. Chaudhari, G. Tomar, & S. Singh (Eds.), *Exploring Enterprise Service Bus in the Service-Oriented Architecture Paradigm* (pp. 116–127). Hershey, PA: IGI Global. doi:10.4018/978-1-5225-2157-0.ch008

Bhushan, S. (2017). System Dynamics Base-Model of Humanitarian Supply Chain (HSCM) in Disaster Prone Eco-Communities of India: A Discussion on Simulation and Scenario Results. *International Journal of System Dynamics Applications, 6*(3), 20–37. doi:10.4018/IJSDA.2017070102

Binder, D., & Miller, J. W. (2021). A Generations' Perspective on Employer Branding in Tourism. In V. Costa, A. Moura, & M. Mira (Eds.), *Handbook of Research on Human Capital and People Management in the Tourism Industry* (pp. 152–174). IGI Global. https://doi.org/10.4018/978-1-7998-4318-4.ch008

Birch Freeman, A. A., Mensah, I., & Antwi, K. B. (2022). Smiling vs. Frowning Faces: Community Participation for Sustainable Tourism in Ghanaian Communities. In I. Mensah & E. Afenyo-Agbe (Eds.), *Prospects and Challenges of Community-Based Tourism and Changing Demographics* (pp. 83–106). IGI Global. https://doi.org/10.4018/978-1-7998-7335-8.ch004

Biswas, A., & De, A. K. (2017). On Development of a Fuzzy Stochastic Programming Model with Its Application to Business Management. In S. Trivedi, S. Dey, A. Kumar, & T. Panda (Eds.), *Handbook of Research on Advanced Data Mining Techniques and Applications for Business Intelligence* (pp. 353–378). Hershey, PA: IGI Global. doi:10.4018/978-1-5225-2031-3.ch021

Boragnio, A., & Faracce Macia, C. (2021). "Taking Care of Yourself at Home": Use of E-Commerce About Food and Care During the COVID-19 Pandemic in the City of Buenos Aires. In M. Korstanje (Ed.), *Socio-Economic Effects and Recovery Efforts for the Rental Industry: Post-COVID-19 Strategies* (pp. 45–71). IGI Global. https://doi.org/10.4018/978-1-7998-7287-0.ch003

Borges, V. D. (2021). Happiness: The Basis for Public Policy in Tourism. In A. Perinotto, V. Mayer, & J. Soares (Eds.), *Rebuilding and Restructuring the Tourism Industry: Infusion of Happiness and Quality of Life* (pp. 1–25). IGI Global. https://doi.org/10.4018/978-1-7998-7239-9.ch001

Bücker, J., & Ernste, K. (2018). Use of Brand Heroes in Strategic Reputation Management: The Case of Bacardi, Adidas, and Daimler. In A. Erdemir (Ed.), *Reputation Management Techniques in Public Relations* (pp. 126–150). Hershey, PA: IGI Global. doi:10.4018/978-1-5225-3619-2.ch007

Buluk Eşitti, B. (2021). COVID-19 and Alternative Tourism: New Destinations and New Tourism Products. In M. Demir, A. Dalgıç, & F. Ergen (Eds.), *Handbook of Research on the Impacts and Implications of COVID-19 on the Tourism Industry* (pp. 786–805). IGI Global. https://doi.org/10.4018/978-1-7998-8231-2.ch038

Bureš, V. (2018). Industry 4.0 From the Systems Engineering Perspective: Alternative Holistic Framework Development. In R. Brunet-Thornton & F. Martinez (Eds.), *Analyzing the Impacts of Industry 4.0 in Modern Business Environments* (pp. 199–223). Hershey, PA: IGI Global. doi:10.4018/978-1-5225-3468-6.ch011

Buzady, Z. (2017). Resolving the Magic Cube of Effective Case Teaching: Benchmarking Case Teaching Practices in Emerging Markets – Insights from the Central European University Business School, Hungary. In D. Latusek (Ed.), *Case Studies as a Teaching Tool in Management Education* (pp. 79–103). Hershey, PA: IGI Global. doi:10.4018/978-1-5225-0770-3.ch005

Camillo, A. (2021). *Legal Matters, Risk Management, and Risk Prevention: From Forming a Business to Legal Representation*. IGI Global. doi:10.4018/978-1-7998-4342-9.ch004

Căpusneanu, S., & Topor, D. I. (2018). Business Ethics and Cost Management in SMEs: Theories of Business Ethics and Cost Management Ethos. In I. Oncioiu (Ed.), *Ethics and Decision-Making for Sustainable Business Practices* (pp. 109–127). Hershey, PA: IGI Global. doi:10.4018/978-1-5225-3773-1.ch007

Chan, R. L., Mo, P. L., & Moon, K. K. (2018). Strategic and Tactical Measures in Managing Enterprise Risks: A Study of the Textile and Apparel Industry. In K. Strang, M. Korstanje, & N. Vajjhala (Eds.), *Research, Practices, and Innovations in Global Risk and Contingency Management* (pp. 1–19). Hershey, PA: IGI Global. doi:10.4018/978-1-5225-4754-9.ch001

Charlier, S. D., Burke-Smalley, L. A., & Fisher, S. L. (2018). Undergraduate Programs in the U.S: A Contextual and Content-Based Analysis. In J. Mendy (Ed.), *Teaching Human Resources and Organizational Behavior at the College Level* (pp. 26–57). Hershey, PA: IGI Global. doi:10.4018/978-1-5225-2820-3.ch002

Chumillas, J., Güell, M., & Quer, P. (2022). The Use of ICT in Tourist and Educational Literary Routes: The Role of the Guide. In C. Ramos, S. Quinteiro, & A. Gonçalves (Eds.), *ICT as Innovator Between Tourism and Culture* (pp. 15–29). IGI Global. https://doi.org/10.4018/978-1-7998-8165-0.ch002

Dahlberg, T., Kivijärvi, H., & Saarinen, T. (2017). IT Investment Consistency and Other Factors Influencing the Success of IT Performance. In S. De Haes & W. Van Grembergen (Eds.), *Strategic IT Governance and Alignment in Business Settings* (pp. 176–208). Hershey, PA: IGI Global. doi:10.4018/978-1-5225-0861-8.ch007

Damnjanović, A. M. (2017). Knowledge Management Optimization through IT and E-Business Utilization: A Qualitative Study on Serbian SMEs. In M. Vemić (Ed.), *Optimal Management Strategies in Small and Medium Enterprises* (pp. 249–267). Hershey, PA: IGI Global. doi:10.4018/978-1-5225-1949-2.ch012

Daneshpour, H. (2017). Integrating Sustainable Development into Project Portfolio Management through Application of Open Innovation. In M. Vemić (Ed.), *Optimal Management Strategies in Small and Medium Enterprises* (pp. 370–387). Hershey, PA: IGI Global. doi:10.4018/978-1-5225-1949-2.ch017

Daniel, A. D., & Reis de Castro, V. (2018). Entrepreneurship Education: How to Measure the Impact on Nascent Entrepreneurs. In A. Carrizo Moreira, J. Guilherme Leitão Dantas, & F. Manuel Valente (Eds.), *Nascent Entrepreneurship and Successful New Venture Creation* (pp. 85–110). Hershey, PA: IGI Global. doi:10.4018/978-1-5225-2936-1.ch004

David, R., Swami, B. N., & Tangirala, S. (2018). Ethics Impact on Knowledge Management in Organizational Development: A Case Study. In N. Baporikar (Ed.), *Global Practices in Knowledge Management for Societal and Organizational Development* (pp. 19–45). Hershey, PA: IGI Global. doi:10.4018/978-1-5225-3009-1.ch002

De Uña-Álvarez, E., & Villarino-Pérez, M. (2022). Fostering Ecocultural Resources, Identity, and Tourism in Inland Territories (Galicia, NW Spain). In G. Fernandes (Ed.), *Challenges and New Opportunities for Tourism in Inland Territories: Ecocultural Resources and Sustainable Initiatives* (pp. 1-16). IGI Global. https://doi.org/10.4018/978-1-7998-7339-6.ch001

Delias, P., & Lakiotaki, K. (2018). Discovering Process Horizontal Boundaries to Facilitate Process Comprehension. *International Journal of Operations Research and Information Systems*, *9*(2), 1–31. doi:10.4018/IJORIS.2018040101

Denholm, J., & Lee-Davies, L. (2018). Success Factors for Games in Business and Project Management. In *Enhancing Education and Training Initiatives Through Serious Games* (pp. 34–68). Hershey, PA: IGI Global. doi:10.4018/978-1-5225-3689-5.ch002

Deshpande, M. (2017). Best Practices in Management Institutions for Global Leadership: Policy Aspects. In N. Baporikar (Ed.), *Management Education for Global Leadership* (pp. 1–27). Hershey, PA: IGI Global. doi:10.4018/978-1-5225-1013-0.ch001

Deshpande, M. (2018). Policy Perspectives for SMEs Knowledge Management. In N. Baporikar (Ed.), *Knowledge Integration Strategies for Entrepreneurship and Sustainability* (pp. 23–46). Hershey, PA: IGI Global. doi:10.4018/978-1-5225-5115-7.ch002

Dezdar, S. (2017). ERP Implementation Projects in Asian Countries: A Comparative Study on Iran and China. *International Journal of Information Technology Project Management*, *8*(3), 52–68. doi:10.4018/IJITPM.2017070104

Domingos, D., Respício, A., & Martinho, R. (2017). Reliability of IoT-Aware BPMN Healthcare Processes. In C. Reis & M. Maximiano (Eds.), *Internet of Things and Advanced Application in Healthcare* (pp. 214–248). Hershey, PA: IGI Global. doi:10.4018/978-1-5225-1820-4.ch008

Dosumu, O., Hussain, J., & El-Gohary, H. (2017). An Exploratory Study of the Impact of Government Policies on the Development of Small and Medium Enterprises in Developing Countries: The Case of Nigeria. *International Journal of Customer Relationship Marketing and Management*, *8*(4), 51–62. doi:10.4018/IJCRMM.2017100104

Durst, S., Bruns, G., & Edvardsson, I. R. (2017). Retaining Knowledge in Smaller Building and Construction Firms. *International Journal of Knowledge and Systems Science*, *8*(3), 1–12. doi:10.4018/IJKSS.2017070101

Edvardsson, I. R., & Durst, S. (2017). Outsourcing, Knowledge, and Learning: A Critical Review. *International Journal of Knowledge-Based Organizations*, *7*(2), 13–26. doi:10.4018/IJKBO.2017040102

Edwards, J. S. (2018). Integrating Knowledge Management and Business Processes. In M. Khosrow-Pour, D.B.A. (Ed.), Encyclopedia of Information Science and Technology, Fourth Edition (pp. 5046-5055). Hershey, PA: IGI Global. doi:10.4018/978-1-5225-2255-3.ch437

Eichelberger, S., & Peters, M. (2021). Family Firm Management in Turbulent Times: Opportunities for Responsible Tourism. In A. Zehrer, G. Glowka, K. Schwaiger, & V. Ranacher-Lackner (Eds.), *Resiliency Models and Addressing Future Risks for Family Firms in the Tourism Industry* (pp. 103–124). IGI Global. https://doi.org/10.4018/978-1-7998-7352-5.ch005

Eide, D., Hjalager, A., & Hansen, M. (2022). Innovative Certifications in Adventure Tourism: Attributes and Diffusion. In R. Augusto Costa, F. Brandão, Z. Breda, & C. Costa (Eds.), *Planning and Managing the Experience Economy in Tourism* (pp. 161-175). IGI Global. https://doi.org/10.4018/978-1-7998-8775-1.ch009

Ejiogu, A. O. (2018). Economics of Farm Management. In *Agricultural Finance and Opportunities for Investment and Expansion* (pp. 56–72). Hershey, PA: IGI Global. doi:10.4018/978-1-5225-3059-6.ch003

Ekanem, I., & Abiade, G. E. (2018). Factors Influencing the Use of E-Commerce by Small Enterprises in Nigeria. *International Journal of ICT Research in Africa and the Middle East, 7*(1), 37–53. doi:10.4018/IJICTRAME.2018010103

Ekanem, I., & Alrossais, L. A. (2017). Succession Challenges Facing Family Businesses in Saudi Arabia. In P. Zgheib (Ed.), *Entrepreneurship and Business Innovation in the Middle East* (pp. 122–146). Hershey, PA: IGI Global. doi:10.4018/978-1-5225-2066-5.ch007

El Faquih, L., & Fredj, M. (2017). Ontology-Based Framework for Quality in Configurable Process Models. *Journal of Electronic Commerce in Organizations, 15*(2), 48–60. doi:10.4018/JECO.2017040104

Faisal, M. N., & Talib, F. (2017). Building Ambidextrous Supply Chains in SMEs: How to Tackle the Barriers? *International Journal of Information Systems and Supply Chain Management, 10*(4), 80–100. doi:10.4018/IJISSCM.2017100105

Fernandes, T. M., Gomes, J., & Romão, M. (2017). Investments in E-Government: A Benefit Management Case Study. *International Journal of Electronic Government Research, 13*(3), 1–17. doi:10.4018/IJEGR.2017070101

Figueira, L. M., Honrado, G. R., & Dionísio, M. S. (2021). Human Capital Management in the Tourism Industry in Portugal. In V. Costa, A. Moura, & M. Mira (Eds.), *Handbook of Research on Human Capital and People Management in the Tourism Industry* (pp. 1–19). IGI Global. doi:10.4018/978-1-7998-4318-4.ch001

Gao, S. S., Oreal, S., & Zhang, J. (2018). Contemporary Financial Risk Management Perceptions and Practices of Small-Sized Chinese Businesses. In I. Management Association (Ed.), Global Business Expansion: Concepts, Methodologies, Tools, and Applications (pp. 917-931). Hershey, PA: IGI Global. doi:10.4018/978-1-5225-5481-3.ch041

Garg, R., & Berning, S. C. (2017). Indigenous Chinese Management Philosophies: Key Concepts and Relevance for Modern Chinese Firms. In B. Christiansen & G. Koc (Eds.), *Transcontinental Strategies for Industrial Development and Economic Growth* (pp. 43–57). Hershey, PA: IGI Global. doi:10.4018/978-1-5225-2160-0.ch003

Gencer, Y. G. (2017). Supply Chain Management in Retailing Business. In U. Akkucuk (Ed.), *Ethics and Sustainability in Global Supply Chain Management* (pp. 197–210). Hershey, PA: IGI Global. doi:10.4018/978-1-5225-2036-8.ch011

Gera, R., Arora, S., & Malik, S. (2021). Emotional Labor in the Tourism Industry: Strategies, Antecedents, and Outcomes. In V. Costa, A. Moura, & M. Mira (Eds.), *Handbook of Research on Human Capital and People Management in the Tourism Industry* (pp. 73–91). IGI Global. https://doi.org/10.4018/978-1-7998-4318-4.ch004

Giacosa, E. (2018). The Increasing of the Regional Development Thanks to the Luxury Business Innovation. In L. Carvalho (Ed.), *Handbook of Research on Entrepreneurial Ecosystems and Social Dynamics in a Globalized World* (pp. 260–273). Hershey, PA: IGI Global. doi:10.4018/978-1-5225-3525-6.ch011

Glowka, G., Tusch, M., & Zehrer, A. (2021). The Risk Perception of Family Business Owner-Manager in the Tourism Industry: A Qualitative Comparison of the Intra-Firm Senior and Junior Generation. In A. Zehrer, G. Glowka, K. Schwaiger, & V. Ranacher-Lackner (Eds.), *Resiliency Models and Addressing Future Risks for Family Firms in the Tourism Industry* (pp. 126–153). IGI Global. https://doi.org/10.4018/978-1-7998-7352-5.ch006

Glykas, M., & George, J. (2017). Quality and Process Management Systems in the UAE Maritime Industry. *International Journal of Productivity Management and Assessment Technologies*, *5*(1), 20–39. doi:10.4018/IJPMAT.2017010102

Glykas, M., Valiris, G., Kokkinaki, A., & Koutsoukou, Z. (2018). Banking Business Process Management Implementation. *International Journal of Productivity Management and Assessment Technologies*, *6*(1), 50–69. doi:10.4018/IJPMAT.2018010104

Gomes, J., & Romão, M. (2017). The Balanced Scorecard: Keeping Updated and Aligned with Today's Business Trends. *International Journal of Productivity Management and Assessment Technologies*, *5*(2), 1–15. doi:10.4018/IJPMAT.2017070101

Gomes, J., & Romão, M. (2017). Aligning Information Systems and Technology with Benefit Management and Balanced Scorecard. In S. De Haes & W. Van Grembergen (Eds.), *Strategic IT Governance and Alignment in Business Settings* (pp. 112–131). Hershey, PA: IGI Global. doi:10.4018/978-1-5225-0861-8.ch005

Goyal, A. (2021). Communicating and Building Destination Brands With New Media. In M. Dinis, L. Bonixe, S. Lamy, & Z. Breda (Eds.), *Impact of New Media in Tourism* (pp. 1-20). IGI Global. https://doi.org/10.4018/978-1-7998-7095-1.ch001

Grefen, P., & Turetken, O. (2017). Advanced Business Process Management in Networked E-Business Scenarios. *International Journal of E-Business Research*, *13*(4), 70–104. doi:10.4018/IJEBR.2017100105

Guasca, M., Van Broeck, A. M., & Vanneste, D. (2021). Tourism and the Social Reintegration of Colombian Ex-Combatants. In J. da Silva, Z. Breda, & F. Carbone (Eds.), *Role and Impact of Tourism in Peacebuilding and Conflict Transformation* (pp. 66-86). IGI Global. https://doi.org/10.4018/978-1-7998-5053-3.ch005

Haider, A., & Saetang, S. (2017). Strategic IT Alignment in Service Sector. In S. Rozenes & Y. Cohen (Eds.), *Handbook of Research on Strategic Alliances and Value Co-Creation in the Service Industry* (pp. 231–258). Hershey, PA: IGI Global. doi:10.4018/978-1-5225-2084-9.ch012

Hajilari, A. B., Ghadaksaz, M., & Fasghandis, G. S. (2017). Assessing Organizational Readiness for Implementing ERP System Using Fuzzy Expert System Approach. *International Journal of Enterprise Information Systems*, *13*(1), 67–85. doi:10.4018/IJEIS.2017010105

Haldorai, A., Ramu, A., & Murugan, S. (2018). Social Aware Cognitive Radio Networks: Effectiveness of Social Networks as a Strategic Tool for Organizational Business Management. In H. Bansal, G. Shrivastava, G. Nguyen, & L. Stanciu (Eds.), *Social Network Analytics for Contemporary Business Organizations* (pp. 188–202). Hershey, PA: IGI Global. doi:10.4018/978-1-5225-5097-6.ch010

Hall, O. P. Jr. (2017). Social Media Driven Management Education. *International Journal of Knowledge-Based Organizations*, *7*(2), 43–59. doi:10.4018/IJKBO.2017040104

Hanifah, H., Halim, H. A., Ahmad, N. H., & Vafaei-Zadeh, A. (2017). Innovation Culture as a Mediator Between Specific Human Capital and Innovation Performance Among Bumiputera SMEs in Malaysia. In N. Ahmad, T. Ramayah, H. Halim, & S. Rahman (Eds.), *Handbook of Research on Small and Medium Enterprises in Developing Countries* (pp. 261–279). Hershey, PA: IGI Global. doi:10.4018/978-1-5225-2165-5.ch012

Hartlieb, S., & Silvius, G. (2017). Handling Uncertainty in Project Management and Business Development: Similarities and Differences. In Y. Raydugin (Ed.), *Handbook of Research on Leveraging Risk and Uncertainties for Effective Project Management* (pp. 337–362). Hershey, PA: IGI Global. doi:10.4018/978-1-5225-1790-0.ch016

Hass, K. B. (2017). Living on the Edge: Managing Project Complexity. In Y. Raydugin (Ed.), *Handbook of Research on Leveraging Risk and Uncertainties for Effective Project Management* (pp. 177–201). Hershey, PA: IGI Global. doi:10.4018/978-1-5225-1790-0.ch009

Hawking, P., & Carmine Sellitto, C. (2017). Developing an Effective Strategy for Organizational Business Intelligence. In M. Tavana (Ed.), *Enterprise Information Systems and the Digitalization of Business Functions* (pp. 222–237). Hershey, PA: IGI Global. doi:10.4018/978-1-5225-2382-6.ch010

Hawking, P., & Sellitto, C. (2017). A Fast-Moving Consumer Goods Company and Business Intelligence Strategy Development. *International Journal of Enterprise Information Systems*, *13*(2), 22–33. doi:10.4018/IJEIS.2017040102

Hawking, P., & Sellitto, C. (2017). Business Intelligence Strategy: Two Case Studies. *International Journal of Business Intelligence Research*, *8*(2), 17–30. doi:10.4018/IJBIR.2017070102

Hee, W. J., Jalleh, G., Lai, H., & Lin, C. (2017). E-Commerce and IT Projects: Evaluation and Management Issues in Australian and Taiwanese Hospitals. *International Journal of Public Health Management and Ethics*, *2*(1), 69–90. doi:10.4018/IJPHME.2017010104

Hernandez, A. A. (2018). Exploring the Factors to Green IT Adoption of SMEs in the Philippines. *Journal of Cases on Information Technology*, *20*(2), 49–66. doi:10.4018/JCIT.2018040104

Hollman, A., Bickford, S., & Hollman, T. (2017). Cyber InSecurity: A Post-Mortem Attempt to Assess Cyber Problems from IT and Business Management Perspectives. *Journal of Cases on Information Technology, 19*(3), 42–70. doi:10.4018/JCIT.2017070104

Ibrahim, F., & Zainin, N. M. (2021). Exploring the Technological Impacts: The Case of Museums in Brunei Darussalam. *International Journal of Tourism and Hospitality Management in the Digital Age, 5*(1), 1–18. https://doi.org/10.4018/IJTHMDA.2021010101

Igbinakhase, I. (2017). Responsible and Sustainable Management Practices in Developing and Developed Business Environments. In Z. Fields (Ed.), *Collective Creativity for Responsible and Sustainable Business Practice* (pp. 180–207). Hershey, PA: IGI Global. doi:10.4018/978-1-5225-1823-5.ch010

Iwata, J. J., & Hoskins, R. G. (2017). Managing Indigenous Knowledge in Tanzania: A Business Perspective. In P. Jain & N. Mnjama (Eds.), *Managing Knowledge Resources and Records in Modern Organizations* (pp. 198–214). Hershey, PA: IGI Global. doi:10.4018/978-1-5225-1965-2.ch012

Jain, P. (2017). Ethical and Legal Issues in Knowledge Management Life-Cycle in Business. In P. Jain & N. Mnjama (Eds.), *Managing Knowledge Resources and Records in Modern Organizations* (pp. 82–101). Hershey, PA: IGI Global. doi:10.4018/978-1-5225-1965-2.ch006

James, S., & Hauli, E. (2017). Holistic Management Education at Tanzanian Rural Development Planning Institute. In N. Baporikar (Ed.), *Management Education for Global Leadership* (pp. 112–136). Hershey, PA: IGI Global. doi:10.4018/978-1-5225-1013-0.ch006

Janošková, M., Csikósová, A., & Čulková, K. (2018). Measurement of Company Performance as Part of Its Strategic Management. In R. Leon (Ed.), *Managerial Strategies for Business Sustainability During Turbulent Times* (pp. 309–335). Hershey, PA: IGI Global. doi:10.4018/978-1-5225-2716-9.ch017

Jean-Vasile, A., & Alecu, A. (2017). Theoretical and Practical Approaches in Understanding the Influences of Cost-Productivity-Profit Trinomial in Contemporary Enterprises. In A. Jean Vasile & D. Nicolò (Eds.), *Sustainable Entrepreneurship and Investments in the Green Economy* (pp. 28–62). Hershey, PA: IGI Global. doi:10.4018/978-1-5225-2075-7.ch002

Joia, L. A., & Correia, J. C. (2018). CIO Competencies From the IT Professional Perspective: Insights From Brazil. *Journal of Global Information Management, 26*(2), 74–103. doi:10.4018/JGIM.2018040104

Juma, A., & Mzera, N. (2017). Knowledge Management and Records Management and Competitive Advantage in Business. In P. Jain & N. Mnjama (Eds.), *Managing Knowledge Resources and Records in Modern Organizations* (pp. 15–28). Hershey, PA: IGI Global. doi:10.4018/978-1-5225-1965-2.ch002

K., I., & A, V. (2018). Monitoring and Auditing in the Cloud. In K. Munir (Ed.), *Cloud Computing Technologies for Green Enterprises* (pp. 318-350). Hershey, PA: IGI Global. https://doi.org/ doi:10.4018/978-1-5225-3038-1.ch013

Kabra, G., Ghosh, V., & Ramesh, A. (2018). Enterprise Integrated Business Process Management and Business Intelligence Framework for Business Process Sustainability. In A. Paul, D. Bhattacharyya, & S. Anand (Eds.), *Green Initiatives for Business Sustainability and Value Creation* (pp. 228–238). Hershey, PA: IGI Global. doi:10.4018/978-1-5225-2662-9.ch010

Kaoud, M. (2017). Investigation of Customer Knowledge Management: A Case Study Research. *International Journal of Service Science, Management, Engineering, and Technology*, *8*(2), 12–22. doi:10.4018/IJSSMET.2017040102

Katuu, S. (2018). A Comparative Assessment of Enterprise Content Management Maturity Models. In N. Gwangwava & M. Mutingi (Eds.), *E-Manufacturing and E-Service Strategies in Contemporary Organizations* (pp. 93–118). Hershey, PA: IGI Global. doi:10.4018/978-1-5225-3628-4.ch005

Khan, M. Y., & Abir, T. (2022). The Role of Social Media Marketing in the Tourism and Hospitality Industry: A Conceptual Study on Bangladesh. In C. Ramos, S. Quinteiro, & A. Gonçalves (Eds.), *ICT as Innovator Between Tourism and Culture* (pp. 213–229). IGI Global. https://doi.org/10.4018/978-1-7998-8165-0.ch013

Kinnunen, S., Ylä-Kujala, A., Marttonen-Arola, S., Kärri, T., & Baglee, D. (2018). Internet of Things in Asset Management: Insights from Industrial Professionals and Academia. *International Journal of Service Science, Management, Engineering, and Technology*, *9*(2), 104–119. doi:10.4018/IJSSMET.2018040105

Klein, A. Z., Sabino de Freitas, A., Machado, L., Freitas, J. C. Jr, Graziola, P. G. Jr, & Schlemmer, E. (2017). Virtual Worlds Applications for Management Education. In L. Tomei (Ed.), *Exploring the New Era of Technology-Infused Education* (pp. 279–299). Hershey, PA: IGI Global. doi:10.4018/978-1-5225-1709-2.ch017

Kővári, E., Saleh, M., & Steinbachné Hajmásy, G. (2022). The Impact of Corporate Digital Responsibility (CDR) on Internal Stakeholders' Satisfaction in Hungarian Upscale Hotels. In M. Valeri (Ed.), *New Governance and Management in Touristic Destinations* (pp. 35–51). IGI Global. https://doi.org/10.4018/978-1-6684-3889-3.ch003

Kożuch, B., & Jabłoński, A. (2017). Adopting the Concept of Business Models in Public Management. In M. Lewandowski & B. Kożuch (Eds.), *Public Sector Entrepreneurship and the Integration of Innovative Business Models* (pp. 10–46). Hershey, PA: IGI Global. doi:10.4018/978-1-5225-2215-7.ch002

Kumar, J., Adhikary, A., & Jha, A. (2017). Small Active Investors' Perceptions and Preferences Towards Tax Saving Mutual Fund Schemes in Eastern India: An Empirical Note. *International Journal of Asian Business and Information Management, 8*(2), 35–45. doi:10.4018/IJABIM.2017040103

Latusi, S., & Fissore, M. (2021). Pilgrimage Routes to Happiness: Comparing the Camino de Santiago and Via Francigena. In A. Perinotto, V. Mayer, & J. Soares (Eds.), *Rebuilding and Restructuring the Tourism Industry: Infusion of Happiness and Quality of Life* (pp. 157–182). IGI Global. https://doi.org/10.4018/978-1-7998-7239-9.ch008

Lavassani, K. M., & Movahedi, B. (2017). Applications Driven Information Systems: Beyond Networks toward Business Ecosystems. *International Journal of Innovation in the Digital Economy, 8*(1), 61–75. doi:10.4018/IJIDE.2017010104

Lazzareschi, V. H., & Brito, M. S. (2017). Strategic Information Management: Proposal of Business Project Model. In G. Jamil, A. Soares, & C. Pessoa (Eds.), *Handbook of Research on Information Management for Effective Logistics and Supply Chains* (pp. 59–88). Hershey, PA: IGI Global. doi:10.4018/978-1-5225-0973-8.ch004

Lechuga Sancho, M. P., & Martín Navarro, A. (2022). Evolution of the Literature on Social Responsibility in the Tourism Sector: A Systematic Literature Review. In G. Fernandes (Ed.), *Challenges and New Opportunities for Tourism in Inland Territories: Ecocultural Resources and Sustainable Initiatives* (pp. 169–186). IGI Global. https://doi.org/10.4018/978-1-7998-7339-6.ch010

Lederer, M., Kurz, M., & Lazarov, P. (2017). Usage and Suitability of Methods for Strategic Business Process Initiatives: A Multi Case Study Research. *International Journal of Productivity Management and Assessment Technologies, 5*(1), 40–51. doi:10.4018/IJPMAT.2017010103

Lee, I. (2017). A Social Enterprise Business Model and a Case Study of Pacific Community Ventures (PCV). In V. Potocan, M. Ünğan, & Z. Nedelko (Eds.), *Handbook of Research on Managerial Solutions in Non-Profit Organizations* (pp. 182–204). Hershey, PA: IGI Global. doi:10.4018/978-1-5225-0731-4.ch009

Leon, L. A., Seal, K. C., Przasnyski, Z. H., & Wiedenman, I. (2017). Skills and Competencies Required for Jobs in Business Analytics: A Content Analysis of Job Advertisements Using Text Mining. *International Journal of Business Intelligence Research*, *8*(1), 1–25. doi:10.4018/IJBIR.2017010101

Levy, C. L., & Elias, N. I. (2017). SOHO Users' Perceptions of Reliability and Continuity of Cloud-Based Services. In M. Moore (Ed.), *Cybersecurity Breaches and Issues Surrounding Online Threat Protection* (pp. 248–287). Hershey, PA: IGI Global. doi:10.4018/978-1-5225-1941-6.ch011

Levy, M. (2018). Change Management Serving Knowledge Management and Organizational Development: Reflections and Review. In N. Baporikar (Ed.), *Global Practices in Knowledge Management for Societal and Organizational Development* (pp. 256–270). Hershey, PA: IGI Global. doi:10.4018/978-1-5225-3009-1.ch012

Lewandowski, M. (2017). Public Organizations and Business Model Innovation: The Role of Public Service Design. In M. Lewandowski & B. Kożuch (Eds.), *Public Sector Entrepreneurship and the Integration of Innovative Business Models* (pp. 47–72). Hershey, PA: IGI Global. doi:10.4018/978-1-5225-2215-7.ch003

Lhannaoui, H., Kabbaj, M. I., & Bakkoury, Z. (2017). A Survey of Risk-Aware Business Process Modelling. *International Journal of Risk and Contingency Management*, *6*(3), 14–26. doi:10.4018/IJRCM.2017070102

Li, J., Sun, W., Jiang, W., Yang, H., & Zhang, L. (2017). How the Nature of Exogenous Shocks and Crises Impact Company Performance?: The Effects of Industry Characteristics. *International Journal of Risk and Contingency Management*, *6*(4), 40–55. doi:10.4018/IJRCM.2017100103

Lopez-Fernandez, M., Perez-Perez, M., Serrano-Bedia, A., & Cobo-Gonzalez, A. (2021). Small and Medium Tourism Enterprise Survival in Times of Crisis: "El Capricho de Gaudí. In D. Toubes & N. Araújo-Vila (Eds.), *Risk, Crisis, and Disaster Management in Small and Medium-Sized Tourism Enterprises* (pp. 103–129). IGI Global. doi:10.4018/978-1-7998-6996-2.ch005

Mahajan, A., Maidullah, S., & Hossain, M. R. (2022). Experience Toward Smart Tour Guide Apps in Travelling: An Analysis of Users' Reviews on Audio Odigos and Trip My Way. In R. Augusto Costa, F. Brandão, Z. Breda, & C. Costa (Eds.), *Planning and Managing the Experience Economy in Tourism* (pp. 255-273). IGI Global. https://doi.org/10.4018/978-1-7998-8775-1.ch014

Malega, P. (2017). Small and Medium Enterprises in the Slovak Republic: Status and Competitiveness of SMEs in the Global Markets and Possibilities of Optimization. In M. Vemić (Ed.), *Optimal Management Strategies in Small and Medium Enterprises* (pp. 102–124). Hershey, PA: IGI Global. doi:10.4018/978-1-5225-1949-2.ch006

Malewska, K. M. (2017). Intuition in Decision-Making on the Example of a Non-Profit Organization. In V. Potocan, M. Üngan, & Z. Nedelko (Eds.), *Handbook of Research on Managerial Solutions in Non-Profit Organizations* (pp. 378–399). Hershey, PA: IGI Global. doi:10.4018/978-1-5225-0731-4.ch018

Maroofi, F. (2017). Entrepreneurial Orientation and Organizational Learning Ability Analysis for Innovation and Firm Performance. In N. Baporikar (Ed.), *Innovation and Shifting Perspectives in Management Education* (pp. 144–165). Hershey, PA: IGI Global. doi:10.4018/978-1-5225-1019-2.ch007

Marques, M., Moleiro, D., Brito, T. M., & Marques, T. (2021). Customer Relationship Management as an Important Relationship Marketing Tool: The Case of the Hospitality Industry in Estoril Coast. In M. Dinis, L. Bonixe, S. Lamy, & Z. Breda (Eds.), Impact of New Media in Tourism (pp. 39-56). IGI Global. https://doi.org/doi:10.4018/978-1-7998-7095-1.ch003

Martins, P. V., & Zacarias, M. (2017). A Web-based Tool for Business Process Improvement. *International Journal of Web Portals*, *9*(2), 68–84. doi:10.4018/IJWP.2017070104

Matthies, B., & Coners, A. (2017). Exploring the Conceptual Nature of e-Business Projects. *Journal of Electronic Commerce in Organizations*, *15*(3), 33–63. doi:10.4018/JECO.2017070103

Mayer, V. F., Fraga, C. C., & Silva, L. C. (2021). Contributions of Neurosciences to Studies of Well-Being in Tourism. In A. Perinotto, V. Mayer, & J. Soares (Eds.), *Rebuilding and Restructuring the Tourism Industry: Infusion of Happiness and Quality of Life* (pp. 108–128). IGI Global. https://doi.org/10.4018/978-1-7998-7239-9.ch006

McKee, J. (2018). Architecture as a Tool to Solve Business Planning Problems. In M. Khosrow-Pour, D.B.A. (Ed.), Encyclopedia of Information Science and Technology, Fourth Edition (pp. 573-586). Hershey, PA: IGI Global. doi:10.4018/978-1-5225-2255-3.ch050

McMurray, A. J., Cross, J., & Caponecchia, C. (2018). The Risk Management Profession in Australia: Business Continuity Plan Practices. In N. Bajgoric (Ed.), *Always-On Enterprise Information Systems for Modern Organizations* (pp. 112–129). Hershey, PA: IGI Global. doi:10.4018/978-1-5225-3704-5.ch006

Meddah, I. H., & Belkadi, K. (2018). Mining Patterns Using Business Process Management. In R. Hamou (Ed.), *Handbook of Research on Biomimicry in Information Retrieval and Knowledge Management* (pp. 78–89). Hershey, PA: IGI Global. doi:10.4018/978-1-5225-3004-6.ch005

Melian, A. G., & Camprubí, R. (2021). The Accessibility of Museum Websites: The Case of Barcelona. In C. Eusébio, L. Teixeira, & M. Carneiro (Eds.), *ICT Tools and Applications for Accessible Tourism* (pp. 234–255). IGI Global. https://doi.org/10.4018/978-1-7998-6428-8.ch011

Mendes, L. (2017). TQM and Knowledge Management: An Integrated Approach Towards Tacit Knowledge Management. In D. Jaziri-Bouagina & G. Jamil (Eds.), *Handbook of Research on Tacit Knowledge Management for Organizational Success* (pp. 236–263). Hershey, PA: IGI Global. doi:10.4018/978-1-5225-2394-9.ch009

Menezes, V. D., & Cavagnaro, E. (2021). Communicating Sustainable Initiatives in the Hotel Industry: The Case of the Hotel Jakarta Amsterdam. In F. Brandão, Z. Breda, R. Costa, & C. Costa (Eds.), *Handbook of Research on the Role of Tourism in Achieving Sustainable Development Goals* (pp. 224-234). IGI Global. https://doi.org/10.4018/978-1-7998-5691-7.ch013

Menezes, V. D., & Cavagnaro, E. (2021). Communicating Sustainable Initiatives in the Hotel Industry: The Case of the Hotel Jakarta Amsterdam. In F. Brandão, Z. Breda, R. Costa, & C. Costa (Eds.), *Handbook of Research on the Role of Tourism in Achieving Sustainable Development Goals* (pp. 224-234). IGI Global. https://doi.org/10.4018/978-1-7998-5691-7.ch013

Mitas, O., Bastiaansen, M., & Boode, W. (2022). If You're Happy, I'm Happy: Emotion Contagion at a Tourist Information Center. In R. Augusto Costa, F. Brandão, Z. Breda, & C. Costa (Eds.), *Planning and Managing the Experience Economy in Tourism* (pp. 122-140). IGI Global. https://doi.org/10.4018/978-1-7998-8775-1.ch007

Mnjama, N. M. (2017). Preservation of Recorded Information in Public and Private Sector Organizations. In P. Jain & N. Mnjama (Eds.), *Managing Knowledge Resources and Records in Modern Organizations* (pp. 149–167). Hershey, PA: IGI Global. doi:10.4018/978-1-5225-1965-2.ch009

Mokoqama, M., & Fields, Z. (2017). Principles of Responsible Management Education (PRME): Call for Responsible Management Education. In Z. Fields (Ed.), *Collective Creativity for Responsible and Sustainable Business Practice* (pp. 229–241). Hershey, PA: IGI Global. doi:10.4018/978-1-5225-1823-5.ch012

Monteiro, A., Lopes, S., & Carbone, F. (2021). Academic Mobility: Bridging Tourism and Peace Education. In J. da Silva, Z. Breda, & F. Carbone (Eds.), *Role and Impact of Tourism in Peacebuilding and Conflict Transformation* (pp. 275-301). IGI Global. https://doi.org/10.4018/978-1-7998-5053-3.ch016

Muniapan, B. (2017). Philosophy and Management: The Relevance of Vedanta in Management. In P. Ordóñez de Pablos (Ed.), *Managerial Strategies and Solutions for Business Success in Asia* (pp. 124–139). Hershey, PA: IGI Global. doi:10.4018/978-1-5225-1886-0.ch007

Murad, S. E., & Dowaji, S. (2017). Using Value-Based Approach for Managing Cloud-Based Services. In A. Turuk, B. Sahoo, & S. Addya (Eds.), *Resource Management and Efficiency in Cloud Computing Environments* (pp. 33–60). Hershey, PA: IGI Global. doi:10.4018/978-1-5225-1721-4.ch002

Mutahar, A. M., Daud, N. M., Thurasamy, R., Isaac, O., & Abdulsalam, R. (2018). The Mediating of Perceived Usefulness and Perceived Ease of Use: The Case of Mobile Banking in Yemen. *International Journal of Technology Diffusion*, *9*(2), 21–40. doi:10.4018/IJTD.2018040102

Naidoo, V. (2017). E-Learning and Management Education at African Universities. In N. Baporikar (Ed.), *Management Education for Global Leadership* (pp. 181–201). Hershey, PA: IGI Global. doi:10.4018/978-1-5225-1013-0.ch009

Naidoo, V., & Igbinakhase, I. (2018). Opportunities and Challenges of Knowledge Retention in SMEs. In N. Baporikar (Ed.), *Knowledge Integration Strategies for Entrepreneurship and Sustainability* (pp. 70–94). Hershey, PA: IGI Global. doi:10.4018/978-1-5225-5115-7.ch004

Naumov, N., & Costandachi, G. (2021). Creativity and Entrepreneurship: Gastronomic Tourism in Mexico. In J. Soares (Ed.), *Innovation and Entrepreneurial Opportunities in Community Tourism* (pp. 90–108). IGI Global. https://doi.org/10.4018/978-1-7998-4855-4.ch006

Nayak, S., & Prabhu, N. (2017). Paradigm Shift in Management Education: Need for a Cross Functional Perspective. In N. Baporikar (Ed.), *Management Education for Global Leadership* (pp. 241–255). Hershey, PA: IGI Global. doi:10.4018/978-1-5225-1013-0.ch012

Nedelko, Z., & Potocan, V. (2017). Management Solutions in Non-Profit Organizations: Case of Slovenia. In V. Potocan, M. Üngan, & Z. Nedelko (Eds.), *Handbook of Research on Managerial Solutions in Non-Profit Organizations* (pp. 1–22). Hershey, PA: IGI Global. doi:10.4018/978-1-5225-0731-4.ch001

Nedelko, Z., & Potocan, V. (2017). Priority of Management Tools Utilization among Managers: International Comparison. In V. Wang (Ed.), *Encyclopedia of Strategic Leadership and Management* (pp. 1083–1094). Hershey, PA: IGI Global. doi:10.4018/978-1-5225-1049-9.ch075

Nedelko, Z., Raudeliūnienė, J., & Črešnar, R. (2018). Knowledge Dynamics in Supply Chain Management. In N. Baporikar (Ed.), *Knowledge Integration Strategies for Entrepreneurship and Sustainability* (pp. 150–166). Hershey, PA: IGI Global. doi:10.4018/978-1-5225-5115-7.ch008

Nguyen, H. T., & Hipsher, S. A. (2018). Innovation and Creativity Used by Private Sector Firms in a Resources-Constrained Environment. In S. Hipsher (Ed.), *Examining the Private Sector's Role in Wealth Creation and Poverty Reduction* (pp. 219–238). Hershey, PA: IGI Global. doi:10.4018/978-1-5225-3117-3.ch010

Obicci, P. A. (2017). Risk Sharing in a Partnership. In *Risk Management Strategies in Public-Private Partnerships* (pp. 115–152). Hershey, PA: IGI Global. doi:10.4018/978-1-5225-2503-5.ch004

Obidallah, W. J., & Raahemi, B. (2017). Managing Changes in Service Oriented Virtual Organizations: A Structural and Procedural Framework to Facilitate the Process of Change. *Journal of Electronic Commerce in Organizations, 15*(1), 59–83. doi:10.4018/JECO.2017010104

Ojo, O. (2017). Impact of Innovation on the Entrepreneurial Success in Selected Business Enterprises in South-West Nigeria. *International Journal of Innovation in the Digital Economy*, *8*(2), 29–38. doi:10.4018/IJIDE.2017040103

Okdinawati, L., Simatupang, T. M., & Sunitiyoso, Y. (2017). Multi-Agent Reinforcement Learning for Value Co-Creation of Collaborative Transportation Management (CTM). *International Journal of Information Systems and Supply Chain Management, 10*(3), 84–95. doi:10.4018/IJISSCM.2017070105

Olivera, V. A., & Carrillo, I. M. (2021). Organizational Culture: A Key Element for the Development of Mexican Micro and Small Tourist Companies. In J. Soares (Ed.), *Innovation and Entrepreneurial Opportunities in Community Tourism* (pp. 227–242). IGI Global. doi:10.4018/978-1-7998-4855-4.ch013

Ossorio, M. (2022). Corporate Museum Experiences in Enogastronomic Tourism. In R. Augusto Costa, F. Brandão, Z. Breda, & C. Costa (Eds.), Planning and Managing the Experience Economy in Tourism (pp. 107-121). IGI Global. https://doi.org/doi:10.4018/978-1-7998-8775-1.ch006

Ossorio, M. (2022). Enogastronomic Tourism in Times of Pandemic. In G. Fernandes (Ed.), *Challenges and New Opportunities for Tourism in Inland Territories: Ecocultural Resources and Sustainable Initiatives* (pp. 241–255). IGI Global. https://doi.org/10.4018/978-1-7998-7339-6.ch014

Özekici, Y. K. (2022). ICT as an Acculturative Agent and Its Role in the Tourism Context: Introduction, Acculturation Theory, Progress of the Acculturation Theory in Extant Literature. In C. Ramos, S. Quinteiro, & A. Gonçalves (Eds.), *ICT as Innovator Between Tourism and Culture* (pp. 42–66). IGI Global. https://doi.org/10.4018/978-1-7998-8165-0.ch004

Pal, K. (2018). Building High Quality Big Data-Based Applications in Supply Chains. In A. Kumar & S. Saurav (Eds.), *Supply Chain Management Strategies and Risk Assessment in Retail Environments* (pp. 1–24). Hershey, PA: IGI Global. doi:10.4018/978-1-5225-3056-5.ch001

Palos-Sanchez, P. R., & Correia, M. B. (2018). Perspectives of the Adoption of Cloud Computing in the Tourism Sector. In J. Rodrigues, C. Ramos, P. Cardoso, & C. Henriques (Eds.), *Handbook of Research on Technological Developments for Cultural Heritage and eTourism Applications* (pp. 377–400). Hershey, PA: IGI Global. doi:10.4018/978-1-5225-2927-9.ch018

Papadopoulou, G. (2021). Promoting Gender Equality and Women Empowerment in the Tourism Sector. In F. Brandão, Z. Breda, R. Costa, & C. Costa (Eds.), Handbook of Research on the Role of Tourism in Achieving Sustainable Development Goals (pp. 152-174). IGI Global. https://doi.org/ doi:10.4018/978-1-7998-5691-7.ch009

Papp-Váry, Á. F., & Tóth, T. Z. (2022). Analysis of Budapest as a Film Tourism Destination. In R. Baleiro & R. Pereira (Eds.), *Global Perspectives on Literary Tourism and Film-Induced Tourism* (pp. 257-279). IGI Global. https://doi.org/10.4018/978-1-7998-8262-6.ch014

Patiño, B. E. (2017). New Generation Management by Convergence and Individual Identity: A Systemic and Human-Oriented Approach. In N. Baporikar (Ed.), *Innovation and Shifting Perspectives in Management Education* (pp. 119–143). Hershey, PA: IGI Global. doi:10.4018/978-1-5225-1019-2.ch006

Patro, C. S. (2021). Digital Tourism: Influence of E-Marketing Technology. In M. Dinis, L. Bonixe, S. Lamy, & Z. Breda (Eds.), *Impact of New Media in Tourism* (pp. 234-254). IGI Global. https://doi.org/10.4018/978-1-7998-7095-1.ch014

Pawliczek, A., & Rössler, M. (2017). Knowledge of Management Tools and Systems in SMEs: Knowledge Transfer in Management. In A. Bencsik (Ed.), *Knowledge Management Initiatives and Strategies in Small and Medium Enterprises* (pp. 180–203). Hershey, PA: IGI Global. doi:10.4018/978-1-5225-1642-2.ch009

Pejic-Bach, M., Omazic, M. A., Aleksic, A., & Zoroja, J. (2018). Knowledge-Based Decision Making: A Multi-Case Analysis. In R. Leon (Ed.), *Managerial Strategies for Business Sustainability During Turbulent Times* (pp. 160–184). Hershey, PA: IGI Global. doi:10.4018/978-1-5225-2716-9.ch009

Perano, M., Hysa, X., & Calabrese, M. (2018). Strategic Planning, Cultural Context, and Business Continuity Management: Business Cases in the City of Shkoder. In A. Presenza & L. Sheehan (Eds.), *Geopolitics and Strategic Management in the Global Economy* (pp. 57–77). Hershey, PA: IGI Global. doi:10.4018/978-1-5225-2673-5.ch004

Pereira, R., Mira da Silva, M., & Lapão, L. V. (2017). IT Governance Maturity Patterns in Portuguese Healthcare. In S. De Haes & W. Van Grembergen (Eds.), *Strategic IT Governance and Alignment in Business Settings* (pp. 24–52). Hershey, PA: IGI Global. doi:10.4018/978-1-5225-0861-8.ch002

Pérez-Uribe, R. I., Torres, D. A., Jurado, S. P., & Prada, D. M. (2018). Cloud Tools for the Development of Project Management in SMEs. In R. Perez-Uribe, C. Salcedo-Perez, & D. Ocampo-Guzman (Eds.), *Handbook of Research on Intrapreneurship and Organizational Sustainability in SMEs* (pp. 95–120). Hershey, PA: IGI Global. doi:10.4018/978-1-5225-3543-0.ch005

Petrisor, I., & Cozmiuc, D. (2017). Global Supply Chain Management Organization at Siemens in the Advent of Industry 4.0. In L. Saglietto & C. Cezanne (Eds.), *Global Intermediation and Logistics Service Providers* (pp. 123–142). Hershey, PA: IGI Global. doi:10.4018/978-1-5225-2133-4.ch007

Pierce, J. M., Velliaris, D. M., & Edwards, J. (2017). A Living Case Study: A Journey Not a Destination. In N. Silton (Ed.), *Exploring the Benefits of Creativity in Education, Media, and the Arts* (pp. 158–178). Hershey, PA: IGI Global. doi:10.4018/978-1-5225-0504-4.ch008

Pipia, S., & Pipia, S. (2021). Challenges of Religious Tourism in the Conflict Region: An Example of Jerusalem. In E. Alaverdov & M. Bari (Eds.), *Global Development of Religious Tourism* (pp. 135-148). IGI Global. https://doi.org/10.4018/978-1-7998-5792-1.ch009

Poulaki, P., Kritikos, A., Vasilakis, N., & Valeri, M. (2022). The Contribution of Female Creativity to the Development of Gastronomic Tourism in Greece: The Case of the Island of Naxos in the South Aegean Region. In M. Valeri (Ed.), *New Governance and Management in Touristic Destinations* (pp. 246–258). IGI Global. https://doi.org/10.4018/978-1-6684-3889-3.ch015

Radosavljevic, M., & Andjelkovic, A. (2017). Multi-Criteria Decision Making Approach for Choosing Business Process for the Improvement: Upgrading of the Six Sigma Methodology. In J. Stanković, P. Delias, S. Marinković, & S. Rochhia (Eds.), *Tools and Techniques for Economic Decision Analysis* (pp. 225–247). Hershey, PA: IGI Global. doi:10.4018/978-1-5225-0959-2.ch011

Radovic, V. M. (2017). Corporate Sustainability and Responsibility and Disaster Risk Reduction: A Serbian Overview. In M. Camilleri (Ed.), *CSR 2.0 and the New Era of Corporate Citizenship* (pp. 147–164). Hershey, PA: IGI Global. doi:10.4018/978-1-5225-1842-6.ch008

Raghunath, K. M., Devi, S. L., & Patro, C. S. (2018). Impact of Risk Assessment Models on Risk Factors: A Holistic Outlook. In K. Strang, M. Korstanje, & N. Vajjhala (Eds.), *Research, Practices, and Innovations in Global Risk and Contingency Management* (pp. 134–153). Hershey, PA: IGI Global. doi:10.4018/978-1-5225-4754-9.ch008

Raman, A., & Goyal, D. P. (2017). Extending IMPLEMENT Framework for Enterprise Information Systems Implementation to Information System Innovation. In M. Tavana (Ed.), *Enterprise Information Systems and the Digitalization of Business Functions* (pp. 137–177). Hershey, PA: IGI Global. doi:10.4018/978-1-5225-2382-6.ch007

Rao, Y., & Zhang, Y. (2017). The Construction and Development of Academic Library Digital Special Subject Databases. In L. Ruan, Q. Zhu, & Y. Ye (Eds.), *Academic Library Development and Administration in China* (pp. 163–183). Hershey, PA: IGI Global. doi:10.4018/978-1-5225-0550-1.ch010

Ravasan, A. Z., Mohammadi, M. M., & Hamidi, H. (2018). An Investigation Into the Critical Success Factors of Implementing Information Technology Service Management Frameworks. In K. Jakobs (Ed.), *Corporate and Global Standardization Initiatives in Contemporary Society* (pp. 200–218). Hershey, PA: IGI Global. doi:10.4018/978-1-5225-5320-5.ch009

Rezaie, S., Mirabedini, S. J., & Abtahi, A. (2018). Designing a Model for Implementation of Business Intelligence in the Banking Industry. *International Journal of Enterprise Information Systems, 14*(1), 77–103. doi:10.4018/IJEIS.2018010105

Richards, V., Matthews, N., Williams, O. J., & Khan, Z. (2021). The Challenges of Accessible Tourism Information Systems for Tourists With Vision Impairment: Sensory Communications Beyond the Screen. In C. Eusébio, L. Teixeira, & M. Carneiro (Eds.), *ICT Tools and Applications for Accessible Tourism* (pp. 26–54). IGI Global. https://doi.org/10.4018/978-1-7998-6428-8.ch002

Rodrigues de Souza Neto, V., & Marques, O. (2021). Rural Tourism Fostering Welfare Through Sustainable Development: A Conceptual Approach. In A. Perinotto, V. Mayer, & J. Soares (Eds.), *Rebuilding and Restructuring the Tourism Industry: Infusion of Happiness and Quality of Life* (pp. 38–57). IGI Global. https://doi.org/10.4018/978-1-7998-7239-9.ch003

Romano, L., Grimaldi, R., & Colasuonno, F. S. (2017). Demand Management as a Success Factor in Project Portfolio Management. In L. Romano (Ed.), *Project Portfolio Management Strategies for Effective Organizational Operations* (pp. 202–219). Hershey, PA: IGI Global. doi:10.4018/978-1-5225-2151-8.ch008

Rubio-Escuderos, L., & García-Andreu, H. (2021). Competitiveness Factors of Accessible Tourism E-Travel Agencies. In C. Eusébio, L. Teixeira, & M. Carneiro (Eds.), *ICT Tools and Applications for Accessible Tourism* (pp. 196–217). IGI Global. https://doi.org/10.4018/978-1-7998-6428-8.ch009

Rucci, A. C., Porto, N., Darcy, S., & Becka, L. (2021). Smart and Accessible Cities?: Not Always – The Case for Accessible Tourism Initiatives in Buenos Aries and Sydney. In C. Eusébio, L. Teixeira, & M. Carneiro (Eds.), *ICT Tools and Applications for Accessible Tourism* (pp. 115–145). IGI Global. https://doi.org/10.4018/978-1-7998-6428-8.ch006

Ruhi, U. (2018). Towards an Interdisciplinary Socio-Technical Definition of Virtual Communities. In M. Khosrow-Pour, D.B.A. (Ed.), Encyclopedia of Information Science and Technology, Fourth Edition (pp. 4278-4295). Hershey, PA: IGI Global. doi:10.4018/978-1-5225-2255-3.ch371

Ryan, L., Catena, M., Ros, P., & Stephens, S. (2021). Designing Entrepreneurial Ecosystems to Support Resource Management in the Tourism Industry. In V. Costa, A. Moura, & M. Mira (Eds.), *Handbook of Research on Human Capital and People Management in the Tourism Industry* (pp. 265–281). IGI Global. https://doi.org/10.4018/978-1-7998-4318-4.ch013

Sabuncu, I. (2021). Understanding Tourist Perceptions and Expectations During Pandemic Through Social Media Big Data. In M. Demir, A. Dalgıç, & F. Ergen (Eds.), *Handbook of Research on the Impacts and Implications of COVID-19 on the Tourism Industry* (pp. 330–350). IGI Global. https://doi.org/10.4018/978-1-7998-8231-2.ch016

Safari, M. R., & Jiang, Q. (2018). The Theory and Practice of IT Governance Maturity and Strategies Alignment: Evidence From Banking Industry. *Journal of Global Information Management, 26*(2), 127–146. doi:10.4018/JGIM.2018040106

Sahoo, J., Pati, B., & Mohanty, B. (2017). Knowledge Management as an Academic Discipline: An Assessment. In B. Gunjal (Ed.), *Managing Knowledge and Scholarly Assets in Academic Libraries* (pp. 99–126). Hershey, PA: IGI Global. doi:10.4018/978-1-5225-1741-2.ch005

Saini, D. (2017). Relevance of Teaching Values and Ethics in Management Education. In N. Baporikar (Ed.), *Management Education for Global Leadership* (pp. 90–111). Hershey, PA: IGI Global. doi:10.4018/978-1-5225-1013-0.ch005

Sambhanthan, A. (2017). Assessing and Benchmarking Sustainability in Organisations: An Integrated Conceptual Model. *International Journal of Systems and Service-Oriented Engineering, 7*(4), 22–43. doi:10.4018/IJSSOE.2017100102

Sambhanthan, A., & Potdar, V. (2017). A Study of the Parameters Impacting Sustainability in Information Technology Organizations. *International Journal of Knowledge-Based Organizations, 7*(3), 27–39. doi:10.4018/IJKBO.2017070103

Sánchez-Fernández, M. D., & Manríquez, M. R. (2018). The Entrepreneurial Spirit Based on Social Values: The Digital Generation. In P. Isaias & L. Carvalho (Eds.), *User Innovation and the Entrepreneurship Phenomenon in the Digital Economy* (pp. 173–193). Hershey, PA: IGI Global. doi:10.4018/978-1-5225-2826-5.ch009

Sanchez-Ruiz, L., & Blanco, B. (2017). Process Management for SMEs: Barriers, Enablers, and Benefits. In M. Vemić (Ed.), *Optimal Management Strategies in Small and Medium Enterprises* (pp. 293–319). Hershey, PA: IGI Global. doi:10.4018/978-1-5225-1949-2.ch014

Sanz, L. F., Gómez-Pérez, J., & Castillo-Martinez, A. (2018). Analysis of the European ICT Competence Frameworks. In V. Ahuja & S. Rathore (Eds.), *Multidisciplinary Perspectives on Human Capital and Information Technology Professionals* (pp. 225–245). Hershey, PA: IGI Global. doi:10.4018/978-1-5225-5297-0.ch012

Sarvepalli, A., & Godin, J. (2017). Business Process Management in the Classroom. *Journal of Cases on Information Technology*, *19*(2), 17–28. doi:10.4018/JCIT.2017040102

Saxena, G. G., & Saxena, A. (2021). Host Community Role in Medical Tourism Development. In M. Singh & S. Kumaran (Eds.), *Growth of the Medical Tourism Industry and Its Impact on Society: Emerging Research and Opportunities* (pp. 105–127). IGI Global. https://doi.org/10.4018/978-1-7998-3427-4.ch006

Saygili, E. E., Ozturkoglu, Y., & Kocakulah, M. C. (2017). End Users' Perceptions of Critical Success Factors in ERP Applications. *International Journal of Enterprise Information Systems*, *13*(4), 58–75. doi:10.4018/IJEIS.2017100104

Saygili, E. E., & Saygili, A. T. (2017). Contemporary Issues in Enterprise Information Systems: A Critical Review of CSFs in ERP Implementations. In M. Tavana (Ed.), *Enterprise Information Systems and the Digitalization of Business Functions* (pp. 120–136). Hershey, PA: IGI Global. doi:10.4018/978-1-5225-2382-6.ch006

Schwaiger, K. M., & Zehrer, A. (2021). The COVID-19 Pandemic and Organizational Resilience in Hospitality Family Firms: A Qualitative Approach. In A. Zehrer, G. Glowka, K. Schwaiger, & V. Ranacher-Lackner (Eds.), *Resiliency Models and Addressing Future Risks for Family Firms in the Tourism Industry* (pp. 32–49). IGI Global. https://doi.org/10.4018/978-1-7998-7352-5.ch002

Scott, N., & Campos, A. C. (2022). Cognitive Science of Tourism Experiences. In R. Augusto Costa, F. Brandão, Z. Breda, & C. Costa (Eds.), Planning and Managing the Experience Economy in Tourism (pp. 1-21). IGI Global. https://doi.org/ doi:10.4018/978-1-7998-8775-1.ch001

Seidenstricker, S., & Antonino, A. (2018). Business Model Innovation-Oriented Technology Management for Emergent Technologies. In M. Khosrow-Pour, D.B.A. (Ed.), Encyclopedia of Information Science and Technology, Fourth Edition (pp. 4560-4569). Hershey, PA: IGI Global. doi:10.4018/978-1-5225-2255-3.ch396

Selvi, M. S. (2021). Changes in Tourism Sales and Marketing Post COVID-19. In M. Demir, A. Dalgıç, & F. Ergen (Eds.), *Handbook of Research on the Impacts and Implications of COVID-19 on the Tourism Industry* (pp. 437–460). IGI Global. doi:10.4018/978-1-7998-8231-2.ch021

Senaratne, S., & Gunarathne, A. D. (2017). Excellence Perspective for Management Education from a Global Accountants' Hub in Asia. In N. Baporikar (Ed.), *Management Education for Global Leadership* (pp. 158–180). Hershey, PA: IGI Global. doi:10.4018/978-1-5225-1013-0.ch008

Sensuse, D. I., & Cahyaningsih, E. (2018). Knowledge Management Models: A Summative Review. *International Journal of Information Systems in the Service Sector, 10*(1), 71–100. doi:10.4018/IJISSS.2018010105

Seth, M., Goyal, D., & Kiran, R. (2017). Diminution of Impediments in Implementation of Supply Chain Management Information System for Enhancing its Effectiveness in Indian Automobile Industry. *Journal of Global Information Management, 25*(3), 1–20. doi:10.4018/JGIM.2017070101

Seyal, A. H., & Rahman, M. N. (2017). Investigating Impact of Inter-Organizational Factors in Measuring ERP Systems Success: Bruneian Perspectives. In M. Tavana (Ed.), *Enterprise Information Systems and the Digitalization of Business Functions* (pp. 178–204). Hershey, PA: IGI Global. doi:10.4018/978-1-5225-2382-6.ch008

Shaqrah, A. A. (2018). Analyzing Business Intelligence Systems Based on 7s Model of McKinsey. *International Journal of Business Intelligence Research, 9*(1), 53–63. doi:10.4018/IJBIR.2018010104

Sharma, A. J. (2017). Enhancing Sustainability through Experiential Learning in Management Education. In N. Baporikar (Ed.), *Management Education for Global Leadership* (pp. 256–274). Hershey, PA: IGI Global. doi:10.4018/978-1-5225-1013-0.ch013

Shetty, K. P. (2017). Responsible Global Leadership: Ethical Challenges in Management Education. In N. Baporikar (Ed.), *Innovation and Shifting Perspectives in Management Education* (pp. 194–223). Hershey, PA: IGI Global. doi:10.4018/978-1-5225-1019-2.ch009

Sinthupundaja, J., & Kohda, Y. (2017). Effects of Corporate Social Responsibility and Creating Shared Value on Sustainability. *International Journal of Sustainable Entrepreneurship and Corporate Social Responsibility, 2*(1), 27–38. doi:10.4018/IJSECSR.2017010103

Škarica, I., & Hrgović, A. V. (2018). Implementation of Total Quality Management Principles in Public Health Institutes in the Republic of Croatia. *International Journal of Productivity Management and Assessment Technologies, 6*(1), 1–16. doi:10.4018/IJPMAT.2018010101

Skokic, V. (2021). How Small Hotel Owners Practice Resilience: Longitudinal Study Among Small Family Hotels in Croatia. In A. Zehrer, G. Glowka, K. Schwaiger, & V. Ranacher-Lackner (Eds.), *Resiliency Models and Addressing Future Risks for Family Firms in the Tourism Industry* (pp. 50–73). IGI Global. doi:10.4018/978-1-7998-7352-5.ch003

Smuts, H., Kotzé, P., Van der Merwe, A., & Loock, M. (2017). Framework for Managing Shared Knowledge in an Information Systems Outsourcing Context. *International Journal of Knowledge Management, 13*(4), 1–30. doi:10.4018/IJKM.2017100101

Sousa, M. J., Cruz, R., Dias, I., & Caracol, C. (2017). Information Management Systems in the Supply Chain. In G. Jamil, A. Soares, & C. Pessoa (Eds.), *Handbook of Research on Information Management for Effective Logistics and Supply Chains* (pp. 469–485). Hershey, PA: IGI Global. doi:10.4018/978-1-5225-0973-8.ch025

Spremic, M., Turulja, L., & Bajgoric, N. (2018). Two Approaches in Assessing Business Continuity Management Attitudes in the Organizational Context. In N. Bajgoric (Ed.), *Always-On Enterprise Information Systems for Modern Organizations* (pp. 159–183). Hershey, PA: IGI Global. doi:10.4018/978-1-5225-3704-5.ch008

Steenkamp, A. L. (2018). Some Insights in Computer Science and Information Technology. In *Examining the Changing Role of Supervision in Doctoral Research Projects: Emerging Research and Opportunities* (pp. 113–133). Hershey, PA: IGI Global. doi:10.4018/978-1-5225-2610-0.ch005

Stipanović, C., Rudan, E., & Zubović, V. (2022). Reaching the New Tourist Through Creativity: Sustainable Development Challenges in Croatian Coastal Towns. In M. Valeri (Ed.), *New Governance and Management in Touristic Destinations* (pp. 231–245). IGI Global. https://doi.org/10.4018/978-1-6684-3889-3.ch014

Tabach, A., & Croteau, A. (2017). Configurations of Information Technology Governance Practices and Business Unit Performance. *International Journal of IT/Business Alignment and Governance, 8*(2), 1–27. doi:10.4018/IJITBAG.2017070101

Talaue, G. M., & Iqbal, T. (2017). Assessment of e-Business Mode of Selected Private Universities in the Philippines and Pakistan. *International Journal of Online Marketing, 7*(4), 63–77. doi:10.4018/IJOM.2017100105

Tam, G. C. (2017). Project Manager Sustainability Competence. In *Managerial Strategies and Green Solutions for Project Sustainability* (pp. 178–207). Hershey, PA: IGI Global. doi:10.4018/978-1-5225-2371-0.ch008

Tambo, T. (2018). Fashion Retail Innovation: About Context, Antecedents, and Outcome in Technological Change Projects. In I. Management Association (Ed.), Fashion and Textiles: Breakthroughs in Research and Practice (pp. 233-260). Hershey, PA: IGI Global. https://doi.org/ doi:10.4018/978-1-5225-3432-7.ch010

Tantau, A. D., & Frăţilă, L. C. (2018). Information and Management System for Renewable Energy Business. In *Entrepreneurship and Business Development in the Renewable Energy Sector* (pp. 200–244). Hershey, PA: IGI Global. doi:10.4018/978-1-5225-3625-3.ch006

Teixeira, N., Pardal, P. N., & Rafael, B. G. (2018). Internationalization, Financial Performance, and Organizational Challenges: A Success Case in Portugal. In L. Carvalho (Ed.), *Handbook of Research on Entrepreneurial Ecosystems and Social Dynamics in a Globalized World* (pp. 379–423). Hershey, PA: IGI Global. doi:10.4018/978-1-5225-3525-6.ch017

Teixeira, P., Teixeira, L., Eusébio, C., Silva, S., & Teixeira, A. (2021). The Impact of ICTs on Accessible Tourism: Evidence Based on a Systematic Literature Review. In C. Eusébio, L. Teixeira, & M. Carneiro (Eds.), *ICT Tools and Applications for Accessible Tourism* (pp. 1–25). IGI Global. doi:10.4018/978-1-7998-6428-8.ch001

Trad, A., & Kalpić, D. (2018). The Business Transformation Framework, Agile Project and Change Management. In M. Khosrow-Pour, D.B.A. (Ed.), Encyclopedia of Information Science and Technology, Fourth Edition (pp. 620-635). Hershey, PA: IGI Global. https://doi.org/ doi:10.4018/978-1-5225-2255-3.ch054

Trad, A., & Kalpić, D. (2018). The Business Transformation and Enterprise Architecture Framework: The Financial Engineering E-Risk Management and E-Law Integration. In B. Sergi, F. Fidanoski, M. Ziolo, & V. Naumovski (Eds.), *Regaining Global Stability After the Financial Crisis* (pp. 46–65). Hershey, PA: IGI Global. doi:10.4018/978-1-5225-4026-7.ch003

Trengereid, V. (2022). Conditions of Network Engagement: The Quest for a Common Good. In R. Augusto Costa, F. Brandão, Z. Breda, & C. Costa (Eds.), *Planning and Managing the Experience Economy in Tourism* (pp. 69-84). IGI Global. https://doi.org/10.4018/978-1-7998-8775-1.ch004

Turulja, L., & Bajgoric, N. (2018). Business Continuity and Information Systems: A Systematic Literature Review. In N. Bajgoric (Ed.), *Always-On Enterprise Information Systems for Modern Organizations* (pp. 60–87). Hershey, PA: IGI Global. doi:10.4018/978-1-5225-3704-5.ch004

Vargas-Hernández, J. G. (2017). Professional Integrity in Business Management Education. In N. Baporikar (Ed.), *Management Education for Global Leadership* (pp. 70–89). Hershey, PA: IGI Global. doi:10.4018/978-1-5225-1013-0.ch004

Varnacı Uzun, F. (2021). The Destination Preferences of Foreign Tourists During the COVID-19 Pandemic and Attitudes Towards: Marmaris, Turkey. In M. Demir, A. Dalgıç, & F. Ergen (Eds.), *Handbook of Research on the Impacts and Implications of COVID-19 on the Tourism Industry* (pp. 285–306). IGI Global. https://doi.org/10.4018/978-1-7998-8231-2.ch014

Vasista, T. G., & AlAbdullatif, A. M. (2017). Role of Electronic Customer Relationship Management in Demand Chain Management: A Predictive Analytic Approach. *International Journal of Information Systems and Supply Chain Management, 10*(1), 53–67. doi:10.4018/IJISSCM.2017010104

Vieru, D., & Bourdeau, S. (2017). Survival in the Digital Era: A Digital Competence-Based Multi-Case Study in the Canadian SME Clothing Industry. *International Journal of Social and Organizational Dynamics in IT, 6*(1), 17–34. doi:10.4018/IJSODIT.2017010102

Vijayan, G., & Kamarulzaman, N. H. (2017). An Introduction to Sustainable Supply Chain Management and Business Implications. In M. Khan, M. Hussain, & M. Ajmal (Eds.), *Green Supply Chain Management for Sustainable Business Practice* (pp. 27–50). Hershey, PA: IGI Global. doi:10.4018/978-1-5225-0635-5.ch002

Vlachvei, A., & Notta, O. (2017). Firm Competitiveness: Theories, Evidence, and Measurement. In A. Vlachvei, O. Notta, K. Karantininis, & N. Tsounis (Eds.), *Factors Affecting Firm Competitiveness and Performance in the Modern Business World* (pp. 1–42). Hershey, PA: IGI Global. doi:10.4018/978-1-5225-0843-4.ch001

Wang, C., Schofield, M., Li, X., & Ou, X. (2017). Do Chinese Students in Public and Private Higher Education Institutes Perform at Different Level in One of the Leadership Skills: Critical Thinking?: An Exploratory Comparison. In V. Wang (Ed.), *Encyclopedia of Strategic Leadership and Management* (pp. 160–181). Hershey, PA: IGI Global. doi:10.4018/978-1-5225-1049-9.ch013

Wang, J. (2017). Multi-Agent based Production Management Decision System Modelling for the Textile Enterprise. *Journal of Global Information Management, 25*(4), 1–15. doi:10.4018/JGIM.2017100101

Wiedemann, A., & Gewald, H. (2017). Examining Cross-Domain Alignment: The Correlation of Business Strategy, IT Management, and IT Business Value. *International Journal of IT/Business Alignment and Governance, 8*(1), 17–31. doi:10.4018/IJITBAG.2017010102

Wolf, R., & Thiel, M. (2018). Advancing Global Business Ethics in China: Reducing Poverty Through Human and Social Welfare. In S. Hipsher (Ed.), *Examining the Private Sector's Role in Wealth Creation and Poverty Reduction* (pp. 67–84). Hershey, PA: IGI Global. doi:10.4018/978-1-5225-3117-3.ch004

Yablonsky, S. (2018). Innovation Platforms: Data and Analytics Platforms. In *Multi-Sided Platforms (MSPs) and Sharing Strategies in the Digital Economy: Emerging Research and Opportunities* (pp. 72–95). Hershey, PA: IGI Global. doi:10.4018/978-1-5225-5457-8.ch003

Yaşar, B. (2021). The Impact of COVID-19 on Volatility of Tourism Stocks: Evidence From BIST Tourism Index. In M. Demir, A. Dalgıç, & F. Ergen (Eds.), *Handbook of Research on the Impacts and Implications of COVID-19 on the Tourism Industry* (pp. 23–44). IGI Global. https://doi.org/10.4018/978-1-7998-8231-2.ch002

Yusoff, A., Ahmad, N. H., & Halim, H. A. (2017). Agropreneurship among Gen Y in Malaysia: The Role of Academic Institutions. In N. Ahmad, T. Ramayah, H. Halim, & S. Rahman (Eds.), *Handbook of Research on Small and Medium Enterprises in Developing Countries* (pp. 23–47). Hershey, PA: IGI Global. doi:10.4018/978-1-5225-2165-5.ch002

Zacher, D., & Pechlaner, H. (2021). Resilience as an Opportunity Approach: Challenges and Perspectives for Private Sector Participation on a Community Level. In A. Zehrer, G. Glowka, K. Schwaiger, & V. Ranacher-Lackner (Eds.), *Resiliency Models and Addressing Future Risks for Family Firms in the Tourism Industry* (pp. 75–102). IGI Global. https://doi.org/10.4018/978-1-7998-7352-5.ch004

Zanin, F., Comuzzi, E., & Costantini, A. (2018). The Effect of Business Strategy and Stock Market Listing on the Use of Risk Assessment Tools. In *Management Control Systems in Complex Settings: Emerging Research and Opportunities* (pp. 145–168). Hershey, PA: IGI Global. doi:10.4018/978-1-5225-3987-2.ch007

Zgheib, P. W. (2017). Corporate Innovation and Intrapreneurship in the Middle East. In P. Zgheib (Ed.), *Entrepreneurship and Business Innovation in the Middle East* (pp. 37–56). Hershey, PA: IGI Global. doi:10.4018/978-1-5225-2066-5.ch003

About the Contributors

Ebtihaj Al A'Ali s an Associate Professor, Department of Management and Marketing, College of Business Administration, University of Bahrain. She holds a Ph.D. degree in industrial psychology and industrial sociology from Lancaster University, United Kingdom. She is a founder of Bahrain management society. working with United Nations Development Programme and UNIDO on project basis. She published many books with IGI. She as well published articles in different journals. Her research interests are women in management, organisational theory, organisational behaviour, research methodology, industrial sociology and industrial psychology.

Meryem Masmoudi is Assistant Professor of Management at the Applied Science University, Kingdom of Bahrain. She holds a PhD in Management from University of Tunis (2013). She has been involved in teaching and research in the areas of management, organizational change and development and management science. Meryem has published research papers in top international refereed journals (ANOR, JORS, ITOR, INFOR). She is a member of the International Society on Multiple Criteria Decision Making, the Tunisian Decision Aid Society and INFORMS Bahrain International Group.

Gardenia AlSaffar is a consultant psychiatrist in Royal Bahrain Hospital. She is a member of the Royal College of the Psychiatrists in the UK. She did her fellowship in Ireland with a special interests in General Adults Psychiatry and Rehabilitation psychiatry. She co-edited a book published by IGI. She attended many seminars and conferences and published different articles. She has been a guest speaker for many events. Her research interests vary between health concerns, psychological and psychiatrical issues in general and corporate psychology.

***

Ramazan Atasoy is an Associate Professor of education management and planning at Harran University in Turkey. He teaches education leadership, education planning-policy and social development and education. His research focuses on education policy and planning, quality of education, PIAAC adult competency, literacy skills, numeracy skills and problem solving skills in technology-rich environments.

Asma Ayari is a Ph.D. holder in Management from IAE University de Lille _ France Assistant Professor at the University of Bahrain teaching management, organizational behavior, and HRM MSc and MBA Thesis supervisor and reviewer

Marisa Cleveland has more than two decades in the education and publishing industries, and Dr. Cleveland is adamant about supporting efforts toward the betterment of the human condition. Cleveland is the executive director for The Seymour Agency, a trustee for Hodges University Board of Trustees, and co-author of the leadership book, There Is No Box. Cleveland holds an Ed.D. in Organizational Leadership from Northeastern University, and an M.A. in Educational Administration and a B.A. in Speech Communication from George Mason University. She is a 2022 graduate of Leadership Collier.

Simon Cleveland is a professor of project management Purdue University Global. Dr. Cleveland is a graduate of George Mason University with Bachelor of Science degree in Business, of the George Washington University with a Master of Science degree in Project Management, of the City University of Seattle with a Master of Arts degree in Leadership, with a Ph.D. in Information Systems from Nova Southeastern University, and with a Ed.D. in Organizational Leadership from Northeastern University. He is also certified as a project management professional (PMP), Six Sigma Black Belt (SSBB) expert, and Information Technology Infrastructure Library (ITIL) foundations expert. Dr. Cleveland is the author of over 50 peer-reviewed publications in journals and conferences, and is a three-time recipient of the prestigious Dr. Harold Kerzner Scholarship which is awarded by the Project Management Institute Educational Foundation. Professionally, Dr. Cleveland has worked as both technology manager, program manager and PMO Director for organizations such as MD Anderson Cancer Center, Department of Homeland Security, NASA, Accenture, and AOL.

Anjali Daisy holds a Ph.D. degree in the field of Emotional Intelligence. She assessed and developed an Emotional Competence Inventory for IT employees in Tamil Nadu as the outcome of her research work. She has done her MBA in PSG Institute of Management, Coimbatore. She secured University second position in B.Sc(Computer Science).She holds a Post Graduate Diploma in Labour Law and

Administrative Law(PGDLL). She conducted EI training programs for diversified working professionals. She has published research papers in SCOPUS and SSCI indexed journals and wrote book chapters as well. She has presented papers at International conferences. She is also a reviewer in IGI Global. She has completed certification courses in the areas of Mind control, Competency Mapping, Strategic Performance Management, Psychology and Teaching in higher education offered by international premier institutes viz the University of Michigan, the University of Toronto, Yale University, and the University of Washington. She is able to incorporate global teaching-learning pedagogies in the courses she handles.

Meryem Masmoudi is Assistant Professor of Management at the University of Bahrain, College of Business Administration. She holds a PhD in Management from University of Tunis (2013). She has been involved in teaching and research in the areas of management, organizational change and development and management science. Meryem has published research papers in top international refereed journals (ANOR, JORS, ITOR, INFOR). She is a member of the International Society on Multiple Criteria Decision Making and the Tunisian Decision Aid Society.

Mehmet Tufan Yalçın is an Assistant Professor at Çankırı Karatekin University in Turkey. His research interests include leadership, school administration, instructional capacity, teacher professional learning, school climate, and organizational learning.

Index

www.ingramcontent.com/pod-product-compliance
Lightning Source LLC
LaVergne TN
LVHW061535290926
849162LV00004B/794